CREATIVE HOMEOWNER®

HILLSIDE
HOME PLANS

CREATIVE HOMEOWNER®, Upper Saddle River, New Jersey

Vice President and Publisher: Timothy O. Bakke
Production Director: Kimberly H. Vivas

Home Plans Editor: Kenneth D. Stuts
Home Plans Designer Liaison: Timothy Mulligan

Design and Layout: Arrowhead Direct (David Kroha, Cindy DiPierdomenico, Judith Kroha); Maureen Mulligan

Cover Design: David Geer

Current Printing (last digit)
10 9 8 7 6 5 4 3 2 1

Hillside Home Plans
Library of Congress Control Number: 2007921255
ISBN-10: 1-58011-360-5
ISBN-13: 978-1-58011-360-1

CREATIVE HOMEOWNER®
A Division of Federal Marketing Corp.
24 Park Way
Upper Saddle River, NJ 07458
www.creativehomeowner.com

Note: The homes as shown in the photographs and renderings in this book may differ from the actual blueprints. When studying the house of your choice, please check the floor plans carefully.

PHOTO CREDITS

Front cover: *main plan* 181036, page 118; *left to right:* plan 551135, page 98; plan 161101, page 232; plan 481021, page 82; plan 481031, page 30 **page 1:** plan 161093, page 253 **page 3:** top to bottom plan 271058, page 16; plan 271054, page 29; plan 161056, page 42 **page 4:** plan 481021, page 82 **page 5:** plan 271077, page 85 **page 6:** *top to bottom* plan 271079, page 255; plan 551182, page 92 **Page 7:** plan 481116, page 86 **page 70:** *top* courtesy of Thomasville; *bottom* both courtesy of Rubbermaid **page 71:** courtesy of IKEA **page 72:** courtesy of Closetmaid **page 73:** *top* courtesy of Closetmaid; *bottom* courtesy of Rubbermaid **pages 74–75:** all courtesy of Rubbermaid **pages 76–77:** courtesy of Diamond Cabinets **page 134:** *top* courtesy of American Olean; *bottom* courtesy of Villeroy & Boch **page 135:** *top* courtesy of Wilsonart; *bottom* courtesy of Kraftmaid Cabinetry **pages 136–137:** *left* courtesy of Silestone; *top center* courtesy of Wilsonart; *top right and bottom right* courtesy of Armstrong **page 138:** courtesy of Kraftmaid Cabinetry **page 139:** *top* courtesy of York Wallcoverings; *bottom* courtesy of Villeroy & Boch *page 184:* Walter Chandoha **page 185:** Carolyn Bates, design & installation: Paul Wieczoreck, Champlain Valley Landscaping **page 186:** Jerry Pavia **page 187:** *top* Jerry Pavia; illustration Elayne Sears, Michele Angle Farrar, Robert LaPointe **page 188:** John Parsekian/CH **page 189:** Carolyn Bates, design & installation: Paul Wieczoreck, Champlain Valley Landscaping **page 190:** *top* Brad Simmons; *bottom right* Positive Images/Patricia Bruno; *bottom left* Jerry Pavia **page 191:** *top* Garden Picture Library/Vaughan Fleming; *bottom* Tony Giammarino/ Giammarino & Dworkin **pages 236-237:** all Phillip H. Ennis Photography, design: Anne Cooper Interiors **pages 238-239:** all Phillip H. Ennis Photography, design: Audio Design Assoc./Justin Baxter **page 240:** *both* Phillip H. Ennis Photography, design: Beverly Ellsley **page 241:** Phillip H. Ennis Photography, design: Blodgett Designs **page 242:** *top* Phillip H. Ennis Photography, design: Siskin-Valls, Inc.; *bottom* Phillip H. Ennis Photography, design: Rita Grants **page 243:** Phillip H. Ennis Photography **page 277:** plan 401029, page 248 **Page 281:** *top to bottom* plan 551074, page 104; plan 141051, page 167; plan 141030, page 218 **Page 288:** *top to bottom* plan 141038, page 182; plan 151007, page 225; plan 161095, **page 266** *back cover: top* plan 551132, page 83; *middle plan* 551179, page 103; *left to right:* plan 161097, page 274; plan 481028, page 223; plan 131030, page 142

Contents

Getting Started

Maybe you can't wait to bang the first nail. Or you may be just as happy leaving town until the windows are cleaned. The extent of your involvement with the construction phase is up to you. Your time, interests, and abilities can help you decide how to get the project from lines on paper to reality. But building a house requires more than putting pieces together. Whoever is in charge of the process must competently manage people as well as supplies, materials, and construction. He or she will have to

- Make a project schedule to plan the orderly progress of the work. This can be a bar chart that shows the time period of activity by each trade.
- Establish a budget for each category of work, such as foundation, framing, and finish carpentry.
- Arrange for a source of construction financing.
- Get a building permit and post it conspicuously at the construction site.
- Line up supply sources and order materials.
- Find subcontractors and negotiate their contracts.
- Coordinate the work so that it progresses smoothly with the fewest conflicts.
- Notify inspectors at the appropriate milestones.
- Make payments to suppliers and subcontractors.

You as the Builder

You'll have to take care of every logistical detail yourself if you decide to act as your own builder or general contractor. But along with the responsibilities of managing the project, you gain the flexibility to do as much of your own work as you want and subcontract out the rest. Before taking this path, however, be sure you have the time and capabilities. Do you also have the

time and ability to schedule the work, hire and coordinate subs, order materials, and keep ahead of the accounting required to manage the project successfully? If you do, you stand to save the amount that a general contractor would charge to take on these responsibilities, normally 15 to 30 percent of the construction cost. If you take this responsibility on but mismanage the project, the potential savings will erode and may even cost you more than if you had hired a builder in the first place. A subcontractor might charge extra for hav-

Acting as the builder, above, requires the ability to hire and manage subcontractors.

Building a home, opposite, includes the need to schedule building inspections at the appropriate milestones.

ing to return to the site to complete work that was originally scheduled for an earlier date. Or perhaps because you didn't order the windows at the beginning, you now have to pay for a recent cost increase. (If you had hired a builder in the first place he or she would absorb the increase.)

Hiring a Builder to Handle Construction

A builder or general contractor will manage every aspect of the construction process. Your role after signing the construction contract will be to make regular progress payments and ensure that the work for which you are paying has been completed. You will also consult with the builder and agree to any changes that may have to be made along the way.

Leads for finding builders might come from friends or neighbors who have had contractors build, remodel, or add to their homes. Real-estate agents and bankers may have some names handy but are more likely familiar with the builder's ability to complete projects on time and budget than the quality of the work itself.

The next step is to narrow your list of candidates to three or four who you think can do a quality job and work harmoniously with you. Phone each builder to see whether he or she is interested in being considered for your project. If so, invite the builder to an interview at your home. The meeting will serve two purposes. You'll be able to ask the candidate about his or her experience, and you'll be able to see whether or not your personalities are compatible. Go over the plans with the builder to make certain that he or she understands the scope of the project. Ask if they have constructed similar houses. Get references, and check the builder's standing with the Better Business Bureau. Develop a short list of builders, say three, and ask them to submit bids for the project.

Contracts

Lump-Sum Contracts

A lump-sum, or fixed-fee, contract lets you know from the beginning just what the project will cost, barring any changes made because of your requests or unforeseen conditions. This form works well for projects that promise few surprises and are well defined from the outset by a complete set of contract documents. You can enter into a fixed-price contract by negotiating with a single builder on your short list or by obtaining bids from three or four builders. If you go the latter route, give each bidder a set of documents and allow at least two weeks for them to submit their bids. When you get the bids, decide who you want and call the others to thank them for their efforts. You don't have to accept the lowest bid, but it probably makes sense to do so since you have already honed the list to builders you trust. Inform this builder of your intentions to finalize a contract.

Cost-Plus-Fee Contracts

Under a cost-plus-fee contract, you agree to pay the builder for the costs of labor and materials, as verified by receipts, plus a fee that represents the builder's overhead and profit. This arrangement is sometimes referred to as "time and materials." The fee can range between 15 and 30 percent of the incurred costs. Because you ultimately pick up the tab—whatever the costs—the contractor is never at risk, as he is with a lump-sum contract. You won't know the final total cost of a cost-plus-fee contract until the project is built and paid for. If you can live with that uncertainty, there are offsetting advantages. First, this form allows you to accommodate unknown conditions much more easily than does a lump-sum contract. And rather than being tied down by the project documents, you will be free to make changes at any point along the way. This can be a trap, though. Watching the project take shape will spark the desire to add something or do something differently. Each change costs more, and the accumulation can easily exceed your budget. Because of the uncertainty of the final tab and the built-in advantage to the contractor, you should think twice before entering into this form of contract.

Contract Content

The conditions of your agreement should be spelled out thoroughly in writing and signed by both parties, whatever contractual arrangement you make with your builder. Your contract should include provisions for the following:

- The names and addresses of the owner and builder.
- A description of the work to be included ("As described in the plans and specifications dated . . .").
- The date that the work will be completed if time is of the essence.
- The contract price for lump-sum contracts and the builder's allowed profit and overhead costs for changes.
- The builder's fee for cost-plus-fee contracts and the method of accounting and requesting payment.
- The criteria for progress payments (monthly, by project milestones) and the conditions of final payment.
- A list of each drawing and specification section that is to be included as part of the contract.
- Requirements for guarantees. (One year is the standard period for which contractors guarantee the entire project, but you may require specific guarantees on

When submitting bids, all of the builders should base their estimates on the same specifications. Once the work begins, communicate with your builder to keep the work proceeding smoothly.

Inspect your newly built home, if possible, before the builder closes it up and finishes it.

certain parts of the project, such as a 20-year guarantee on the roofing.)
■ Provisions for insurance.
■ A description of how changes in the work orders will be handled.

The builder may have a standard contract that you can tailor to the specifics of your project. These contain complete specific conditions with blanks that you can fill in to fit your project and a set of "general conditions" that cover a host of issues from insurance to termination provisions. It's always a good idea to have an attorney review the draft of your completed contract before signing it.

Working with Your Builder

The construction phase officially begins when you have a signed copy of the contract and copies of any insurance required from the builder. It's not unheard of for a builder to request an initial payment of 10 to 20 percent of the total cost to cover mobilization costs, those costs associated with obtaining permits and getting set up to begin the actual construction. If you agree to this, keep a careful eye on the progress of the work to ensure that the total paid out at any one time doesn't get too far out of sync with the actual work completed.

What about changes? From here on, it's up to you and your builder to proceed in good faith and to keep the channels of communication open. Even so, changes of one sort or another beset every project, and they usually add to its cost.

Light at the End of the Tunnel.

The builder's request for a final inspection marks the end of the construction phase—almost. At the final inspection meeting, you and the builder will inspect the work, noting any defects or incomplete items on a "punch list." When the builder tidies up the punch list items, you should reinspect. Sometimes, builders go on to another job and take forever to clean up the last few details, so only after all items on the list have been completed satisfactorily should you release the final payment, which often accounts for the builder's profit.

Some Final Words

Having a positive attitude is important when undertaking a project as large as building a home. A positive attitude can help you ride out the rigors and stress of the construction process.

Stay Flexible. Expect problems, because they certainly will occur. Weather can upset the schedule you have established for subcontractors. A supplier may get behind on deliveries, which also affects the schedule. An unexpected pipe may surprise you during excavation. Just as certain, every problem that comes along has a solution if you are open to it.

Be Patient. The extra days it may take to resolve a construction problem will be forgotten once the project is completed.

Express Yourself. If what you see isn't exactly what you thought you were getting, don't be afraid to look into changing it. Or you may spot an unforeseen opportunity for an improvement. Changes usually cost more money, though, so don't make frivolous decisions.

Finally, watching your home go up is exciting, so stay upbeat. Get away from your project from time to time. Dine out. Take time to relax. A positive attitude will make for smoother relations with your builder. An optimistic outlook will yield better-quality work if you are doing your own construction. And though the project might seem endless while it is under way, keep in mind that all the planning and construction will fade to a faint memory at some time in the future, and you will be getting a lifetime of pleasure from a home that is just right for you.

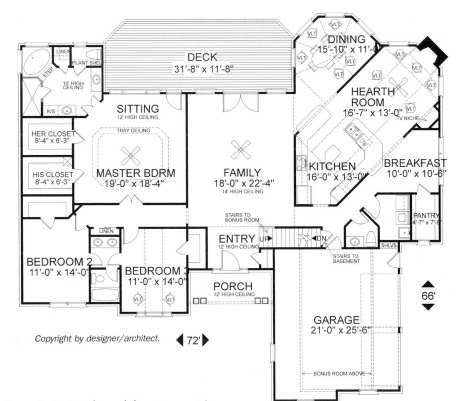

Plan #101013

Dimensions: 72' W x 66' D

Levels: 1

Square Footage: 2,564

Bedrooms: 3

Bathrooms: 2½

Foundation: Crawl space, slab, basement, or walkout

Materials List Available: Yes

Price Category: F

This exciting design combines a striking classic exterior with a highly functional floor plan.

Features:

- Ceiling Height: 9 ft. unless otherwise noted.

- Family Room: This warm and inviting room measures 18 ft. x 22 ft. It features a 14-ft. ceiling and a rear wall of windows. French doors lead to an enormous deck.

- Kitchen: This unique angled kitchen is open to the hearth room and eating areas, all of which enjoy vaulted ceilings and are surrounded by windows. The hearth room has a TV niche.

- Master Suite: This 19-ft. x 18-ft. master suite is truly sumptuous, with its 12-ft. ceiling, sitting area, two walk-in closets, and full-featured bath.

- Secondary Bedrooms: Each of the secondary bedrooms measures 11 ft. x 14 ft. and has direct access to a shared bath.

- Bonus Room: Just beyond the entry are stairs leading to this bonus room, which measures approximately 12 ft. x 21 ft.—plenty of room for storage or future expansion.

Dining Room

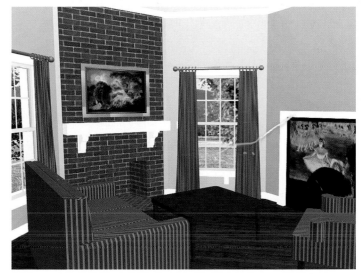

Hearth Room

Kitchen

Family Room

Master Bedroom

Master Bath

Plan #281031

Dimensions: 48' W x 58' D
Levels: 1
Square Footage: 1,493
Bedrooms: 3
Bathrooms: 2
Foundation: Basement or walkout
Material List Available: Yes
Price Category: B

This Country-style home has a beautiful brick exterior, with large bay windows that add to its charm.

Features:

- Porch: Enter the home through this covered porch and into the foyer, which features a vaulted ceiling.

- Great Room: This generously sized great room is attached to a dining room, creating possibilities for either entertaining large groups or hosting intimate dinners.

- Kitchen: This kitchen, with its attached breakfast nook, spills onto the sundeck, providing the perfect escape for sunny mornings or a quiet place to entertain guests.

- Master Suite: This master suite features a large walk-in closet and a whirlpool tub to melt away stress.

- Additional Bedrooms: Two other bedrooms can be converted into guest rooms or a study.

- Garage: A two-car garage offers you the option of storage for your cars or equipment.

Sundeck

Nook
11-0 x 8-0

Master Br
14-0 x 14-0

Kitchen
11-4 x 12-0

Great Room
23-0 x 17-0

Dining

China

WIC

Hall

Ens.   Util.   Bath

Double Garage
21-0 x 21-0

Br #2
10-0 x 10-4

Foyer
vaulted clg.

Br #3/Study
10-0 x 11-4

Porch

Rear Elevation

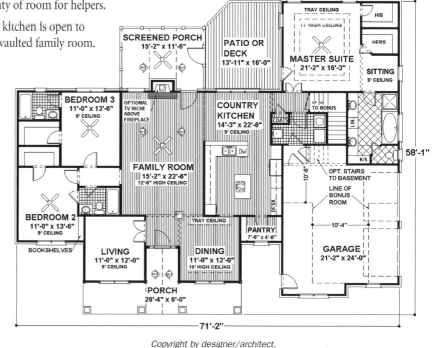

Plan #101011

Dimensions: 71'2" W x 58'1" D
Levels: 1
Square Footage: 2,184
Bedrooms: 3
Bathrooms: 3
Foundation: Crawl space, slab, basement, or walkout
Materials List Available: Yes
Price Category: E

Images provided by designer/architect.

A classic design and spacious interior add up to a flexible design suitable to any modern lifestyle.

CAD FILE AVAILABLE

Features:

- Ceiling Height: 9 ft. unless otherwise noted.
- Formal Dining Room: A decorative square column and a tray ceiling adorn this elegant dining room.

- Screened Porch: Enjoy summer breezes in style by stepping out of the French doors into this vaulted screened porch.
- Kitchen: Does everyone want to hang out in the kitchen while you are cooking? No problem. True to the home's country style, this huge 14-ft.-3-in. x 22-ft.-6-in. has plenty of room for helpers.
- The kitchen is open to the vaulted family room.

- Patio or Deck: This pleasant outdoor area is accessible from both the screened porch and the master bedroom.
- Master Suite: This luxurious suite includes a double tray ceiling, a sitting area, two walk-in closets, and an exquisite bath.

Kitchen

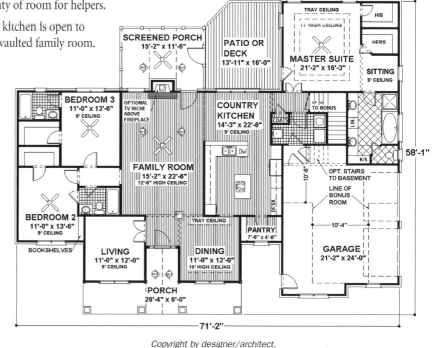

Copyright by designer/architect.

Plan #151050

Dimensions: 69'2" W x 74'10" D

Levels: 1

Square Footage: 2,096

Bedrooms: 3

Bathrooms: 2½

Foundation: Crawl space, slab, or basement

CompleteCost List Available: Yes

Price Category: D

Images provided by designer/architect.

You'll love this spacious home for both its elegance and its convenient design.

Features:

- Ceiling Height: 8 ft.

- Great Room: A 9-ft. boxed ceiling complements this large room, which sits just beyond the front gallery. A fireplace and door to the rear porch make it a natural gathering spot.

- Kitchen: This well-designed kitchen includes a central work island and shares an angled eating bar with the adjacent breakfast room.

- Breakfast Room: This room's bay window is gorgeous, and the door to the garage is practical.

- Master Suite: You'll love the 9-ft. boxed ceiling in the bedroom and the vaulted ceiling in the bath, which also includes two walk-in closets, a corner whirlpool tub, split vanities, a shower, and a compartmentalized toilet.

- Workshop: A huge workshop with half-bath is ideal for anyone who loves to build or repair.

Optional Front View

Plan #101012

Dimensions: 69'4" W x 62'9" D

Levels: 1

Square Footage: 2,288

Bedrooms: 3

Bathrooms: 2½

Foundation: Crawl space, slab, basement, or walkout

Materials List Available: No

Price Category: E

Images provided by designer/architect.

This classic brick ranch boasts traditional styling and an exciting up-to-date floor plan.

Features:

- Ceiling Height: 9 ft. unless otherwise noted.

- Front Porch: Guests will be welcome by this inviting front porch, which features a 12-ft. ceiling.

- Family Room: This warm and inviting room measures 16 ft. x 19 ft. It features a 14-ft. ceiling and a rear wall of windows. French doors lead to an enormous deck.

- Kitchen: This unique angled kitchen is open to the hearth room and eating areas, all of which enjoy vaulted ceilings and are surrounded by windows. The hearth room has a TV niche.

- Master Suite: This 16-ft. x 15-ft. master suite is truly sumptuous, with its 12-ft. ceiling, sitting area, two walk-in closets, and full-featured bath.

- Bonus Room: Here is plenty of storage or room for future expansion. Just beyond the entry are stairs leading to a bonus room measuring approximately 12 ft. x 21 ft.

Copyright by designer/architect.

Living Room

Plan #151008

Dimensions: 42' W x 66'10" D

Levels: 1

Square Footage: 1,892

Bedrooms: 3

Bathrooms: 2

Foundation: Crawl space, slab, basement, or daylight basement

CompleteCost List Available: Yes

Price Category: D

Images provided by designer/architect.

This home, as shown in the photograph, may differ from the actual blueprints. For more detailed information, please check the floor plans carefully.

CAD FILE AVAILABLE CAD

Copyright by designer/architect.

Main Level Floor Plan

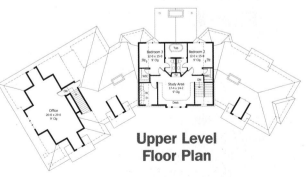

Upper Level Floor Plan

Copyright by designer/architect.

Plan #481032

Images provided by designer/architect.

Dimensions: 139' W x 73'4" D

Levels: 2

Square Footage: 4,113

Main Level Sq. Ft.: 3,033

Upper Level Sq. Ft.: 1,080

Bedrooms: 3

Bathrooms: 2 full, 2 half

Foundation: Walkout

Material List Available: No

Price Category: I

Plan #161063

Dimensions: 81'8" W x 51' D

Levels: 2

Square Footage: 3,168

Main Level Sq. Ft.: 2,144

Upper Level Sq. Ft.: 1,024

Bedrooms: 5

Bathrooms: 3½

Foundation: Basement, walkout basement

Materials List Available: Yes

Price Category: G

Images provided by designer/architect.

Rear Elevation

Main Level Floor Plan

Copyright by designer/architect.

Upper Level Floor Plan

Plan #151169

Dimensions: 51'6" W x 49'10" D

Levels: 1

Square Footage: 1,525

Bedrooms: 3

Bathrooms: 2

Foundation: crawl space, slab, basement, or daylight basement

CompleteCost List Available: Yes

Price Category: C

Images provided by designer/architect.

CAD FILE AVAILABLE

Copyright by designer/architect.

Rear Elevation

Main Level Floor Plan

- GREAT RM 19' X 14'
- DINING 19' X 12'
- PORCH 14' X 11'
- KITCHEN 18' X 13'
- SHED
- STUDY 11' X 12'
- ENTRY
- LAUN
- MUD
- GARAGE 36' X 28'

Plan #271058

Dimensions: 68' W x 53' D

Levels: 2

Square Footage: 2,924

Main Level Sq. Ft.: 1,579

Upper Level Sq. Ft.: 1,345

Bedrooms: 3

Bathrooms: 2½

Foundation: Daylight basement

Materials List Available: No

Price Category: F

Images provided by designer/architect.

CAD FILE AVAILABLE CAD

Upper Level Floor Plan

Copyright by designer/architect.

- OWNER'S SUITE 17' X 17'
- BATH
- BED RM 13' X 13'
- W.I. CL.
- LOFT
- BED RM 11' X 16'

75'-8"

58'-4"

- Master Suite 13-8 x 16-0 11' Tray Clg
- Great Rm 16-8 x 14-10 10' Clg
- Built-In
- FP
- Hearth/Kitchen 22-4 x 21-8 9' Clg
- DW
- Built-In
- Pantry
- Ref
- WIC
- Niche
- DN
- Buffet
- P
- D W
- Foyer 10' Clg
- Dining Rm 11-8 x 14-0 10' Clg
- WIC
- Study 13-0 x 11-6 13' Vault Clg
- Porch
- Garage 34-0 x 24-4
- Slp Slp

Plan #481029

Dimensions: 75'8" W x 58'4" D

Levels: 1

Square Footage: 4,048

Main Level Sq. Ft.: 2,147

Lower Level Sq. Ft.: 1,901

Bedrooms: 4

Bathrooms: 3½

Foundation: Walkout basement

Material List Available: No

Price Category: I

Images provided by designer/architect.

Lower Level Floor Plan

Copyright by designer/architect.

- Billiards 20-8 x 18-4
- Family Rm 13-6 x 18-8
- FP
- Bedroom 14-10 x 15-2
- Built-In
- L
- UP
- Games 19-4 x 13-6
- F
- WH
- Mechanical
- WIC
- Ref
- Bedroom 12-6 x 13-6

Plan #341294

Dimensions: 38'5" W x 42'8" D

Levels: 1

Square Footage: 1,418

Bedrooms: 3

Bathrooms: 2

Foundation: Crawl space, slab, basement or walkout

Material List Available: No

Price Category: B

Images provided by designer/architect.

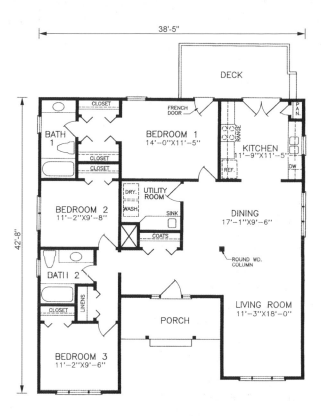

Copyright by designer/architect.

Plan #101003

Dimensions: 50' W x 55' D

Levels: 1

Square Footage: 1,593

Bedrooms: 3

Bathrooms: 2

Foundation: Crawl space, slab, or basement

Materials List Available: Yes

Price Category: D

Images provided by designer/architect.

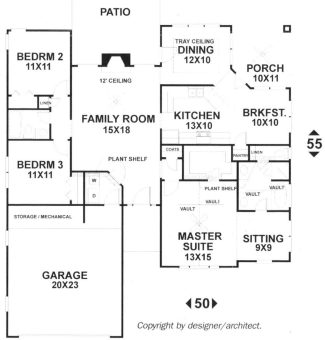

Copyright by designer/architect.

Plan #151034

Dimensions: 58'6" W x 64'6" D
Levels: 1
Square Footage: 2,133
Bedrooms: 3
Bathrooms: 2
Foundation: Crawl space, slab, or basement
CompleteCost List Available: Yes
Price Category: D

This home, as shown in the photograph, may differ from the actual blueprints. For more detailed information, please check the floor plans carefully.

Images provided by designer/architect.

You'll love the high ceilings, open floor plan, and contemporary design features in this home.

Features:

- **Great Room:** A pass-through tiled fireplace between this lovely large room and the adjacent hearth room allows you to notice the mirror effect created by the 10-ft. boxed ceilings in both rooms.

- **Dining Room:** An 11-ft. ceiling and 8-in. boxed column give formality to this lovely room, where you're certain to entertain.

- **Kitchen:** If you're a cook, this room may become your favorite spot in the house, thanks to its great design, which includes plenty of work and storage space, and a very practical layout.

- **Master Suite:** A 10-ft. boxed ceiling gives elegance to this room. A pocket door opens to the private bath, with its huge walk-in closet, glass-blocked whirlpool tub, separate glass shower, and private toilet room.

Copyright by designer/architect.

Rendering reflects floor plan

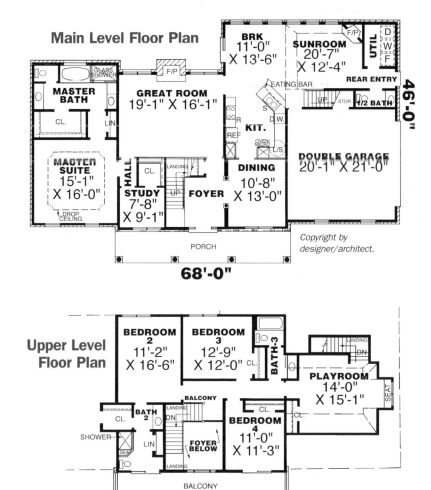

Plan #241013

Dimensions: 68' W x 46' D

Levels: 2

Square Footage: 3,033

Main Level Sq. Ft.: 1,918

Upper Level Sq. Ft.: 1,115

Bedrooms: 4

Bathrooms: 3½

Foundation: Crawl space, slab, or walkout

Materials List Available: No

Price Category: G

Images provided by designer/architect.

The generous front porch and balcony of this home signal its beauty and comfortable design.

Features:

- **Great Room:** A large fireplace is the focal point of this spacious room, which opens from the foyer.

- **Kitchen:** Open to the dining room and breakfast room, the kitchen is designed for convenience.

- **Sunroom:** A fireplace and tray ceiling highlight this room that's just off the breakfast room.

- **Study:** Positioned for privacy, the study is ideal for quiet time alone.

- **Master Suite:** You'll love the decorative drop ceiling, huge walk-in closet, and bath with two vanities, a tub, and separate shower.

- **Playroom:** This enormous space gives ample room for play on rainy afternoons. Set up a media center here when the children have outgrown the need for a playroom.

Main Level Floor Plan

BRK 11'-0" X 13'-6"

SUNROOM 20'-7" X 12'-4"

UTIL

REAR ENTRY

MASTER BATH

GREAT ROOM 19'-1" X 16'-1"

EATING BAR

1/2 BATH

KIT.

MASTER SUITE 15'-1" X 16'-0"

HALL

STUDY 7'-8" X 9'-1"

FOYER

DINING 10'-8" X 13'-0"

DOUBLE GARAGE 20'-1" X 21'-0"

DROP CEILING

PORCH

46'-0"

68'-0"

Copyright by designer/architect.

Upper Level Floor Plan

BEDROOM 2 11'-2" X 16'-6"

BEDROOM 3 12'-9" X 12'-0"

BATH-3

LANDING

DN

PLAYROOM 14'-0" X 15'-1"

SEAT

SHOWER

BATH 2

LIN

DN

BALCONY

LANDING

FOYER BELOW

BEDROOM 4 11'-0" X 11'-3"

LANDING

BALCONY

Plan #321001

Dimensions: 83' W x 42' D

Levels: 1

Square Footage: 1,721

Bedrooms: 3

Bathrooms: 2

Foundation: Crawl space, slab, or basement

Materials List Available: Yes

Price Category: C

Images provided by designer/architect.

Rear View

You'll love the atrium, which creates a warm, naturally lit space inside this gracious home, as well as the roof dormers that give the house wonderful curb appeal from the outside.

Features:

- Great Room: Bathed in light from the atrium window wall, this room, with its vaulted ceiling, will be the hub of your family life.

- Dining Room: This room also has a vaulted ceiling and is lit by the atrium, but you can draw drapes at night to create a cozy, warm feeling.

- Kitchen: Designed for functionality, this step-saving kitchen is easy to organize and makes cooking a pleasure.

- Breakfast Room: For convenience, this room is located between the kitchen and the rear covered porch.

- Master Suite: Retire with pleasure to this lovely retreat, with its luxurious bath.

Copyright by designer/architect.

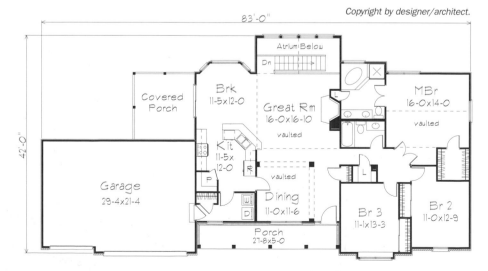

Plan #161105

Dimensions: 90'2" W x 104'5" D
Levels: 2
Square Footage: 6,806
Main Level Sq. Ft.: 4,511
Upper Level Sq. Ft.: 2,295
Bedrooms: 4
Bathrooms: 4 full, 2 half
Foundation: Walkout basement
Material List Available: No
Price Category: K

The opulence and drama of this European inspired home features a solid brick exterior with limestone detail, arched dormers, and a parapet.

Features:

- **Foyer:** A large octagonal skylight tops a water fountain feature displayed in this exquisite entryway. The formal dining room and library flank the entry and enjoy a 10-ft. ceiling height.

- **Family Living Area:** The gourmet kitchen, breakfast area, and cozy hearth room comprise this family activity center of the home. Wonderful amenities such as a magnificent counter with seating, a celestial ceiling over the dining table, an alcove for an entertainment center, a stone-faced wood-burning fireplace, and access to the rear porch enhance the informal area.

- **Master Suite:** This luxurious suite enjoys a raised ceiling, a seating area with bay window, and access to the terrace. The dressing room pampers the homeowner with a whirlpool tub, a ceramic tile shower enclosure, two vanities, and a spacious walk-in closet.

- **Upper Level:** Elegant stairs lead to the second-floor study loft and two additional bedrooms, each with a private bathroom and large walk-in closet. On the same level, and located for privacy, the third bedroom serves as a guest suite, showcasing a cozy sitting area and private bathroom.

Upper Level Floor Plan

Main Level Floor Plan

Optional Basement Level Floor Plan

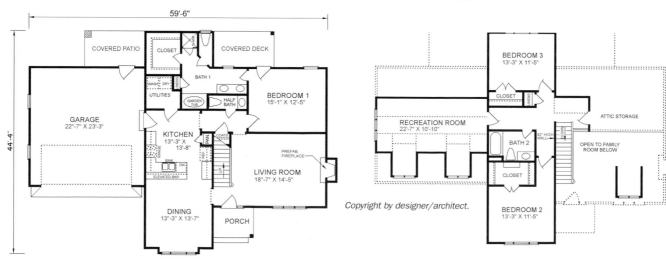

Plan #341216

Dimensions: 59'6" W x 44'4" D
Levels: 2
Square Footage: 1,881
Main Level Sq. Ft.: 1,237
Upper Level Sq. Ft.: 644
Bedrooms: 3
Bathrooms: 2½
Foundation: Crawl space, slab, basement or walkout
Material List Available: No
Price Category: D

Find your dream home within the walls of this traditional-style house.

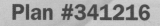

Images provided by designer/architect.

Features:

- Outdoor Living Space: Enjoy a summer breeze in the shade-minus the mosquitoes.

- Living Room: Cozy up to the fire in this large living room with its prefabricated fireplace.

- Kitchen: This is the perfect space for throwing a dinner party where the guests have the option of enjoying your company while you cook or relaxing in the dining room.

- Secondary Bedrooms: Three bedrooms and the nearby bathrooms are perfect for your growing family.

- Storage: Large utility closets have plenty of space to store out-of-season clothing, or canned goods.

Main Level Floor Plan

59'-6"

COVERED PATIO
CLOSET
COVERED DECK
BATH 1
WASH/DRY
LINENS
UTILITIES
GARDEN TUB
HALF BATH
BEDROOM 1
15'-1" X 12'-5"
GARAGE
22'-7" X 23'-3"
KITCHEN
13'-3" X 13'-8"
PAN
COATS
PREFAB FIREPLACE
SINK
DW
ELEVATED BAR
UP
LIVING ROOM
18'-7" X 14'-5"
44'-4"
DINING
13'-3" X 13'-7"
PORCH

Upper Level Floor Plan

BEDROOM 3
13'-3" X 11'-5"
CLOSET
LINENS
RECREATION ROOM
22'-7" X 10'-10"
BATH 2
42" HIGH WALL
DOWN
ATTIC STORAGE
OPEN TO FAMILY ROOM BELOW
CLOSET
BEDROOM 2
13'-3" X 11'-5"

Copyright by designer/architect.

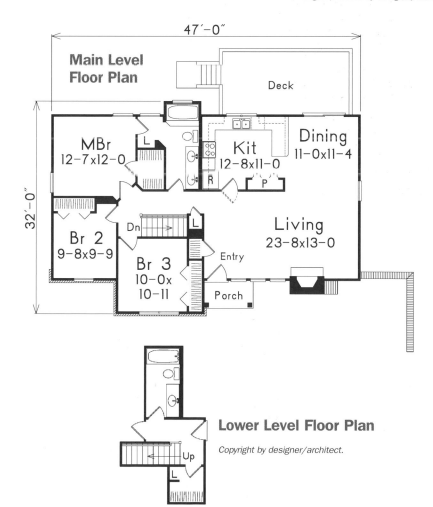

Plan #321024

Dimensions: 47' W x 32' D
Levels: 1
Square Footage: 1,403
Main Level Sq. Ft: 1,252
Lower Level Sq. Ft: 151
Bedrooms: 3
Bathrooms: 1-2
Foundation: Daylight basement
Materials List Available: Yes
Price Category: B

With its sleek lines and eye-catching exterior, this well-designed compact home is perfect for couples just starting out.

Features:

- **Living Area:** Enter into this spacious living room, which flows directly to the dining room. The openness of rooms is wonderful for a busy house with a lot of traffic, and the exit to the deck allows summertime company to pass in and out easily.

- **Kitchen:** This room features a large pantry, a well-designed work area, and entries to both the living and dining rooms for convenient access.

- **Master Suite:** With his and her sinks and a large closet, the generous size of this master suite makes getting ready in the morning a breeze.

- **Additional Bedrooms:** Enjoy the option of turning a spare bedroom into a home office or study.

Images provided by designer/architect.

Main Level Floor Plan

47'-0"

32'-0"

Deck

MBr
12-7x12-0

Kit
12-8x11-0

Dining
11-0x11-4

Br 2
9-8x9-9

Dn

Living
23-8x13-0

Br 3
10-0x
10-11

Entry

Porch

Lower Level Floor Plan

Up

Copyright by designer/architect.

Plan #151319

Dimensions: 69'11" W x 75'6" D
Levels: 1.5
Square Footage: 4,231
Main Level Sq. Ft.: 1,329
Upper Level Sq. Ft.: 2,902
Bedrooms: 5
Bathrooms: 4½
Foundation: Crawl space, slab, basement or walkout
CompleteCost List Available: Yes
Price Category: I

This classic brick home will be the highlight of any neighborhood.

CAD FILE AVAILABLE

Images provided by designer/architect.

Features:

- Foyer: This entry with its 12-ft.-high ceiling extends an open welcome to all. The foyer affords a view into the great room.

- Great Room: The high ceiling and cozy fire place strike a balance that creates the perfect gathering place for family and friends. An abundance of space allows you to tailor this room to your needs.

- Master Suite: Away from the busy areas of the home, this master suite is ideal for shedding your daily cares and relaxing in a romantic atmosphere. It includes a full master bath with his and her sinks, a stall shower, and a whirlpool tub.

- Upper Level: At the top of the stairs you will find attic storage to your right and an optional bedroom to your left. The bedroom boasts a large walk-in closet and a full bathroom.

Copyright by designer/architect.

Main Level Floor Plan

Upper Level Floor Plan

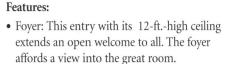

Basement Level Floor Plan

Plan #321009

Dimensions: 55'8" W x 46'4" D

Levels: 1

Square Footage: 2,295

Bedrooms: 3

Bathrooms: 2

Foundation: Walkout

Materials List Available: Yes

Price Category: E

If you've got a site with great views, you'll love this home, which is designed to make the most of them.

Images provided by designer/architect.

Features:

- **Porch:** This wraparound porch is an ideal spot to watch the sun come up or go down. Add potted plants to create a lush atmosphere or grow some culinary herbs.
- **Great Room:** You couldn't ask for more luxury than this room provides, with its vaulted ceiling, large bay window, fireplace, dining balcony, and atrium window wall.
- **Kitchen:** No matter whether you're an avid cook or not, you'll relish the thoughtful design of this room.
- **Master Suite:** This suite is truly a retreat you'll treasure. It has two large walk-in closets for good storage space, and sliding doors that open to an exterior balcony where you can sit out to enjoy the stars. The amenity-filled bath adds to your enjoyment of this suite.

Rear View

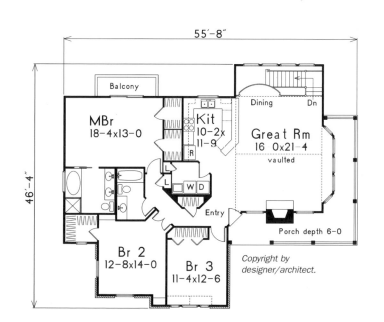

Copyright by designer/architect.

Optional Basement Level Floor Plan

Plan #151168

Dimensions: 66' W x 65'2" D

Levels: 1

Square Footage: 2,261

Bedrooms: 4

Bathrooms: 2½

Foundation: Crawl space, slab, basement, or daylight basement

CompleteCost List Available: Yes

Price Category: E

Images provided by designer/architect.

The well-planned layout of this home will delight your family if you want plenty of space for group activities, as well as private times.

Features:

- Great Room: Natural light flows into this room, with its door to the covered porch and fireplace.

- Outdoor Areas: Relax and enjoy the rear covered porch, the patio, and the front covered porch.

- Dining Room: An 11-ft. boxed ceiling and entry columns let you decorate for formality here.

- Kitchen: The central island has space for working as well as a snack bar, and you'll love the pantry.

- Breakfast Room: Set the table in the deep bay to enjoy the morning light.

- Master Suite: A 9-ft. boxed ceiling and door to the rear porch make the bedroom luxurious, and the bath has two walk-in closets and a whirlpool tub, separate shower, and dual vanity.

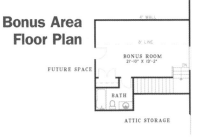

Bonus Area Floor Plan

Plan #341176

Dimensions: 76'6" W x 34' D
Levels: 2
Square Footage: 2,170
Main Level Sq. Ft.: 1,550
Lower Level Sq. Ft: 620
Bedrooms: 3
Bathrooms: 2½
Foundation: Crawl space, slab, basement, or walkout
Materials List Available: Yes
Price Category: D

Images provided by designer/architect.

A columned entry and brick steps combine to create this classically beautiful home, which has an ideal design for the modern family.

Features:

- Foyer: Double doors swing into this welcoming space, with closets ready to take your guests' coats and an attached formal living room that introduces them comfortably to your home.

- Family Room: With built-in entertainment and storage space and an unfettered connection with the dining room and kitchen, this

is a space where the whole family can gather and enjoy each other's company.

- Kitchen: The sweeping design of this space is both efficient and attractive. It features a working island with a range and stands open to the dining room. And whether it's a cool, sunny day or a warm, rainy one, you'll enjoy relaxing meals on the screened porch that is just a few steps away.

- Master Suite: In this space, a walk-in closet and full master bath adorn the bedroom, all waiting to be transformed into your personal retreat.

Main Level Floor Plan

Upper Level Floor Plan

Copyright by designer/architect.

Plan #161018

Dimensions: 74'4" W x 69'11" D

Levels: 2

Square Footage: 2,816
+ 325 Sq. Ft. bonus room

Main Level Sq. Ft.: 2,231

Upper Level Sq. Ft.: 624

Bedrooms: 3

Bathrooms: 2 full, 2 half

Foundation: Basement

Materials List Available: No

Price Category: F

Images provided by designer/architect.

If you love classic European designs, look closely at this home with its multiple gables and countless conveniences and luxuries.

Features:

- Foyer: Open to the great room, the 2-story foyer offers a view all the way to the rear windows.

- Great Room: A fireplace makes this room cozy in any kind of weather.

- Kitchen: This large room features an island with a sink, and an angled wall with French doors to the back yard.

- Dining Room: The furniture alcove and raised ceiling make this room both formal and practical.

- Master Suite: You'll love the quiet in the bedroom and the luxuries—a whirlpool tub, separate shower, and double vanities—in the bath.

- Basement: The door from the basement to the side yard adds convenience to outdoor work.

Rear View

Main Level Floor Plan

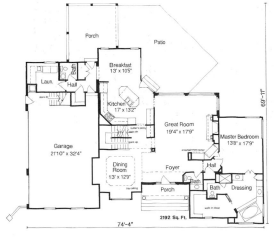

Upper Level Floor Plan

Copyright by designer/architect.

Foyer/Dining Room

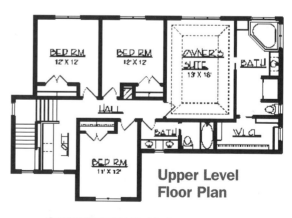

Plan #271054

Dimensions: 63' W x 49' D
Levels: 2
Square Footage: 2,654
Main Level Sq. Ft.: 1,384
Upper Level Sq. Ft.: 1,270
Bedrooms: 4
Bathrooms: 2½
Foundation: Daylight basement
Materials List Available: No
Price Category: F

This updated farmhouse attracts comments from passersby with its shuttered windows and welcoming wraparound porch.

Images provided by designer/architect.

Features:

- **Great Room:** This popular gathering spot includes a fireplace flanked by a media center and abundant shelves, and a wall of windows.

- **Dining Room:** This formal dining room is closed off with a pocket door for peace and quiet during meals. The bayed window facing the front is a nice touch.

- **Kitchen:** This thoroughly modern kitchen boasts an island with two sinks, a good-sized pantry, and a bayed dinette with sliding doors to the backyard.

- **Sun Porch:** Accessed via double doors from the dinette, this warm getaway spot flaunts a wood floor, ample angled windows, and a French door to the backyard.

- **Owner's Suite:** This master bedroom has a gorgeous tray ceiling in the sleeping chamber, plus a private bath with a corner whirlpool tub, a separate shower, and an endless walk-in closet.

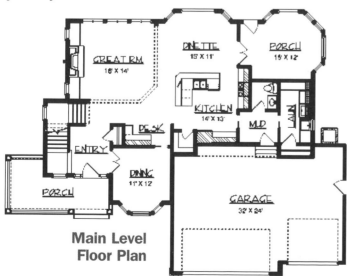

Main Level Floor Plan

Upper Level Floor Plan

Copyright by designer/architect.

Plan #151060

Dimensions: 80'11" W x 95'8" D

Levels: 1

Square Footage: 3,554

Bedrooms: 3

Bathrooms: 3

Foundation: Crawl space, slab basement, or walkout

CompleteCost List Available: Yes

Price Category: F

Images provided by designer/architect.

CAD FILE AVAILABLE CAD

Copyright by designer/architect.

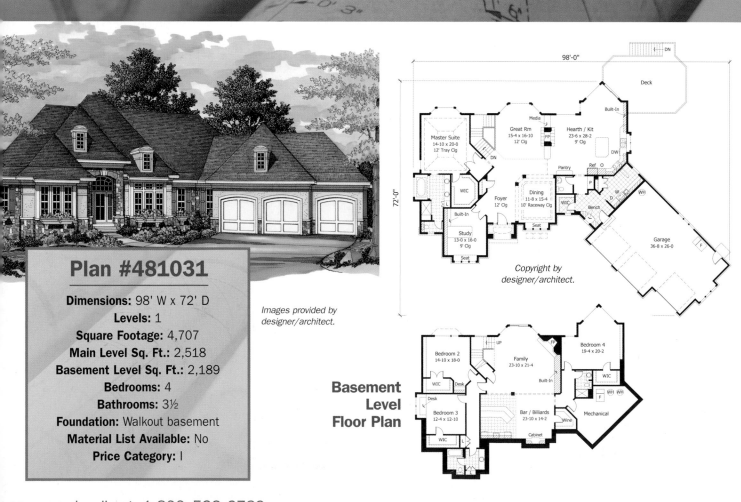

Plan #481031

Dimensions: 98' W x 72' D

Levels: 1

Square Footage: 4,707

Main Level Sq. Ft.: 2,518

Basement Level Sq. Ft.: 2,189

Bedrooms: 4

Bathrooms: 3½

Foundation: Walkout basement

Material List Available: No

Price Category: I

Images provided by designer/architect.

Copyright by designer/architect.

Basement Level Floor Plan

Plan #151125

Dimensions: 67'6" W x 73'10" D

Levels: 1.5

Square Footage: 2,606

Bedrooms: 4

Bathrooms: 2½

Foundation: Crawl space, slab, basement, or walkout

CompleteCost List Available: Yes

Price Category: F

Images provided by designer/architect.

CAD FILE AVAILABLE

Optional Bonus Area Floor Plan

Copyright by designer/architect.

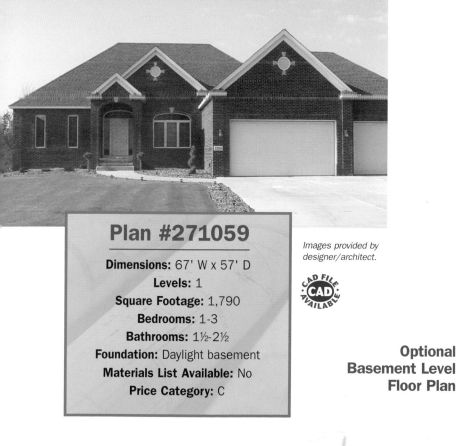

Plan #271059

Dimensions: 67' W x 57' D

Levels: 1

Square Footage: 1,790

Bedrooms: 1-3

Bathrooms: 1½-2½

Foundation: Daylight basement

Materials List Available: No

Price Category: C

Images provided by designer/architect.

CAD FILE AVAILABLE

Copyright by designer/architect.

Optional Basement Level Floor Plan

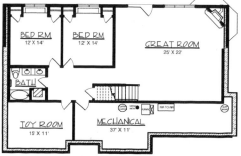

Plan #161066

Dimensions: 62'8" W x 57'11" D

Levels: 1

Square Footage: 2,078

Bedrooms: 3

Bathrooms: 2

Foundation: Basement, walkout basement

Materials List Available: Yes

Price Category: D

Images provided by designer/architect.

Rear Elevation

Copyright by designer/architect.

Plan #341287

Dimensions: 55'1" W x 39' D

Levels: 1

Square Footage: 1,217

Bedrooms: 3

Bathrooms: 2

Foundation: Crawl space, slab, basement, or walkout

Material List Available: Yes

Price Category: B

Images provided by designer/architect.

CAD FILE AVAILABLE · CAD

Copyright by designer/architect.

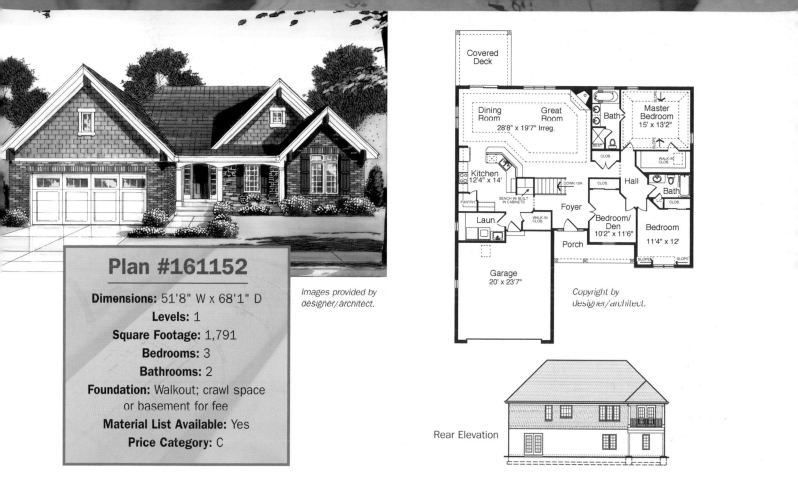

Plan #161152

Dimensions: 51'8" W x 68'1" D

Levels: 1

Square Footage: 1,791

Bedrooms: 3

Bathrooms: 2

Foundation: Walkout; crawl space or basement for fee

Material List Available: Yes

Price Category: C

Images provided by designer/architect.

Copyright by designer/architect.

Rear Elevation

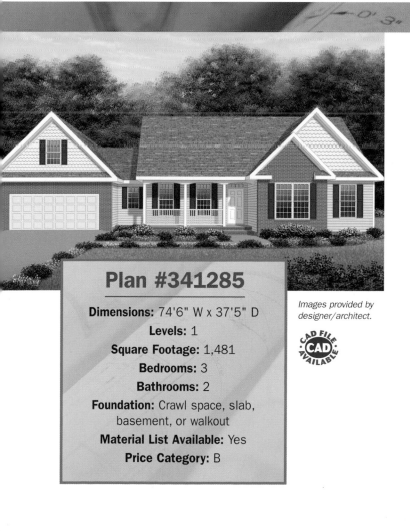

Plan #341285

Dimensions: 74'6" W x 37'5" D

Levels: 1

Square Footage: 1,481

Bedrooms: 3

Bathrooms: 2

Foundation: Crawl space, slab, basement, or walkout

Material List Available: Yes

Price Category: B

Images provided by designer/architect.

CAD FILE AVAILABLE

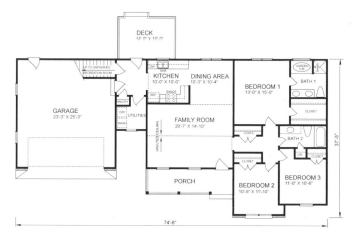

Copyright by designer/architect.

Plan #151173

Dimensions: 58' W x 53'6" D
Levels: 1
Square Footage: 1,739
Bedrooms: 3
Bathrooms: 2
Foundation: Crawl space, slab, basement, or walkout
CompleteCost List Available: Yes
Price Category: C

You'll love the charming architectural features and practical contemporary design of this ranch-style home.

CAD FILE AVAILABLE

Features:

- Great Room: Perfect for entertaining guests or just cozying up to the glowing fireplace with loved-ones, this great room is conveniently located in the center of everything.

- Kitchen: This highly efficient design, complete with island and plenty of workspace and storage, is just steps away from the sunlit breakfast room and the formal dining room, simplifying meal transitions.

- Master Suite: A romantic getaway in itself, this spacious master bedroom adjoins his and her walk-in closets, and a large compartmentalized master bath with a whirlpool tub, dual vanities, and a standing shower. The room also includes a private entrance to the back porch.

- Secondary Bedrooms: In a remote space of their own, these two nicely sized bedrooms share access to a full bathroom.

Plan #161160

Dimensions: 73'10" W x 58' D

Levels: 1

Square Footage: 2,230

Bedrooms: 3

Bathrooms: 2½

Foundation: Walkout

Material List Available: Yes

Price Category: E

This charming home will draw the warm affection of its occupants, guests, and neighbors alike.

CAD FILE AVAILABLE

Features:

- **Great Room:** Find peace at the center of your home with this comfortable space, which is perfect for entertaining friends or just quietly lounging by the fireplace.

- **Kitchen:** This efficiently designed space is situated between the sunlit breakfast area and the formal dining room for simple mealtime transitions. On warm days, move your meal out onto the screened-in deck.

- **Master Suite:** This master suite features a walk-in closet and a compartmentalized full bath with his and her vanities, large tub, and separate standing shower.

- **Secondary Bedrooms:** Two additional bedrooms feature wide closets and proximity to a full bathroom. Don't need three bedrooms? Use the third as a library.

Rear Elevation

Main Level Floor Plan

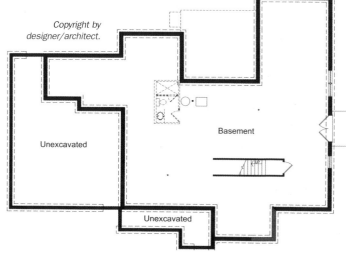

Basement Level Floor Plan

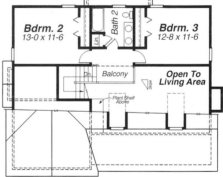

Plan #141010

Dimensions: 43'4" W x 37' D

Levels: 2

Square Footage: 1,765

Main Level Sq. Ft.: 1,210

Upper Level Sq. Ft.: 555

Bedrooms: 3

Bathrooms: 2½

Foundation: Basement

Materials List Available: Yes

Price Category: C

A Palladian window in a stone gable adds a new twist to a classical cottage design.

Features:

• Ceiling Height: 8 ft. unless otherwise noted.

• Living Area: Dormers open into this handsome living area, which is designed to accommodate gatherings of any size.

• Master Suite: This beautiful master bedroom opens off the foyer. It features a modified cathedral ceiling that makes the front Palladian window a focal point inside as well as out. The master bath offers a dramatic cathedral ceiling over the tub and vanity.

• Balcony: U-shaped stairs lead to this elegant balcony, which overlooks the foyer while providing access to two additional bedrooms.

• Garage: This garage is tucked under the house to improve the appearance from the street. It offers two bays for plenty of parking and storage space.

Images provided by designer/architect.

Main Level Floor Plan

Upper Level Floor Plan

Copyright by designer/architect.

Basement Floor Plan

SMARTtip
Stone Tables

Marble- and stone-topped tables with plants are perfect for use in light-filled rooms. Warmed by the sun during the day, the tabletops catch leaf droppings and can stand up to the splatters of watering cans and plant sprayers.

Plan #271056

Dimensions: 73' W x 52' D
Levels: 2
Square Footage: 2,850
Main Level Sq. Ft.: 1,596
Upper Level Sq. Ft.: 1,254
Bedrooms: 3
Bathrooms: 2½
Foundation: Daylight basement
Materials List Available: No
Price Category: F

Images provided by designer/architect.

Classic and gracious outside and functionally elegant inside, this expansive home will be the envy of the neighborhood.

CAD FILE AVAILABLE

Features:

- **Great Room:** Use this wide-open space for entertaining, easily transferring hors d'oeuvres from the adjacent kitchen, or for family game night in front of the fireplace.

- **Kitchen:** It's hard to have too many cooks in the kitchen with this design. There is plenty of space for helpers, and more for spectators on the other side of the snack bar.

- **Master Suite:** Away from the bustle of every-day life on the upper floor, this sprawling

master suite includes a private study and storage space. The master bath has his and her sinks, a spacious tub, separate standing shower, and access to a large walk-in closet.

- **Secondary Bedrooms:** Also restfully situated on the upper floor, these bedrooms have plenty of closet space and access to a nicely sized full bathroom.

Main Level Floor Plan

Upper Level Floor Plan

Copyright by designer/architect.

Plan #341170

Dimensions: 34' W x 42' D
Levels: 2
Square Footage: 1,704
Main Level Sq. Ft.: 852
Upper Level Sq. Ft.: 852
Bedrooms: 3
Bathrooms: 2½
Foundation: Crawl space, slab, basement or walkout
Material List Available: Yes
Price Category: C

This generously sized traditional-style home with its unique architecture and visual appeal is sure to be a beautiful addition to any block.

Images provided by designer/architect.

Features:

• Entry: Enter through this impressive foyer, which features ornate columns for a luxurious look.

• Family Room: This attractive room features ample space and the option of combining it with the dining room to create a large entertainment area.

• Kitchen: This kitchen has the added bonus of an elevated bar for preparing cocktails at a dinner party or enjoying a quick snack.

The breakfast nook is a sweet escape for reading the morning paper.

• Recreation Room: This recreation room affords a number of options-create an entertainment center, an impressive library, or a game room for the kids.

• Additional Bedrooms: All three bedrooms contain large closets and share two bathrooms to alleviate congestion on busy mornings.

Copyright by designer/architect.

Main Level Floor Plan

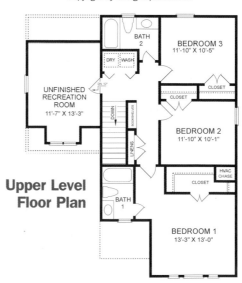

Upper Level Floor Plan

Plan #161092

Dimensions: 92'6" W x 56'8" D
Levels: 1
Square Footage: 2,110
Bedrooms: 3
Bathrooms: 2
Foundation: Walkout basement
Material List Available: Yes
Price Category: D

Brick and Stone, multiple windows, and a boxed window decorate the exterior of this one-level home.

Features:

- **Great Room:** This entertaining area boasts a sloped ceiling and a large fireplace. The area is open to the kitchen and breakfast area.

- **Kitchen:** This fully equipped island kitchen features a built-in pantry and a raised bar that looks into the breakfast area.

- **Master Suite:** This private area features a sloped ceiling in the sleeping area and a large window for backyard views. The master bath boasts a large bathtub, a standup shower, and dual vanities.

- **Lower Level:** This optional finished lower level offers a fourth bedroom, media area, wet bar, and billiards for added enjoyment.

Images provided by designer/architect.

Main Level Floor Plan
Copyright by designer/architect.

Rear Elevation

Basement Level Floor Plan

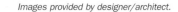

Images provided by designer/architect.

Plan #151741

Dimensions: 73'8" W x 68' D
Levels: 1
Square Footage: 5,632
Main Level Sq. Ft.: 2,816
Lower Level Sq. Ft.: 2,816
Bedrooms: 4
Bathrooms: 3½
Foundation: Crawl space, slab, basement or walkout
CompleteCost List Available: Yes
Price Category: J

A graceful stone exterior and elegantly designed interior make for luxurious living in this spacious home.

Features:

- **Great Room:** Everything you need for an evening in, this great room features a gas fireplace, built-in shelving and entertainment center, and vaulted ceilings.

- **Kitchen:** This open layout offers plenty of storage and workspace and includes a walk-in pantry and a snack bar that transitions into the breakfast room.

- **Master Suite:** This luxurious space includes access to the deck, a window-flanked sitting area, two walk-in closets, and a fully equipped master bath.

- **Secondary Bedrooms:** Of the three additional bedrooms, two have direct access to a compartmentalized full bathroom and their own walk-in closet and vanity. The third has vaulted ceilings, built-in bookshelves, and a walk-in closet. This room would make an ideal study or home office.

Main Level Floor Plan

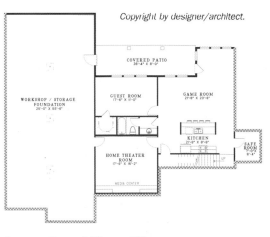

Copyright by designer/architect.

Lower Level Floor Plan

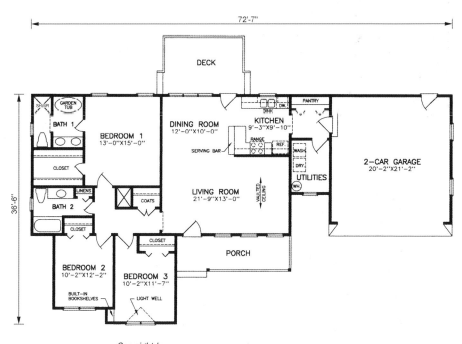

Plan #341071

Dimensions: 72'7" W x 38'6" D
Levels: 1
Square Footage: 1,500
Bedrooms: 3
Bathrooms: 2
Foundation: Crawl space, slab, basement, or walkout
Materials List Available: Yes
Price Category: C

Images provided by designer/architect.

A contemporary ranch design with classic features and country charm, this home promises a relaxing environment that is sure to please.

Features:

- **Vaulted Ceilings:** The living room and dining room feature vaulted ceilings, giving these rooms the feeling of spaciousness.

- **Master Suite:** This private area is located toward the rear of the home to add to its seclusion. The walk-in closet has an abundance of space. The master bath boasts dual vanities and a garden tub.

- **Secondary Bedrooms:** Bedroom 2 makes the perfect child's room and is in close proximity to the second full bathroom. Bedroom 3 has built-in bookshelves and a light well for natural illumination.

- **Garage:** A front-loading two-car garage has easy access to the pantry in the kitchen, making grocery unloading simple. The washer and dryer are also close by.

Copyright by designer/architect.

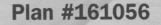

Plan #161056

Dimensions: 86'2" W x 63'8" D
Levels: 1
Square Footage: 5,068
Main Level Sq. Ft.: 3,171
Basement Level Sq. Ft.: 1,897
Bedrooms: 4
Bathrooms: 3½
Foundation: Basement or walkout
Material List Available: Yes
Price Category: J

This home is dedicated to comfort and high lifestyle and sets the standard for excellence.

Images provided by designer/architect.

Features:

- **Open Plan:** A wraparound island with seating is adorned with pillars and arched openings, and it separates the kitchen from the great room and breakfast room. This design element allows the rooms to remain visually open and, paired with a 9-ft. ceiling height, creates a spacious area.

- **Great Room:** A gas fireplace warms this gathering area, and the wall of windows across the rear brings the outdoors in. The built-in entertainment center will be a hit with the entire family.

- **Master Suite:** Delighting you with its size and luxury, this retreat enjoys a stepped ceiling in the sleeping area. The master bath features a garden bathtub and an oversized walk-in closet.

- **Lower Level:** Open stairs introduce this lower level, which mimics the size of the first floor, and, with a 9-ft. ceiling height, offers the same elegant feel of the first floor. Additional bedrooms, a game room, an exercise area, and storage are available options.

Copyright by designer/architect.

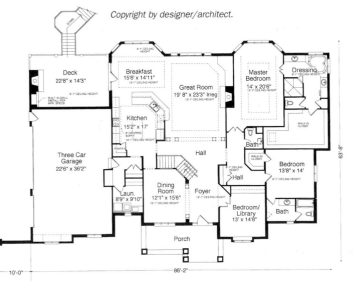

Optional Basement Level Floor Plan

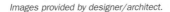

Plan #341073

Dimensions: 74'4" W x 34'4" D

Levels: 1

Square Footage: 1,486

Bedrooms: 3

Bathrooms: 2

Foundation: Crawl space, slab, basement or walkout

Material List Available: No

Price Category: B

This pretty home has classy appeal.

Images provided by designer/architect.

Features:

- **Living Room:** This formal living room is appealing to a family that enjoys spending time relaxing together.

- **Kitchen:** This spacious kitchen features a full cooking center, including built-in ovens.

- **Additional Bedrooms:** Three large bedrooms offer generous closet space, and one has a dressing area with a large walk-in closet that

is perfect for the girl on the go or for getting ready for a night out.

- **Storage Space:** A basement and large closets offer great places to store outdoor equipment and keepsakes.

- **Basement:** As an added feature, the design affords you the opportunity to finish the basement, adding extra space for an entertainment room or extra bedrooms.

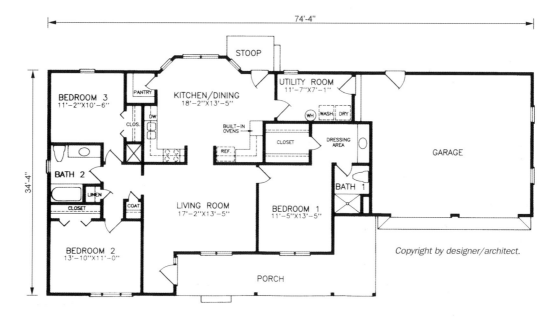

Copyright by designer/architect.

Plan #151703

Dimensions: 69'2" W x 74'10" D

Levels: 1

Square Footage: 2,096

Bedrooms: 3

Bathrooms: 2½

Foundation: Crawl space, slab, basement or walkout

CompleteCost List Available: Yes

Price Category: D

Features:

- **Kitchen:** Situated between both the dining room and breakfast area, this kitchen simplifies mealtime transitions. It even has a snack bar for meals on the go.

- **Master Suite:** Uniquely and conveniently designed, this master suite includes his and her walk-in closets and a master bath with separate vanities, a whirlpool tub sandwiched between them, and a large stall shower.

- **Secondary Bedrooms:** Two additional bedrooms are sequestered on the opposite side of the house and share access to their own full bathroom.

- **Workshop:** A third garage bay that includes a powder room and access to the backyard can function as a workshop.

Your guests will marvel at the gallery lined with built-in bookshelves and the spacious great room with its elegant fireplace and high ceilings in this comfortable home.

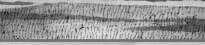

Plan #161085

Dimensions: 67'2" W x 46'2" D

Levels: 1

Square Footage: 1,979

Bedrooms: 3

Bathrooms: 2

Foundation: Walk-out Basement

Materials List Available: No

Price Category: D

Images provided by designer/architect.

This nicely designed floor plan features step-saving convenience, high ceilings, furniture alcoves, and a delightful outdoor living space.

Features:

• **Dining Room:** This formal room and the great room form a large gathering space, and a grand opening to the breakfast area expands the living area.

• **Kitchen:** The snack bar defines this kitchen and offers additional seating. The breakfast area is surrounded by windows and provides a bright and cheery place to start the day.

• **Master Suite:** This suite enjoys a luxurious bath, and two additional bedrooms complete the main floor.

• **Basement:** This house comes with a full walk-out basement, which can be finished for additional square footage.

Rear Elevation

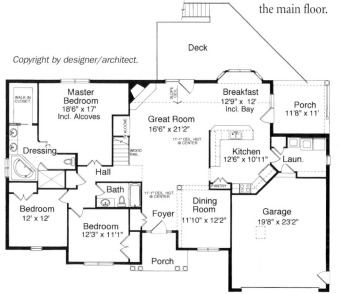

Copyright by designer/architect.

Left Side Elevation

Right Side Elevation

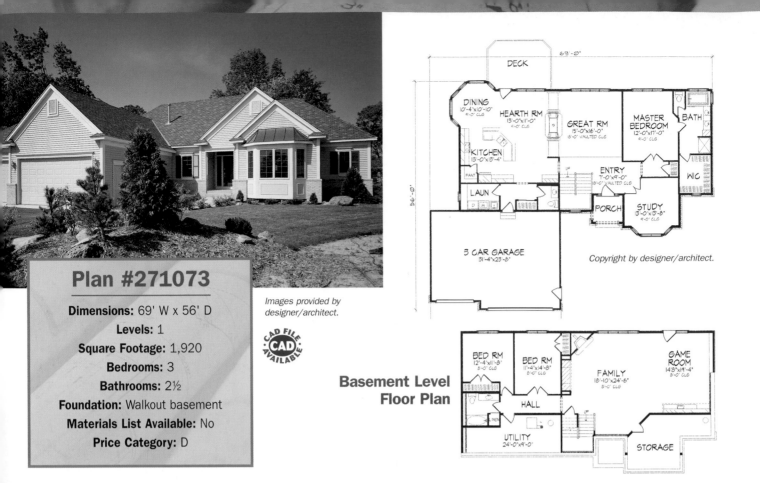

Plan #271073

Dimensions: 69' W x 56' D

Levels: 1

Square Footage: 1,920

Bedrooms: 3

Bathrooms: 2½

Foundation: Walkout basement

Materials List Available: No

Price Category: D

Images provided by designer/architect.

CAD FILE AVAILABLE

Copyright by designer/architect.

Basement Level Floor Plan

Plan #341224

Dimensions: 51'6" W x 49'10" D

Levels: 1

Square Footage: 1,534

Bedrooms: 3

Bathrooms: 2

Foundation: Crawl space, slab, basement or walkout

Material List Available: No

Price Category: C

Images provided by designer/architect.

CAD FILE AVAILABLE

Copyright by designer/architect.

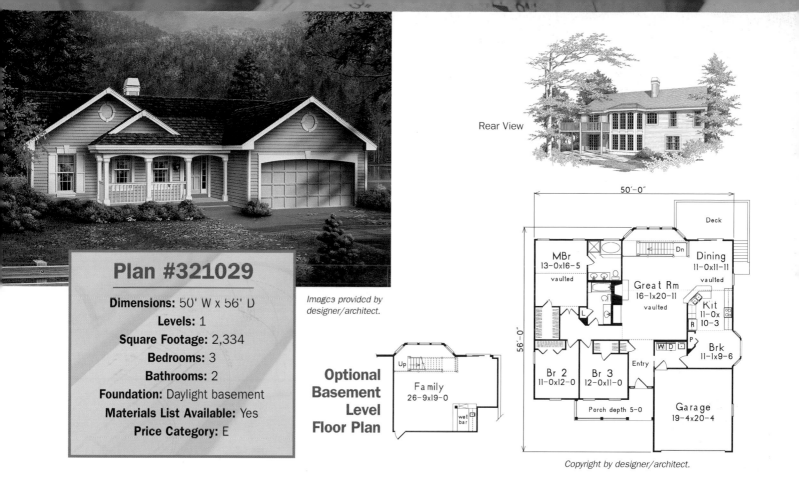

Plan #321029

Dimensions: 50' W x 56' D

Levels: 1

Square Footage: 2,334

Bedrooms: 3

Bathrooms: 2

Foundation: Daylight basement

Materials List Available: Yes

Price Category: E

Rear View

Images provided by designer/architect.

Optional Basement Level Floor Plan

Family 26-9x19-0

wet bar

Up

50'-0"

56'-0"

Deck

MBr 13-0x16-5 vaulted

Dining 11-0x11-11 vaulted

Great Rm 16-1x20-11 vaulted

Kit 11-0x 10-3

Br 2 11-0x12-0

Br 3 12-0x11-0

Entry

Brk 11-1x9-6

WD

Porch depth 5-0

Garage 19-4x20-4

Copyright by designer/architect.

Plan #151372

Dimensions: 50'4" W x 73' D

Levels: 2

Square Footage: 2,676

Main Level Sq. Ft.: 1,797

Upper Level Sq. Ft.: 879

Bedrooms: 4

Bathrooms: 2½

Foundation: Crawl space, slab, basement or walkout

CompleteCost List Available: Yes

Price Category: F

Images provided by designer/architect.

CAD FILE AVAILABLE

Main Level Floor Plan

Copyright by designer/architect.

COVERED PORCH

GARAGE

GREAT ROOM

LAU.

SIDE ENTRY

KITCHEN

BREAKFAST ROOM

M. BATH

FOYER

DINING

MASTER SUITE

COVERED PORCH

SITTING

OPT. BONUS ROOM

BEDROOM 3

BEDROOM 4

OPT. BALCONY WALK

BATH

BEDROOM 2

Upper Level Floor Plan

Copyright by designer/architect.

Images provided by designer/architect.

Plan #341081

Dimensions: 44' W x 36' D

Levels: 1

Square Footage: 1,365

Bedrooms: 3

Bathrooms: 2

Foundation: Crawl space, slab, basement or walkout

Material List Available: No

Price Category: B

Copyright by designer/architect.

Images provided by designer/architect.

Plan #341121

Dimensions: 59' W x 40'8" D

Levels: 1

Square Footage: 1,429

Bedrooms: 3

Bathrooms: 2

Foundation: Crawl space, slab, basement or walkout

Material List Available: Yes

Price Category: B

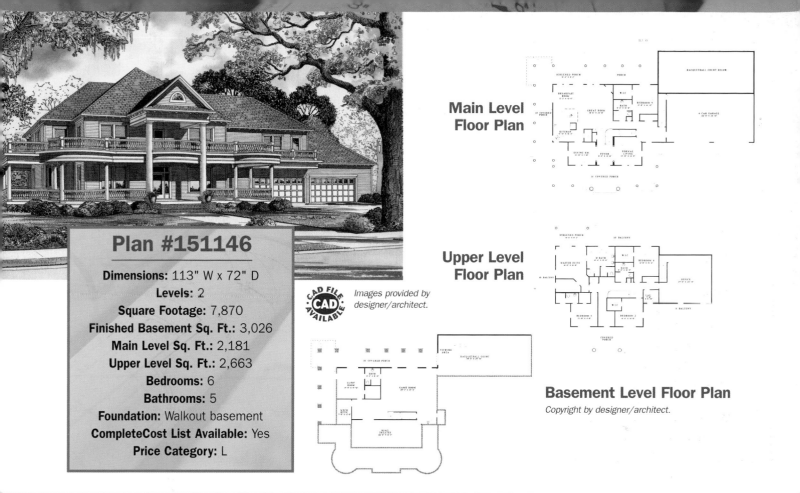

Main Level Floor Plan

Upper Level Floor Plan

Basement Level Floor Plan

Images provided by designer/architect.

Copyright by designer/architect.

Plan #151146

Dimensions: 113" W x 72" D

Levels: 2

Square Footage: 7,870

Finished Basement Sq. Ft.: 3,026

Main Level Sq. Ft.: 2,181

Upper Level Sq. Ft.: 2,663

Bedrooms: 6

Bathrooms: 5

Foundation: Walkout basement

CompleteCost List Available: Yes

Price Category: L

Images provided by designer/architect.

Optional Basement Level Floor Plan

Copyright by designer/architect.

Plan #271076

Dimensions: 69' W x 57' D

Levels: 1

Square Footage: 2,188

Bedrooms: 2-4

Bathrooms: 1½-2½

Foundation: Daylight basement

Materials List Available: No

Price Category: D

Plan #151062

Dimensions: 70'6" W x 48' D

Levels: 2

Square Footage: 3,052

Main Level Sq. Ft.: 2,005

Lower Level Sq. Ft.: 1,047

Bedrooms: 4

Bathrooms: 3

Foundation: Walkout; basement for fee

CompleteCost List Available: Yes

Price Category: E

Images provided by designer/architect.

CAD FILE AVAILABLE

Main Level Floor Plan

Lower Level Floor Plan

Copyright by designer/architect.

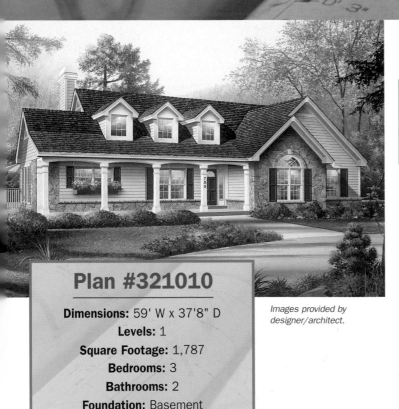

Plan #321010

Dimensions: 59' W x 37'8" D

Levels: 1

Square Footage: 1,787

Bedrooms: 3

Bathrooms: 2

Foundation: Basement

Materials List Available: Yes

Price Category: C

Images provided by designer/architect.

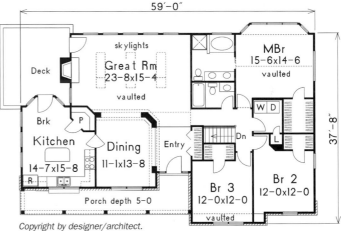

Copyright by designer/architect.

SMARTtip

Country Décor in Your Bathroom

Collections are often part of a country decor, even in the bathroom. All you need is three or more of anything that have size, shape, or color in common. You can mass them on walls, on shelves, on the windowsills, or even along the edge of the tub.

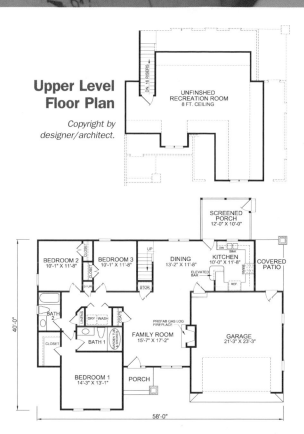

Upper Level Floor Plan

Copyright by designer/architect.

Plan #341084

Dimensions: 58' W x 40' D

Levels: 1.5

Square Footage: 1,429

Bedrooms: 3

Bathrooms: 2

Foundation: Crawl space, slab, basement or walkout

Material List Available: No

Price Category: B

Images provided by designer/architect.

Main Level Floor Plan

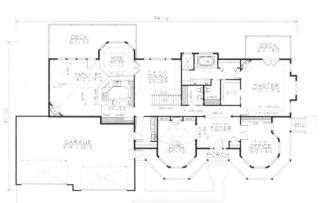

Main Level Floor Plan

Plan #541045

Dimensions: 98'6" W x 51'10" D

Levels: 1

Square Footage: 5,120

Main Level Sq. Ft.: 2,560

Lower Level Sq. Ft.: 2,560

Bedrooms: 5

Bathrooms: 3½

Foundation: Walkout

Material List Available: No

Price Category: J

Images provided by designer/architect.

CAD FILE AVAILABLE

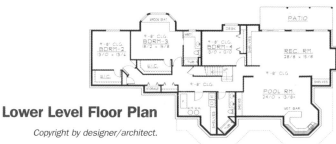

Lower Level Floor Plan

Copyright by designer/architect.

Plan #161068

Dimensions: 61'6" W x 44'6" D
Levels: 2
Square Footage: 3,084
Main Level Sq. Ft.: 1,676
Upper Level Sq. Ft.: 1,408
Bedrooms: 4
Bathrooms: 2½
Foundation: Walkout
Material List Available: Yes
Price Category: G

This beautiful solid brick home's exterior is adorned with brick quoins and limestone keys.

Images provided by designer/architect.

Features:

- Foyer: The angled stairs decorate this two-story foyer. The two coat closets are an added bonus.

- Dining Room: The dropped soffit at the perimeter of this room adds a distinctive design touch. A butler's pantry between the kitchen and dining room will come in handy at mealtime.

- Master Suite: The second floor balcony over looks the foyer and leads to this master suite. The luxurious bath includes a double vanity, linen cabinet, whirlpool tub, and a shower enclosure.

- Secondary Bedrooms: Three additional bedrooms, each with a walk-in closet, complete this family home.

Rear Elevation

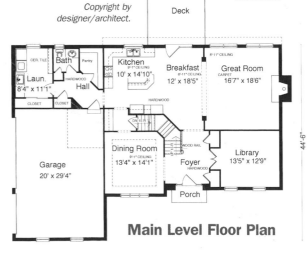

Main Level Floor Plan

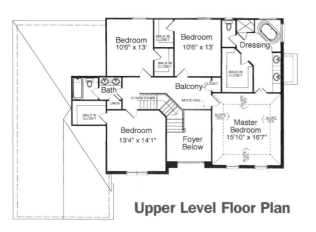

Upper Level Floor Plan

Plan #151702

Dimensions: 54'2" W x 56'4" D
Levels: 1
Square Footage: 1,798
Bedrooms: 3
Bathrooms: 2
Foundation: Basement or walkout
Complete Cost List Available: Yes
Price Category: C

Images provided by designer/architect.

The cozy appearance of this almost 1,800-square-foot home belies the stylish and spacious design of the interior.

Features:

- **Great Room:** Find peace at the center of your home with this large space, which is perfect for entertaining or just quietly reading by the fireplace.

- **Kitchen:** Filled with natural light from the adjacent breakfast room, which is flanked by windows, this kitchen is efficiently designed with ample workspace and storage for the family chef.

- **Master Suite:** French doors and a 9-foot boxed ceiling highlight this master suite. The attached master bath includes his and her sinks, a luxurious walk-in closet, a whirlpool tub, and separate shower.

- **Secondary Bedrooms:** Two additional bedrooms are sequestered on the opposite side of the house and share access to their own full bathroom. The bedroom at the front of the house also features a beautiful bay window.

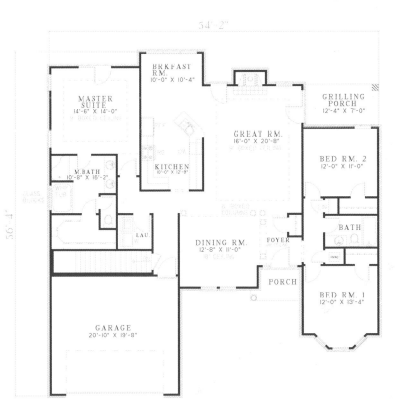

Copyright by designer/architect.

Plan #161163

Dimensions: 83'4" W x 57'4" D

Levels: 1

Square Footage: 2,619

Bedrooms: 2

Bathrooms: 2

Foundation: Walkout; crawl space, slab or basement for fee

Material List Available: No

Price Category: F

Images provided by designer/architect.

This traditional brick home blends an updated exterior with a contemporary interior design.

Features:

- **Porches:** Two porches, one with a fireplace, are great places to relax on lazy days and warm evenings.

- **Great Room:** This spacious great room is great for relaxing in front of the fire at the end of the day or watching Saturday-morning cartoons with the kids.

- **Kitchen:** This highly efficient design, complete with island, snack bar, and plenty of workspace and storage, is just steps away from the sunlit breakfast room and the formal dining room, simplifying meal transitions.

- **Master Suite:** This master suite has enough space for something extra, such as an entertainment or sitting area. The full bath features his and her vanities, a whirlpool tub, separate stall shower, and a sizeable walk-in closet.

Rear Elevation

Copyright by designer/architect.

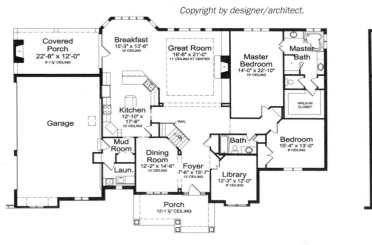

Main Level Floor Plan

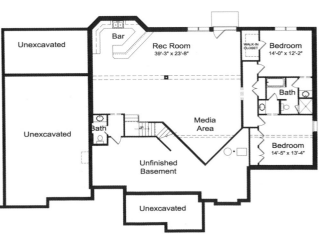

Basement Level Floor Plan

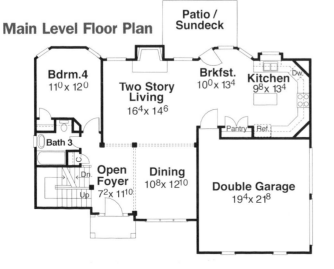

Plan #141028

Dimensions: 48' W x 36'4" D
Levels: 2
Square Footage: 2,215
Main Level Sq. Ft.: 1,075
Upper Level Sq. Ft.: 1,140
Bedrooms: 4
Bathrooms: 3
Foundation: Basement
Materials List Available: Yes
Price Category: E

Don't let appearances fool you. Designed to make efficient use of space without sacrificing style, this charming cottage offers more room than you might expect.

This home, as shown in the photograph, may differ from the actual blueprints. For more detailed information, please check the floor plans carefully.

Images provided by designer/architect.

Features:

- **Living Area:** A delightful foyer with a U-shaped staircase that leads to the second floor welcomes you and introduces you to this comfortable living area, perfect for intimate gatherings of family or friends.

- **Kitchen:** Designed with convenience in mind, incorporating ample counter space and cabinets, this kitchen is a pleasure in which to work.

- **Master Suite:** This second-floor master suite, with windows overlooking the rear of the house, offers the option of a dramatic ceiling treatment. You will appreciate the closet behind the master bath, well-suited for clothing and low storage.

- **Garage:** An attached two-bay garage offers additional storage space.

Main Level Floor Plan

Copyright by designer/architect.

Upper Level Floor Plan

Plan #151092

Dimensions: 27' W x 45' D

Levels: 2

Square Footage: 1,251

Main Level Sq. Ft.: 609

Upper Level Sq. Ft.: 642

Bedrooms: 3

Bathrooms: 2½

Foundation: Crawl space, slab, basement or walkout

CompleteCost List Available: Yes

Price Category: A

Images provided by designer/architect.

Main Level Floor Plan

Copyright by designer/architect.

Upper Level Floor Plan

Plan #151457

Dimensions: 84'2" W x 62' D

Levels: 2

Square Footage: 4,828

Main Level Sq. Ft.: 1,766

Lower Level Sq. Ft.: 3,062

Bedrooms: 4

Bathrooms: 4

Foundation: Basement or walkout

CompleteCost List Available: Yes

Price Category: I

Images provided by designer/architect.

Main Level Floor Plan

Lower Level Floor Plan

Copyright by designer/architect.

Main Level Floor Plan

Upper Level Floor Plan

Copyright by designer/architect.

Images provided by designer/architect.

Plan #151315

Dimensions: 68'2" W x 61' D

Levels: 2

Square Footage: 3,556

Main Level Sq. Ft.: 1,583

Upper Level Sq. Ft.: 1,973

Bedrooms: 3

Bathrooms: 3½

Foundation: Crawl space, slab, basement or walkout

CompleteCost List Available: Yes

Price Category: H

Plan #481020

Dimensions: 74'8" W x 54' D

Levels: 1

Square Footage: 3,141

Main Level Sq. Ft.: 1,794

Lower Level Sq. Ft.: 1,347

Bedrooms: 5

Bathrooms: 3

Foundation: Walkout basement

Material List Available: No

Price Category: G

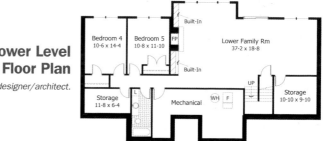

Lower Level Floor Plan

Copyright by designer/architect.

Images provided by designer/architect.

Main Level Floor Plan

DINING 11'-0" X 10'-0"
KITCHEN 17'-5" X 10'-0"
BKFST. AREA
REF.
COATS
LIVING ROOM 14'-6" X 14'-8"
BATH 1
CLOSET
BEDROOM 1 14'-6" X 10'-9"
GARAGE
29'-10"
STOOP

Upper Level Floor Plan

58'-6"

BATH 3
LIN.
BEDROOM 3 12'-5" X 11'-6"
BATH 2
BEDROOM 2 18'-2" X 15'-0"
BEDROOM 4 12'-0" X 18'-6"
CLOSET
CLOSET
CLOSET

Copyright by designer/architect.

Plan #341291

Dimensions: 58'6" W x 29'10" D

Levels: 1.5

Square Footage: 2,147

Main Level Sq. Ft.: 977

Upper Level Sq. Ft.: 1,170

Bedrooms: 4

Bathrooms: 3

Foundation: Crawl space, slab, basement or walkout

Material List Available: Yes

Price Category: D

Images provided by designer/architect.

CAD FILE AVAILABLE

100'-2"

Master Suite 11'-0 x 15-4 14' Vault Clg
Built-In
Great Rm 17'-0 x 15-6 12' Clg
Kit/Dinette 20-4 x 17-4 9' Clg
DW
FP
Built-In
Foyer 12' Clg
Study 11-0 x 10-10 9' Clg
DN
O
Ref
W D
Plant Shelf
WIC
61'-8"
Garage 38-0 x 26-0

Lower Level Floor Plan

Copyright by designer/architect.

Bedroom 2 10-6 x 10-10
Bedroom 3 10-8 x 10-10
Family Rm 25-10 x 17-4
Built-In
UP
Bar Ref
Mechanical
WH F

Plan #481014

Dimensions: 100'2" W x 61'8" D

Levels: 1

Square Footage: 2,706

Main Level Sq. Ft.: 1,623

Lower Level Sq. Ft.: 1,083

Bedrooms: 4

Bathrooms: 2½

Foundation: Walkout basement

Material List Available: No

Price Category: F

Images provided by designer/architect.

Plan #151668

Dimensions: 39' W x 72'4" D

Levels: 1

Square Footage: 1,750

Bedrooms: 3

Bathrooms: 2

Foundation: Crawl space, slab, basement or walkout

CompleteCost List Available: Yes

Price Category: C

Images provided by designer/architect.

CAD FILE AVAILABLE

Copyright by designer/architect.

Plan #481015

Dimensions: 72'4" W x 50' D

Levels: 2

Square Footage: 2,790

Main Level Sq. Ft.: 1,492

Upper Level Sq. Ft.: 1,298

Bedrooms: 4

Bathrooms: 2½

Foundation: Walkout

Material List Available: No

Price Category: F

Images provided by designer/architect.

Rear Elevation

Copyright by designer/architect.

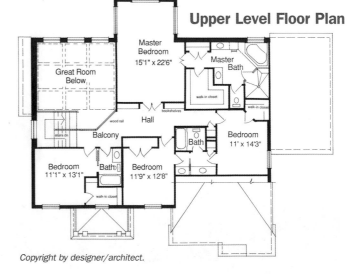

Plan #161094

Dimensions: 68'8" W x 56'8" D
Levels: 2
Square Footage: 3,366
Main Level Sq. Ft.: 1,759
Upper Level Sq. Ft.: 1,607
Bedrooms: 5
Bathrooms: 4
Foundation: Walkout basement
Material List Available: No
Price Category: G

This home, as shown in the photograph, may differ from the actual blueprints. For more detailed information, please check the floor plans carefully.

Images provided by designer/architect.

This luxurious two-story home combines a stately exterior style with a large, functional floor plan.

Features:

- **Great Room:** The volume ceiling in this room is decorated with wood beams and reaches a two-story height, while 9-ft. ceiling heights prevail throughout the rest of the first floor.

- **Bright and Open:** Split stairs lead to the second-floor balcony, which offers a dramatic view of the great room. Light radiates through the multiple rear windows

to flood the great room, breakfast area, and kitchen with natural daylight.

- **Master Suite:** Built-in bookshelves flank the entrance to this lavish retreat, with its large sitting area, which is surrounded by windows, and deluxe master bath, which sports spacious closets, dual vanities, and an oversized whirlpool tub.

- **Bedrooms:** Three more bedrooms, each with large closets and private access to the bathroom, complete this family-friendly home.

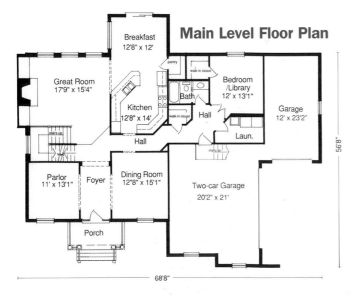

Copyright by designer/architect.

Great Room

Kitchen

Plan #551042

Dimensions: 32' W x 56' D
Levels: 2
Square Footage: 2,127
Main Level Sq. Ft.: 965
Upper Level Sq. Ft.: 1,162
Bedrooms: 3
Bathrooms: 2½
Foundation: Crawl space or walkout; slab or basement for fee
Material List Available: No
Price Category: D

Images provided by designer/architect.

The design of this home reflects the attention to detail of the Craftsman style.

Features:

- Foyer: The porch shelters you from the elements as you enter into this foyer. A large coat closet is conveniently located to your right.

- Great Room: A large fireplace is the focal point of this gathering area. Windows provide a great view into the backyard.

- Kitchen: This efficiently designed island kitchen, with a pass-through to the great room, will be an added plus for the chef in the family. The open floor plan makes the area seem bright and airy.

- Upper Level: The master suite and two bedrooms, with walk-in closets, occupy this level. A bonus room, or fourth bedroom, is also located on this level.

Main Level Floor Plan

PATIO

DINING 12-8 x 13-4

GREAT ROOM 15-8 x 18-4

KITCHEN 13-4 x 15-8

UP   FOYER

UTIL   PDR

COV'D PORCH

2-CAR GARAGE 19-4 x 19-8

Upper Level Floor Plan

WIC

MSTR BEDRM 13-4 x 15-8

BEDRM 2 11-4 x 11-8

WIC

MBA

BEDRM 3 10-4 x 11-8

WIC

DN   OPEN

BA2

BONUS/ BEDRM 4 15-4 x 14-0

Copyright by designer/architect.

Plan #161164

Dimensions: 65'3" W x 49' D

Levels: 1

Square Footage: 1,776

Bedrooms: 3

Bathrooms: 2

Foundation: Basement or walkout; crawl space or slab for fee

Material List Available: Yes

Price Category: C

Images provided by designer/architect.

A Craftsman-style exterior and a well-designed interior makes this home perfect.

Features:

- **Foyer:** Double doors open from the covered front porch into this elegant foyer. The handy closet is an added plus.

- **Great Room:** This perfect gathering area features a sloped ceiling, which creates an open feeling; the fireplace adds a cozy intimacy to the room.

- **Kitchen:** There is plenty of room for all the chefs in the family to cook in this large kitchen. The open counter into the dining area can serve as a buffet table.

- **Master Suite:** Located on the opposite side of the home from the secondary bedrooms for privacy, the bath in this master suite boasts a whirlpool tub, stall shower, and dual vanities.

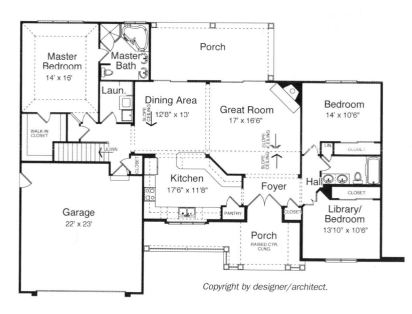

Copyright by designer/architect.

Rear Elevation

Plan #341105

Dimensions: 42' W x 44'6" D
Levels: 2
Square Footage: 1,822
Main Level Sq. Ft.: 911
Upper Level Sq. Ft.: 911
Bedrooms: 3
Bathrooms: 2½
Foundation: Crawl space, slab, basement or walkout
Material List Available: No
Price Category: D

Images provided by designer/architect.

This lovely transitional design greets you with classic Craftsman-style forms and then offers a welcoming embrace with its custom features.

Features:

- Family Room: Illuminated by a bay of windows during the day, and glowing with the light of a fire at night, this space is perfect for entertaining family and friends.

- Kitchen: Featuring plenty of workspace and storage, this kitchen is also adjacent to both the sunny breakfast nook and formal dining room, simplifying mealtime transitions.

- Master Suite: Situated on the upper floor away from the daily tumult, this relaxing retreat boasts bay windows, a walk-in closet, and a full bath with a garden tub.

- Secondary Bedrooms: Both of the two additional bedrooms have ample closet space and access to a full bathroom.

- Bonus Room: This unfinished space can be anything you dream up, including home office, an entertainment area, or a study space.

Main Level Floor Plan

Upper Level Floor Plan

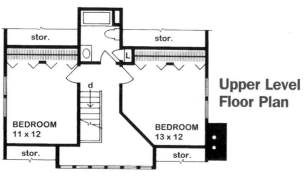

Plan #381046

Dimensions: 32' W x 36' D

Levels: 2

Square Footage: 1,605

Main Level Sq. Ft.: 1,010

Upper Level Sq. Ft.: 595

Bedrooms: 3

Bathrooms: 2

Foundation: Basement or walkout

Material List Available: Yes

Price Category: C

Images provided by designer/architect.

Natural stone and craftsman-style columns dress up this traditional exterior.

Features:

- **Living Room:** Welcome guests from the covered entry and into this inviting living room, illuminated by several windows and a glowing fireplace.

- **Kitchen:** Surrounded by workspace and storage, this efficient kitchen also provides three options for simple mealtime transitions.

Enjoy dining out on the screened porch, in the breakfast nook, or in the formal dining room.

- **Master Suite:** This spacious area features a walk-in closet to simplify the process of getting ready in the morning. There is also private access to the screened porch through French doors.

- **Secondary Bedrooms:** Tucked away in the quiet space on the second floor, two comparably sized bedrooms include wide closets and access to a shared bathroom.

Main Level Floor Plan

Upper Level Floor Plan

Copyright by designer/architect.

Main Level Floor Plan

Images provided by designer/architect.

Upper Level Floor Plan

Copyright by designer/architect.

Plan #551084

Dimensions: 40' W x 52' D

Levels: 2

Square Footage: 2,520

Main Level Sq. Ft.: 1,365

Upper Level Sq. Ft.: 1,155

Bedrooms: 3

Bathrooms: 2½

Foundation: Crawl space or walkout; slab or basement for fee

Material List Available: No

Price Category: E

Main Level Floor Plan

Images provided by designer/architect.

Lower Level Floor Plan

Copyright by designer/architect.

Plan #451140

Dimensions: 78'7" W x 38'6" D

Levels: 2

Square Footage: 2,733

Main Level Sq. Ft.: 1,420

Lower Level Sq. Ft.: 1,313

Bedrooms: 2

Bathrooms: 2½

Foundation: Walkout

Material List Available: No

Price Category: F

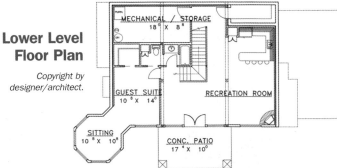

Main Level Floor Plan

Upper Level Floor Plan

Images provided by designer/architect.

Copyright by designer/architect.

Plan #551086

Dimensions: 40' W x 54'8" D

Levels: 2

Square Footage: 2,673

Main Level Sq. Ft.: 1,378

Upper Level Sq. Ft.: 1,295

Bedrooms: 3

Bathrooms: 2½

Foundation: Crawl space or walkout; slab or basement for fcc

Material List Available: No

Price Category: F

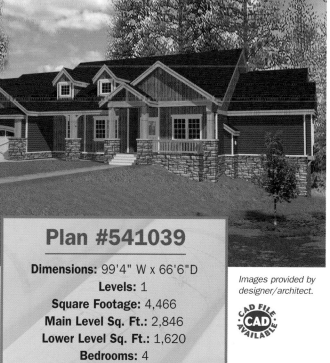

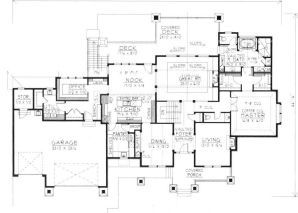

Main Level Floor Plan

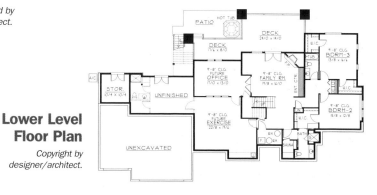

Lower Level Floor Plan

Copyright by designer/architect.

Plan #541039

Dimensions: 99'4" W x 66'6"D

Levels: 1

Square Footage: 4,466

Main Level Sq. Ft.: 2,846

Lower Level Sq. Ft.: 1,620

Bedrooms: 4

Bathrooms: 3½

Foundation: Walkout; basement for fee

Material List Available: No

Price Category: I

Images provided by designer/architect.

CAD FILE AVAILABLE

Plan #551080

Dimensions: 26' W x 62' D
Levels: 2
Square Footage: 3,506
Main Level Sq. Ft.: 1,419
Upper Level Sq. Ft.: 1,328
Lower Level Sq. Ft.: 759
Bedrooms: 4
Bathrooms: 3½
Foundation: Basement or walkout
Material List Available: No
Price Category: H

Images provided by designer/architect.

This Craftsman-style home with its cozy porch fits a relaxed lifestyle perfectly.

Features:

- Den: This private den, located off of the foyer, would make an ideal home office.

- Kitchen: This open kitchen with island is every cook's dream. It contains a walk-in pantry and plenty of room to move around.

- Master Suite: Relax in this luxury master suite, which includes a five-fixture bath and private deck. It is the perfect place to unwind after a long day.

- Flexible Spaces: A bonus room upstairs and an additional room in the basement create lots of useable space for a game room, a rec room, a home theatre, or just great places to relax with the family.

- Garage: Placing the garage under the porch is perfect for sloped lots; while the porch and stone columns add curb appeal, they also serve to draw attention away from the garage doors.

Copyright by designer/architect.

Main Level Floor Plan

Upper Level Floor Plan

Lower Level Floor Plan

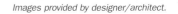

Plan #451380

Dimensions: 37' W x 42' D
Levels: 2
Square Footage: 2,823
Main Level Sq. Ft.: 1,512
Upper Level Sq. Ft.: 1,311
Bedrooms: 4
Bathrooms: 2½
Foundation: Basement and walkout
Material List Available: No
Price Category: F

This stunning design is beautiful on the outside, and lovely and functional on the inside.

CAD FILE AVAILABLE

Images provided by designer/architect.

Features:

- **Living Room:** Bask in the quiet glow of abundant natural light; cozy up to a crackling fire; or gather with the family in this large, relaxing area.

- **Kitchen:** From culinary expert to family cook, everyone will find this kitchen's workspaces and storage just what they need to create special meals. A sun-drenched family area shares the space and opens onto the porch.

- **Master Suite:** This retreat features a large sleeping area and a walk-in closet. The master bath boasts dual vanities, a separate shower, and a spa tub.

- **Secondary Bedrooms:** Three additional bedrooms share the upper level with the master suite. They share a common full bathroom.

Copyright by designer/architect.

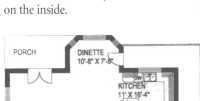

Main Level Floor Plan

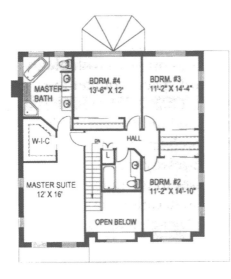

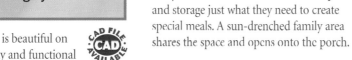

Upper Level Floor Plan

Optional Basement Level Floor Plan

Storage Options for Your Home

O ne of the great things about moving into a new home is all that new, uncluttered closet space you gain. But if you are like most homeowners, storage of all types will quickly become scarce, especially in a smaller home. Here are some tips for expanding and organizing storage space.

Shelving Types

Shelving is an easy and economical way to add extra storage space in almost any part of your home—along walls, inside closets, and even in the basement or garage. Building shelves doesn't usually require a lot of skill or specialized tools, so this is one project just about any do-it-yourselfer can handle. And unless you decide to use hardwood—which looks great but costs a bundle—it won't cost a lot to install them either.

Solid wood shelving is the way to go when you want to show off the wood or your work.

Plywood and particleboard offer a couple of advantages when it comes to shelving, though. They cost less than solid wood, and can be bought faced with decorative surfaces. They also come in sheets, which makes them ideal for a really wide

Home offices require a mix of storage options: open shelving, drawers, and file cabinets.

shelf. Inexpensive, manufactured storage units ready for assembly often are made from melamine-coated particleboard.

Wood trim will help match your new shelves to the rest of the room or add some interesting detail. Trim is also a handy way to hide seams, gaps, exposed edges of plywood, and other blemishes. You can get trim in either hardwood or softwood. If you plan on finishing a project with stain or sealer, make sure the trim

matches the wood you used for the rest of the project.

Bracket Options

There are two basic types of ready-to-hang shelving supports: stationary shelf brackets and shelving standards. Stationary brackets come in many sizes and styles, and range from utilitarian to decorative. Shelving standards are slotted metal strips that support various types of shelf brackets.

Mounting Brackets

For maximum strength, anchor shelf supports to wall studs. If your shelf will carry a light load, you can anchor its supports between studs with mollies or toggle bolts. Attaching supports directly to the studs is always better, though, because sooner or later something heavy will wind up on the shelf. Use masonry anchors to attach shelf supports to brick or concrete. You can also attach shelf supports to a ledger attached to wall studs with 3-inch drywall screws.

Ready-made shelving offers a quick alternative to building your own shelves.

Mud rooms and areas near the entrance the family uses most should have storage for coats, hats, and boots.

Shelf Standards. Metal shelf standards can be mounted directly to walls or, for a more decorative look, you can insert the standards in grooves routed into the wood itself or into hardwood strips.

Cut the standards to fit with a hacksaw, and attach them to wall studs with 3-inch drywall screws. Use a carpenter's level to make sure that both standards are plumb and that the corresponding mounting slots are level. Mount standards 6 inches from the ends of shelving to prevent sagging. For long wall shelves, install standards every 48 inches.

Many kitchen and closet storage systems use wire grids that attach to walls with molded plastic brackets. If you anticipate light loads, you can mount these brackets to drywall using the screws and expansion anchors usually included with such systems. But for heavier loads, use drywall screws to fasten the brackets directly to the wall studs.

Customized Storage

Built-in storage units are an excellent way to make the most of existing storage space in your home. Ready-made or custom-made built-in shelving units, entertainment centers, kitchen cabinets, medicine cabinets, window seats, and under-bed drawers are not only inexpensive and easy to assemble, they allow you to add a unique, personalized touch to your living spaces.

Built-in Shelving

A built-in shelving unit can create valuable storage capacity from an overlooked wall space, such as the area between windows or between a door and its adjacent corner. To construct the shelving, you'll need 1×10 or 1×12 lumber for side panels, top and base panels, and shelves; four 2×2 strips for spreaders; trim molding to conceal gaps along the top and bottom of the unit; 12d

common nails and 6d finishing nails. If the unit will be bearing heavy loads, use hardwood boards, and make sure that the shelves span no more than 36 inches. To make installation easier, cut the side pieces an inch shorter than the ceiling height. (This way, you'll be able to tilt the unit into position without scraping the ceiling.) Paint or stain the wood pieces before assembling the unit. Hang the shelves from pegs or end clips inserted into holes drilled in the side pieces.

Adding Closet Space

What homeowner, even a new homeowner, hasn't complained about having too little closet space? Fortunately, there are almost always ways to find a bit more closet space or to make the closet space you have more efficient. Often, it isn't the space that is lacking but how the space is organized that is the problem. The trick is to find ways to help you organize the space.

Ventilated closet systems help keep your belongings neat and within easy reach.

Organizing Systems. The easiest and most obvious solution is one of the many commercial closet organizing systems now on the market. There are a number of configurations available, and you can customize most systems to meet your needs. Constructing your own version of a commercial closet organizer is another option. With a combination of shelves and plywood partitions, you can divide a closet into storage zones, with a single clothes pole on one side for full-length garments; double clothes poles on the other side for half-length garments like jackets, skirts, or slacks; a column of narrow shelves between the two for folded items or shoes; and one or more closet-wide shelves on top.

Before designing a closet system, above, inventory all of the items you want to store in the closet.

Metal shelf standards, left, can provide a quick solution for creating shelving in areas where it is needed.

Cedar Closets

Both solid cedar boards and composite cedar panels have only moderate resistance to insects, and are used more for their pleasant aroma and appearance. The sheets of pressed red and tan particles are no less aromatic than solid wood, but the panels are 40 to 50 percent less expensive, and are easier to install. Solid boards require more carpentry work, and are likely to produce a fair amount of waste unless you piece the courses and create more joints. To gain the maximum effect, every inside surface should be covered, including the ceiling and the back of the door. The simplest option is to use ¼-inch-thick panels, which are easy to cut into big sections that cover walls in one or two pieces. Try to keep cedar seams in boards or panels from falling over drywall seams. No stain, sealer, or clear finish is needed; just leave the wood raw. The cedar aroma will fade over the years as natural oils crystallize on the surface. But you can easily regenerate the

For garages and basements, you'll find a combination of shelving and hanging hooks keeps tools and equipment organized, opposite top.

Storage for basements, garages, and workshops, opposite bottom, should include a cabinet that locks for storage of dangerous chemicals.

Specialized storage accessories, such as the sports storage system shown at right, not only keeps items organized but they also keep them in ready-to-play condition.

scent from the panels by scuffing the surface with fine sandpaper.

Ideas for Basements, Garages, and Workshops

Workshops and other utility areas such as garages, attics, and basements can benefit from storage upgrades as much as any other room in the home—perhaps even more so, as utility areas are prone to clutter. Convenience, flexibility, and safety are the things to keep in mind when reorganizing your work space. Try to provide storage space for tools and hardware as near as possible to where they'll be used. In addition to a sturdy workbench, utility shelving

is a mainstay in any workshop. You can buy ready-to-assemble units or make your own using ¾-inch particleboard or plywood shelves and ¾ × 1½-inch (1×2) hardwood stock for cleats (nailed to the wall), ribs (nailed to the front underside of the shelves), and vertical shelf supports.

DIY Utility Storage. Don't forget about pegboard. To make a pegboard tool rack, attach washers to the back of the pegboard with hot glue, spacing the washers to coincide with wall studs. Position the pegboard so that the rear washers are located over studs. Drive drywall screws through finish washers and the pegboard into studs. (Use masonry anchors for concrete walls.)

Finally, try to take advantage of any oth-

erwise wasted space. The area in your garage above your parked car is the ideal spot for a U-shaped lumber storage rack, made of 1×4 stock and connecting plates. The space in front of the car could be used for a storage cabinet or even a workbench.

Instant Storage. To utilize the overhead space in your garage, build deep storage platforms supported by ledgers screwed to wall studs and threaded rods hooked to ceiling joists or rafters. You can also hang tools from the walls by mounting pegboard. You can buy sets with a variety of hooks and brackets for tools. For small items, such as jars of nails, make shallow shelves by nailing 1×4 boards between the exposed studs.

Suit storage to your needs. The narrow pullout pantry above is located between the refrigerator and a food-preparation area. Notice how you can access the shelves from both sides of the pantry when it is extended.

Kitchen Storage

The type of storage in a kitchen is almost as important as the amount. Some people like at least a few open shelves for displaying attractive china or glassware; others want absolutely everything tucked away behind doors.

What are your storage needs? The answer depends partly on your food shopping habits and partly on how many pots, pans, and other pieces of kitchen equipment you have or would like to have. A family that goes food shopping several times a week and prepares mostly fresh foods needs more refrigerator space, less freezer capacity, and fewer cabinets than a family that prefers packaged or prepared foods and makes only infrequent forays to the local supermarket.

Planning

To help clarify your needs, mentally walk yourself through a typical meal and list the utensils used to prepare food, where you got them, and your progress throughout the work area. And don't limit yourself to full-scale meals. Much kitchen work is devoted to preparing snacks, reheating leftovers, and making lunches for the kids to take to school.

Food Preparation. During food preparation, the sink and stove come into use. Some families rely heavily on the microwave for reheating. Using water means repeated trips to the sink, so that area might be the best place to keep a steamer, salad spinner, and coffee and tea canisters, as well as glassware and cups. Near the stove you may want storage for odd-shaped items such as a fish poacher or wok. You can hang frequently used pans and utensils from a convenient rack; stow other items in cabinets so that they do not collect grease.

During the Meal. When the food is ready, you must take it to the table. If the eating space is nearby, a work counter might turn into a serving counter. If the dining space is in another room, a pass-through facilitates serving.

Storage accessories, such as the pullout pot holder above, come as options from some cabinet manufacturers, or you can install them later yourself. Notice how the side rails hold the pot lids in place. The cabinet below features space for small baskets.

After the Meal. When the meal ends, dishes must go from the table to the sink or dishwasher, and leftovers to storage containers and the refrigerator. Now the stove and counters need to be wiped down and the sink scoured. When the dishwasher finishes its cycle, everything must be put away.

Open versus Closed Storage.
Shelves, pegboards, pot racks, cup hooks, magnetic knife racks, and the like put your utensils on view, which is a good way to personalize your kitchen.

But open storage has drawbacks. Items left out in the open can look messy unless they are kept neatly arranged. Another option is to install glass doors on wall cabinets. This handily solves the dust problem but often costs more than solid doors.

Plan #161102

Dimensions: 99'6" W x 84'2" D
Levels: 1
Square Footage: 6,659
Main Level Sq. Ft.: 3,990
Lower Level Sq. Ft: 2,669
Bedrooms: 4
Bathrooms: 4 full, 2 half
Foundation: Walkout; basement for fee
Material List Available: Yes
Price Category: K

Images provided by designer/architect.

A brick-and-stone exterior with limestone trim and arches decorates the exterior, while the interior explodes with design elements and large spaces to dazzle all who enter.

Features:

- **Great Room:** The 14-ft. ceiling height in this room is defined with columns and a fireplace wall. Triple French doors with an arched transom create the rear wall, and built-in shelving adds the perfect spot to house your big-screen TV.

- **Kitchen:** This spacious gourmet kitchen opens generously to the great room and allows everyone to enjoy the daily activities. A two-level island with cooktop provides casual seating and additional storage.

- **Breakfast Room:** This room is surrounded by windows, creating a bright and cheery place to start your day. Sliding glass doors to the covered porch in the rear add a rich look for outdoor entertaining, and the built-in fire place provides a cozy, warm atmosphere.

- **Master Suite:** This master bedroom suite is fit for royalty, with its stepped ceiling treatment, spacious dressing room, and private exercise room.

- **Lower Level:** This lower level is dedicated to fun and entertaining. A large media area, billiards room, and wet bar are central to sharing this spectacular home with your friends.

Front View

Rear Elevation

Right Side Elevation

Left Side Elevation

Main Level Floor Plan

Lower Level Floor Plan

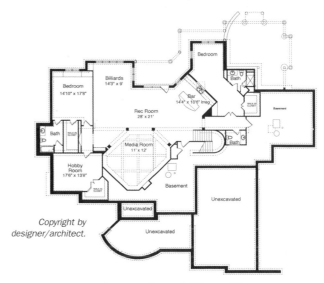

Copyright by designer/architect.

Foyer/Dining Room

Kitchen

Great Room

Porch

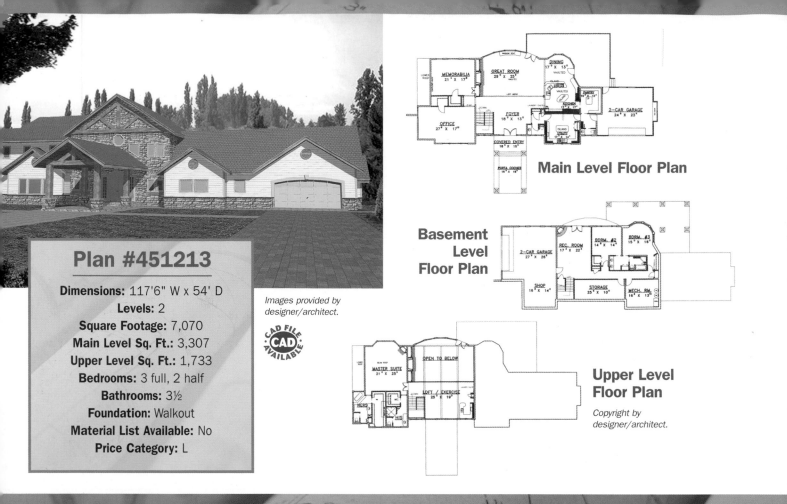

Main Level Floor Plan

Basement Level Floor Plan

Upper Level Floor Plan

Images provided by designer/architect.

Copyright by designer/architect.

Plan #451213

Dimensions: 117'6" W x 54' D
Levels: 2
Square Footage: 7,070
Main Level Sq. Ft.: 3,307
Upper Level Sq. Ft.: 1,733
Bedrooms: 3 full, 2 half
Bathrooms: 3½
Foundation: Walkout
Material List Available: No
Price Category: L

CAD FILE AVAILABLE

Upper Level Floor Plan

Main Level Floor Plan

Images provided by designer/architect.

Copyright by designer/architect.

Plan #481017

Dimensions: 80' W x 49'8" D
Levels: 2
Square Footage: 2,982
Main Level Sq. Ft.: 1,563
Upper Level Sq. Ft.: 1,419
Bedrooms: 4
Bathrooms: 2½
Foundation: Basement
Material List Available: No
Price Category: F

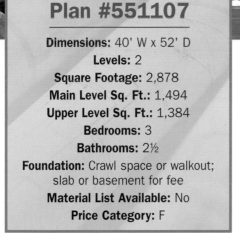

Main Level
Floor Plan

*Copyright by
designer/architect.*

*Images provided by
designer/architect.*

Plan #551107

Dimensions: 40' W x 52' D

Levels: 2

Square Footage: 2,878

Main Level Sq. Ft.: 1,494

Upper Level Sq. Ft.: 1,384

Bedrooms: 3

Bathrooms: 2½

Foundation: Crawl space or walkout; slab or basement for fee

Material List Available: No

Price Category: F

Upper Level
Floor Plan

Basement Level
Floor Plan

Main Level Floor Plan

*Images provided by
designer/architect.*

Plan #551088

Dimensions: 62' W x 41' D

Levels: 2

Square Footage: 2,560

Main Level Sq. Ft.: 1,250

Upper Level Sq. Ft.: 1,310

Bedrooms: 3

Bathrooms: 2½

Foundation: Crawl space or walkout; slab or basement for fee

Material List Available: No

Price Category: E

Upper Level
Floor Plan

*Copyright by
designer/architect.*

Plan #481021

Dimensions: 98'4" W x 55'8" D
Levels: 2
Square Footage: 3,289
Main Level Sq. Ft.: 1,680
Upper Level Sq. Ft.: 1,609
Bedrooms: 3
Bathrooms: 2½
Foundation: Walkout
Material List Available: No
Price Category: G

A large front porch welcomes visitors to this luxury home.

Features:

- **Family Room:** This two-story entertaining area features a beautiful fireplace and is open to the kitchen. The wall of windows will make the space feel light and airy.

- **Dining Room:** A stepped ceiling adds to the elegance of this formal dining area. The butler's pantry is a welcome amenity when it comes to entertaining.

- **Master Suite:** This retreat features a vaulted ceiling and built-in cabinets in the sleeping area. The master bath boasts dual vanities and a private toilet enclosure.

- **Bedrooms:** Two secondary bedrooms share the upper level with the master suite. Both of these bedrooms feature built-in desks.

Images provided by designer/architect.

Family Room

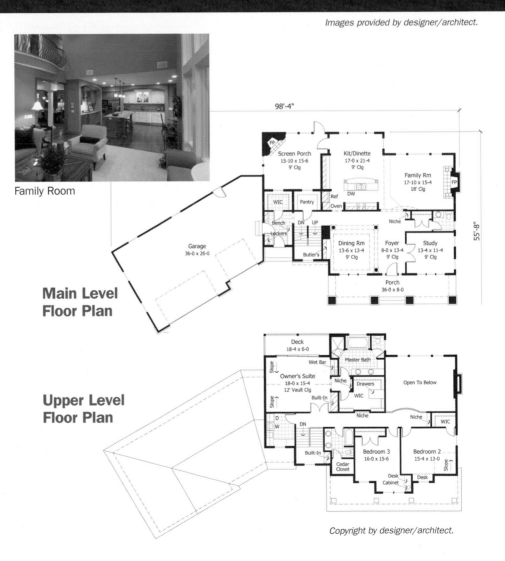

Main Level Floor Plan

Upper Level Floor Plan

Copyright by designer/architect.

Plan #551132

Dimensions: 42' W x 52'6" D
Levels: 2
Square Footage: 2,520
Main Level Sq. Ft.: 1,365
Upper Level Sq. Ft.: 1,155
Bedrooms: 3
Bathrooms: 2½
Foundation: Crawl space, slab or walkout
Material List Available: No
Price Category: E

The exterior of this Craftsman-style home is unmatched. Slanted gables and varying textures make the house a stylish addition to any neighborhood.

Features:

- **Entry:** Cross the threshold through a formal entryway and foyer, and enjoy the view of the open living and dining rooms.

- **Family Room:** Snuggle by the fire in this comfortable family room.

- **Den:** Located off of the kitchen, this quaint room is the perfect accent for making a large home cozier. Use the den as an area for homework or a place where unsightly computer cords and electronics can be concealed.

- **Master Suite:** This bedroom features a vaulted ceiling and walk-in closet. Enter into a luxurious spa-like bathroom, with a whirlpool tub and his and her sinks. Storage space is ample, and a loft overlooks the lower level for a dramatic effect.

- **Garage:** A three-car garage is great for keeping cars out of the elements.

Main Level Floor Plan

Upper Level Floor Plan

Plan #451385

Dimensions: 69' W x 64'6" D

Levels: 1

Square Footage: 1,659

Bedrooms: 2

Bathrooms: 2½

Foundation: Walkout – insulated concrete form

Material List Available: No

Price Category: C

This well-appointed exterior teams up with a straightforward and efficient interior layout.

CAD FILE AVAILABLE

Features:

- **Foyer:** As you enter the home from a covered porch, this foyer offers the convenience of a half bath and a coat closet. The office is close by, allowing business to be conducted without disturbing the rest of the house.

- **Great Room:** This large gathering area boasts a cathedral ceiling and a wall of glass. The rear porch is accessible through the sliding glass doors.

- **Kitchen:** Great for the busy family, this kitchen has all the workspace and storage that the family chef needs, as well as a snack bar that serves as a transition into the large dining room.

- **Lower Level:** A large family room, with a sitting area, occupies most of this level. There is also a second bedroom located on this level.

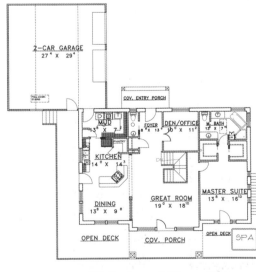

Main Level Floor Plan

Rear Elevation

Lower Level Floor Plan

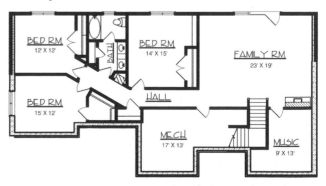

Plan #271077

Dimensions: 69'6" W x 53' D
Levels: 1
Square Footage: 1,786
Bedrooms: 1
Bathrooms: 1½
Foundation: Basement or daylight basement
Materials List Available: No
Price Category: C

Images provided by designer/architect.

This wonderful home has an optional finished basement plan to add three more bedrooms ideal for a growing family.

Features:

- **Great Room:** This large gathering room has a fireplace with built-in cabinets on either side.

- **Kitchen:** This island kitchen, with dinette area, is open to the great room.

- **Master Bedroom:** This luxurious room provides a view of the backyard.

- **Master Bath:** This private bathroom has a walk-in closet and double vanities.

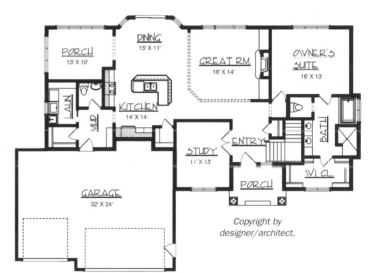

Copyright by designer/architect.

Optional Basement Level Floor Plan

Plan #481116

Dimensions: 70'6" W x 57' D

Levels: 2

Square Footage: 3,249

Main Level Sq. Ft.: 1,620

Upper Level Sq. Ft.: 1,629

Bedrooms: 4

Bathrooms: 2½

Foundation: Walkout

Material List Available: No

Price Category: G

Images provided by designer/architect.

This Country-style home is a gorgeous addition to any neighborhood. The elaborate gables and numerous windows are decorative touches that distinguish the house.

Features:

• Foyer: Enter through this foyer into to a cozy family room.

• Kitchen: This large kitchen is a cooking aficionado's dream, with its island and the option of serving your meals in a dinette or formal dining area.

• Owner's Suite: This owner's suite-featuring vaulted ceilings, a walk-in closet, and a full bath-provides privacy in a luxurious amount of space.

• Secondary Bedrooms: Three additional bedrooms and two walk-in closets accommodate a growing family and create storage for clothes or sports equipment.

• Loft: This captivating loft opens up to the lower floor, adding to the charm of the beautiful home.

• Garage: This three-car garage with a work shop is great for the do-it-yourselfer or crafting enthusiast.

Rear Elevation

Copyright by designer/architect.

Main Level Floor Plan

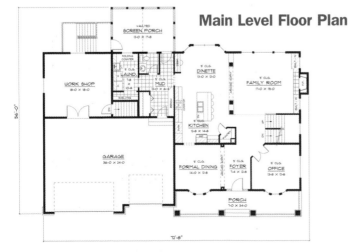

Upper Level Floor Plan

Plan #541037

Dimensions: 93'10" W x 89'5" D

Levels: 1

Square Footage: 4,219

Main Level Sq. Ft.: 2,500

Lower Level Sq. Ft.: 1,719

Bedrooms: 4

Bathrooms: 3

Foundation: Walkout; crawl space, slab, basement for fee

Material List Available: No

Price Category: I

You'll love making this cozy Craftsman-style house into your home.

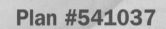

Images provided by designer/architect.

Features:

- **Entry:** Enter through a porch into a stunning foyer with 10-ft.-high ceilings.

- **Great Room:** Vaulted ceilings and a quick exit to a covered deck make this great room ideal for entertaining guests indoors and out. A built-in bookshelf and elegant entertainment center are additive elements that make the room not only beautiful, but also practical.

- **Study:** The options are endless with this quaint room. Located on the end of the home for quiet and privacy, you can turn the room into a study and work from your house, or construct an inviting space for guests to feel at home.

- **Master Suite:** With vaulted ceilings and access to a private covered deck, this master bedroom is perhaps the most enticing space in the home. Equipped with a tub and spa, dual vanity sinks, and a walk-in closet, this suite is an amazing retreat for busy moms and dads.

Main Level Floor Plan

Lower Level Floor Plan

Copyright by designer/architect.

Plan #481086

Dimensions: 71'8" W x 50' D
Levels: 2
Square Footage: 2,795
Main Level Sq. Ft.: 1,392
Upper Level Sq. Ft.: 1,403
Bedrooms: 4
Bathrooms: 2½
Foundation: Walkout
Material List Available: No
Price Category: F

Images provided by designer/architect.

Craftsman in style, this house is a large family's dream. With plenty of space on two levels, the home is beautiful inside and out.

Features:

- **Porches:** Enter through this lovely porch that adds a beautiful touch to the exterior of the house.
- **Family Room:** A built-in fireplace adds a beautiful element to the room.
- **Dining Area:** Enjoy dinner in the dinette, or the more formal dining room which has a racetrack ceiling.
- **Kitchen:** A central island range with appliances set in an L-shape make dual-chef cooking possible and enjoyable.

- **Master Suite:** This master suite features a vaulted ceiling and walk-in closet. Enter into a luxurious spa-like bath, with a full whirlpool tub and his and her sinks.

Rear Elevation

Main Level Floor Plan

Upper Level Floor Plan

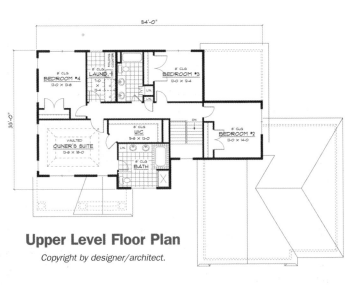

Copyright by designer/architect.

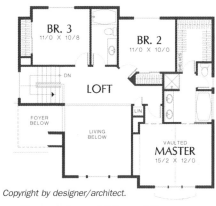

Plan #441019

Dimensions: 38' W x 35' D
Levels: 3
Square Footage: 2,044
Main Level Sq. Ft.: 1,106
Upper Level Sq. Ft.: 872
Lower Level Sq. Ft.: 66
Bedrooms: 3
Bathrooms: 2½
Foundation: Slab
Materials List Available: No
Price Category: D

Designed for a sloping lot, this tri-level home intrigues the eye and lifts the spirits.

Features:

- **Open Plan:** Sunlight filters into the grand two-story foyer and living room from tall windows.

- **Living Room:** From the loft overlooking this room you can view flames dancing in the fireplace, which is shared by the family room.

- **Dining Room:** From the windows or optional French doors in this space you can behold the outdoor vista.

- **Kitchen:** This spacious kitchen houses an island with a downdraft cooktop. Serve food informally in front of the breakfast-nook windows or at the island.

- **Master Suite:** This master bedroom is embellished with a vaulted ceiling and elegant front-facing windows; the attached master bath has a separate tub and shower and a private toilet enclosure.

Images provided by designer/architect.

Main Level Floor Plan

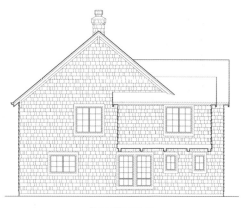

Garage Level Floor Plan

Copyright by designer/architect.

Upper Level Floor Plan

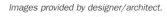

Rear Elevation

Plan #551100

Dimensions: 51'6" W x 40' D
Levels: 2
Square Footage: 2,645
Main Level Sq. Ft.: 1,204
Upper Level Sq. Ft.: 1,441
Bedrooms: 4
Bathrooms: 2½
Foundation: Crawl space or walkout; slab or basement for fee
Material List Available: No
Price Category: F

Images provided by designer/architect.

A traditional facade coupled with an open floor plan make this a perfect home for families.

Features:

- **Foyer:** This two-story room with a curved staircase creates a dramatic space upon entry.

- **Kitchen:** A butler's pantry offers a traditional touch, while a hidden pantry behind the mudroom offers plenty of storage.

- **Master Suite:** This spacious master suite with his and her walk-in closets and a luxurious bath invites you to unwind and relax.

- **Loft:** This roomy loft has many possibilities: home office, bonus room, or if needed, a fourth bedroom.

- **Utility/Laundry Room:** This room is conveniently located upstairs close to all bedrooms and baths, making doing laundry a breeze.

Copyright by designer/architect.

**Main Level
Floor Plan**

**Upper Level
Floor Plan**

Plan #551089

Dimensions: 62' W x 41' D
Levels: 2
Square Footage: 2,560
Main Level Sq. Ft.: 1,235
Upper Level Sq. Ft.: 1,325
Bedrooms: 3
Bathrooms: 2½
Foundation: Crawl space, basement or walkout
Material List Available: No
Price Category: E

Images provided by designer/architect.

The exterior amenities of this Craftsman-style home are ornate and eye-catching.

Features:

- Family Room: This spacious family room is a beautiful space to enjoy time with family and friends, or cozy up by the fireplace.

- Kitchen: Cooking enthusiast will fall in love with this kitchen. The generously sized room offers a centered range and plenty of space to move around. A nook for setting up a table and chairs sits next to the kitchen, while access to a covered patio is available—the perfect setup for outdoor summer meals.

- Master Suite: Perhaps the most enticing element of the home, this master suite is fully equipped. The bedroom features a walk-in closet and sitting area, which can be converted into a dressing space. The master bath features a whirlpool tub, double vanities, and room for extending the layout.

Main Level Floor Plan

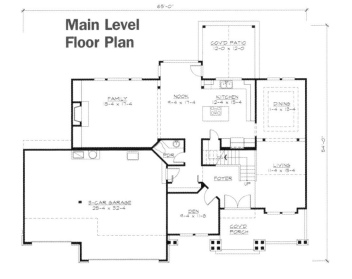

Upper Level Floor Plan

Copyright by designer/architect.

Plan #551182

Dimensions: 58' W x 46' D
Levels: 2
Square Footage: 3,970
Main Level Sq. Ft.: 1,269
Upper Level Sq. Ft.: 901
Lower Level Sq. Ft.: 1,800
Bedrooms: 4
Bathrooms: 3½
Foundation: Crawl space; slab, basement or walkout for fee
Material List Available: No
Price Category: H

This home, as shown in the photograph, may differ from the actual blueprints. For more detailed information, please check the floor plans carefully.

This gorgeous home is a growing family's ideal retreat.

Features:

- Living Room: Spacious and strategically placed, this family area opens up to a covered deck. The adjoining rooms make this section of the home ideal for entertaining or for cozying up with loved ones after dinner.

- Dining Room: Featuring the ideal amount of space for a large table to accommodate all members of your family, this room offers a beautiful retreat from the hustle and bustle of kitchen activity. A bar area, where high-backed chairs can be added, is perfect for less-formal dining.

- Kitchen: This kitchen offers a design that contains everything a cook needs. The range is placed so that reaching for a quick item from the fridge won't interfere with the busy chef. The range and sink are located across from each other, making the setup great for no-fuss food preparation and cooking.

- Loft: The unique design of this upstairs level has added appeal for a couple that enjoys space and privacy. The area affords a view of the lower level.

- Master Suite: Featuring a sitting area that doubles as a comfortable retreat or an ideal place for a vanity, this master bedroom opens into a generously sized bath with a whirlpool tub. Dual sinks and a large walk-in closet make the master suite the perfect haven for carefree mornings.

Main Level Floor Plan

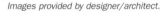

Upper Level Floor Plan

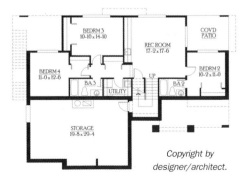

Copyright by designer/architect.

Lower Level Floor Plan

Plan #271090

Dimensions: 78' W x 49' D
Levels: 2
Square Footage: 2,708
Main Level Sq. Ft.: 1,430
Upper Level Sq. Ft.: 1,278
Bedrooms: 3
Bathrooms: 2½
Foundation: Daylight basement
Materials List Available: No
Price Category: F

This traditional home blends an updated exterior with a contemporary interior design.

CAD FILE AVAILABLE

Features:

- **Great Room:** The first thing your guests will see upon entering the house in the evening is glowing light from the fireplace competing with streaming moonlight from the flanking windows. Look deeply enough into the flames and you'll see the study on the other side of the through-the-wall fireplace.

- **Kitchen:** The open design of this kitchen allows for multiple cooks to work comfortably together.

- **Master Suite:** Great for hectic mornings or relaxing evenings, this spacious master suite includes his and her walk-in closets and a compartmentalized master bath with dual vanities, a standing shower, and a separate tub. The room also includes a private entrance to the balcony.

- **Secondary Bedrooms:** Both of these rooms enjoy walk-in closets and access to a compartentalized bathroom with dual sinks, which makes it easier for two people to get ready in the morning.

Main Level Floor Plan

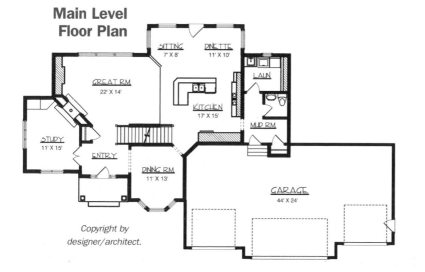

Copyright by designer/architect.

Upper Level Floor Plan

Main Level Floor Plan

Upper Level Floor Plan

Plan #541043

Dimensions: 80'10" W x 53'10" D
Levels: 2
Square Footage: 2,435
Main Level Sq. Ft.: 1,249
Upper Level Sq. Ft.: 1,186
Bedrooms: 3
Bathrooms: 2½
Foundation: Walkout
Material List Available: No
Price Category: E

Images provided by designer/architect.

CAD FILE AVAILABLE

Rear Elevation

Copyright by designer/architect.

Main Level Floor Plan

Lower Level Floor Plan

Plan #541046

Dimensions: 120'2" W x 73' D
Levels: 1
Square Footage: 4,704
Main Level Sq. Ft.: 2,610
Lower Level Sq. Ft.: 2,094
Bedrooms: 3
Bathrooms: 4½
Foundation: Basement or walkout
Material List Available: No
Price Category: I

Images provided by designer/architect.

CAD FILE AVAILABLE

Copyright by designer/architect.

Plan #481133

Dimensions: 98' W x 63'10" D
Levels: 2
Square Footage: 4,171
Main Level Sq. Ft.: 1,701
Upper Level Sq. Ft.: 2,470
Bedrooms: 5
Bathrooms: 3½
Foundation: Walkout
Material List Available: No
Price Category: I

Images provided by designer/architect.

Main Level Floor Plan

Upper Level Floor Plan

Copyright by designer/architect.

Plan #551132

Dimensions: 42' W x 52'6" D
Levels: 2
Square Footage: 2,520
Main Level Sq. Ft.: 1,365
Upper Level Sq. Ft.: 1,155
Bedrooms: 3
Bathrooms: 2½
Foundation: Crawl space, slab or walkout
Material List Available: No
Price Category: E

Images provided by designer/architect.

Main Level Floor Plan

Upper Level Floor Plan

Copyright by designer/architect.

Plan #341282

Dimensions: 35' W x 50' D

Levels: 1.5

Square Footage: 1,404

Main Level Sq. Ft.: 996

Upper Level Sq. Ft.: 408

Bedrooms: 3

Bathrooms: 2 full, 1 half

Foundation: Crawl space, slab, basement or walkout

Material List Available: No

Price Category: B

Images provided by designer/architect.

CAD FILE AVAILABLE

Upper Level Floor Plan

Copyright by designer/architect.

Main Level Floor Plan

Plan #481097

Dimensions: 86' W x 48' D

Levels: 2

Square Footage: 2,945

Main Level Sq. Ft.: 1,650

Upper Level Sq. Ft.: 1,295

Bedrooms: 3

Bathrooms: 2½

Foundation: Walkout

Material List Available: No

Price Category: F

Images provided by designer/architect.

Main Level Floor Plan

Upper Level Floor Plan

Copyright by designer/architect.

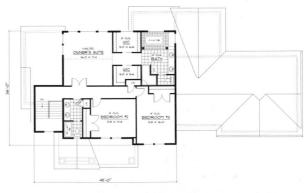

Plan #541044

Dimensions: 73'6" W x 56'6" D

Levels: 1

Square Footage: 4,533

Main Level Sq. Ft.: 2,485

Lower Level Sq. Ft.: 2,048

Bedrooms: 5

Bathrooms: 4½

Foundation: Walkout

Material List Available: No

Price Category: I

Images provided by designer/architect.

CAD FILE AVAILABLE

Rear Elevation

Main Level Floor Plan

Lower Level Floor Plan

Copyright by designer/architect.

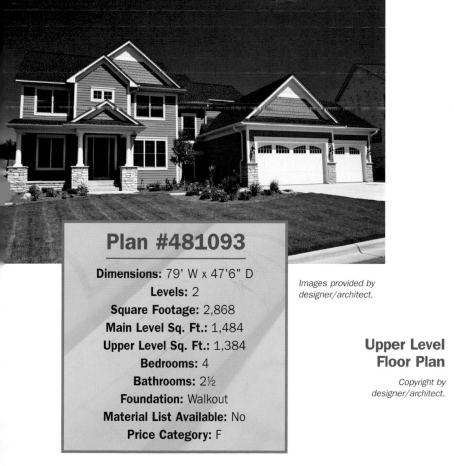

Plan #481093

Dimensions: 79' W x 47'6" D

Levels: 2

Square Footage: 2,868

Main Level Sq. Ft.: 1,484

Upper Level Sq. Ft.: 1,384

Bedrooms: 4

Bathrooms: 2½

Foundation: Walkout

Material List Available: No

Price Category: F

Images provided by designer/architect.

Main Level Floor Plan

Upper Level Floor Plan

Copyright by designer/architect.

Plan #551135

Dimensions: 49' W x 40' D
Levels: 2
Square Footage: 2,575
Main Level Sq. Ft.: 1,368
Upper Level Sq. Ft.: 1,135
Lower Level Sq. Ft.: 72
Bedrooms: 3
Bathrooms: 2½
Foundation: Crawl space; slab, basement or walkout for fee
Material List Available: No
Price Category: E

Images provided by designer/architect.

The exterior of this gorgeous home features two porches-great retreats for enjoying the fresh air while still in the comfort of your own home.

Features:

- **Family Room:** This large room is efficiently located near the kitchen for a cozy effect. A patio is attached.

- **Dining Room:** Experience formal dining and entertaining in this centrally located room, which transitions into the living room.

- **Kitchen:** Featuring an eating bar and a sunny breakfast nook, this room is sure to be a place where family congregates over a light meal or cooks for enjoyment. A full pantry and an offset utility room make the area functional, and the unique design adds flair.

- **Master Suite:** Enjoy the luxury of dual vanities, a separate bath and shower, and a walk-in closet in the spacious, personalized area.

Copyright by designer/architect.

Main Level Floor Plan

Upper Level Floor Plan

Lower Level Floor Plan

Plan #441015

Dimensions: 130'3" W x 79'3" D
Levels: 1
Square Footage: 4,732
Main Level Sq. Ft.: 2,902
Lower Level Sq. Ft.: 1,830
Bedrooms: 4
Bathrooms: 3 full, 2 half
Foundation: Walkout basement
Materials List Available: No
Price Category: I

Images provided by designer/architect.

An artful use of stone was employed on the exterior of this rustic hillside home to complement other architectural elements, such as the angled, oversize four-car garage and the substantial roofline.

CAD FILE AVAILABLE

Features:

- **Great Room:** This massive vaulted room features a large stone fireplace at one end and a formal dining area at the other. A built-in media center and double doors separate the great room from a home office with its own hearth and built-ins.

- **Kitchen:** This kitchen features a walk-in pantry and snack counter and opens to a skylighted outdoor kitchen. Its appointments include a cooktop and a corner fireplace.

- **Home Theatre:** This space has a built-in viewing screen, a fireplace, and double terrace access.

- **Master Suite:** This private space is found at the other side of the home. Look closely for

expansive his and her walk-in closets, a spa tub, a skylighted double vanity area, and a corner fireplace in the salon.

- **Bedrooms:** Three family bedrooms are on the lower level; bedroom 4 has a private bathroom and walk-in closet.

- **Garage:** This large garage has room for four cars; don't miss the dog shower and grooming station just off the garage.

Entry

Main Level Floor Plan

Copyright by designer/architect.

Lower Level Floor Plan

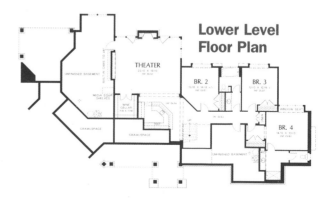

Plan #481018

Dimensions: 90'8" W x 61'10" D
Levels: 2
Square Footage: 3,071
Main Level Sq. Ft.: 1,705
Upper Level Sq. Ft.: 1,366
Bedrooms: 3
Bathrooms: 2½
Foundation: Walkout
Material List Available: No
Price Category: G

This home, as shown in the photograph, may differ from the actual blueprints. For more detailed information, please check the floor plans carefully.

This beautiful Craftsman-style home has an impressive exterior consisting of stone, brick, and wood siding for varying texture and decorative appeal.

Images provided by designer/architect.

Features:

- Porch: This front porch is the perfect area to setup a swing where you can enjoy warm summer nights without leaving the comfort of your home.

- Family Room: Perhaps the most impressive room in this lovely home, this family room boasts 18-ft. ceilings, and a beautiful built-in fireplace.

- Dining Room: The dining room, with 9-ft.-high ceilings, features a window seat where you can relax and enjoy coffee after dinner.

- Computer Room: The home is not only gorgeous, it's functional as well. A computer room is located right off of the kitchen,

making bill paying and homework help convenient.

- Mudroom: Lockers and a built-in bench are located right off of the garage; the perfect places for keeping wet shoes or storing outdoor gear.

- Master Suite: Up the stairs, a large master suite has a whirlpool tub, walk-in closet, and console for the TV.

- Garage: This three-car garage is large enough to house your cars and outdoor power equipment, such as lawn mowers.

Main Level Floor Plan

Copyright by designer/architect.

Upper Level Floor Plan

Plan #271089

Dimensions: 66' W x 51' D
Levels: 2
Square Footage: 2,476
Main Level Sq. Ft.: 1,266
Upper Level Sq. Ft.: 1,210
Bedrooms: 3
Bathrooms: 2½
Foundation: Daylight basement
Materials List Available: No
Price Category: E

This traditional-looking home is filled with modern amenities that will charm any family.

Features:

• Great Room: A handsome fireplace flanked with windows creates the focal point in this room, where the whole family will relax and entertain.

• Dining Room: A huge bay window makes an ideal frame for a table, and the door to the backyard makes outdoor entertaining easy. friends.

• Study: Separated from the great room by the office, this study can be a quiet retreat.

• Kitchen: Here, you'll find a walk-in pantry, ample counter space, and a central island.

• Owner's Suite: The large bedroom is complemented by the bath with a tub in the bay, two vanities, and a walk-in closet.

• Additional Bedrooms: Both rooms have a walk-in closet and a large window area for natural light.

Main Level Floor Plan

Upper Level Floor Plan

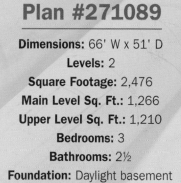

Copyright by designer/architect.

Upper Level Floor Plan

BEDRM 4
10-2 x 12-4

MSTR BA

MSTR BEDRM
12-8 x 16-4

BEDRM 3
10-6 x 13-0

WIC

BEDRM 2
11-6 x 13-4

OPEN TO BELOW

BONUS
12-8 x 15-8

Main Level Floor Plan

Copyright by designer/architect.

FAMILY
13-8 x 15-8

NOOK
11-0 x 11-8

KITCHEN
12-8 x 13-8

LAUNDRY

DINING
11-0 x 13-0

2-CAR GARAGE
19-4 x 19-4

FOYER

LIVING
13-0 x 13-8

COV'D PORCH

Plan #551095

Dimensions: 42' W x 42' D

Levels: 2

Square Footage: 2,651

Main Level Sq. Ft.: 1,190

Upper Level Sq. Ft.: 1,461

Bedrooms: 4

Bathrooms: 2½

Foundation: Crawl space or walkout; slab or basement for fee

Material List Available: No

Price Category: F

Images provided by designer/architect.

Plan #481023

Dimensions: 67' W x 60' D

Levels: 2

Square Footage: 3,253

Main Level Sq. Ft.: 1,797

Upper Level Sq. Ft.: 1,456

Bedrooms: 3

Bathrooms: 2½

Foundation: Walkout

Material List Available: No

Price Category: G

Images provided by designer/architect.

Main Level Floor Plan

Copyright by designer/architect.

Screen Porch
11-6 x 13-6

Laundry
12-4 x 10-4

Pantry

Dinette
15-0 x 11-8
9' Clg

Family Room
20-6 x 16-10
18' Clg

Storage

WIC

Lockers

Kitchen
17-2 x 9-2

Built-In

Dining Room
14-0 x 14-0
9' Clg

Foyer
8-0 x 14-0
9' Clg

Books

Garage
32-0 x 24-0

Study
12-0 x 11-10
9' Clg

Porch
35-0 x 8-0

Upper Level Floor Plan

Great Room

Master Bath

Master Suite
15-0 x 20-10
Vault Clg

Open To Below

Storage

WIC

Niche

Hall

Bonus Room
15-0 x 23-6

Desk

Bedroom 3
11-10 x 11-2

Desk

Bedroom 2
12-0 x 11-4

Seat

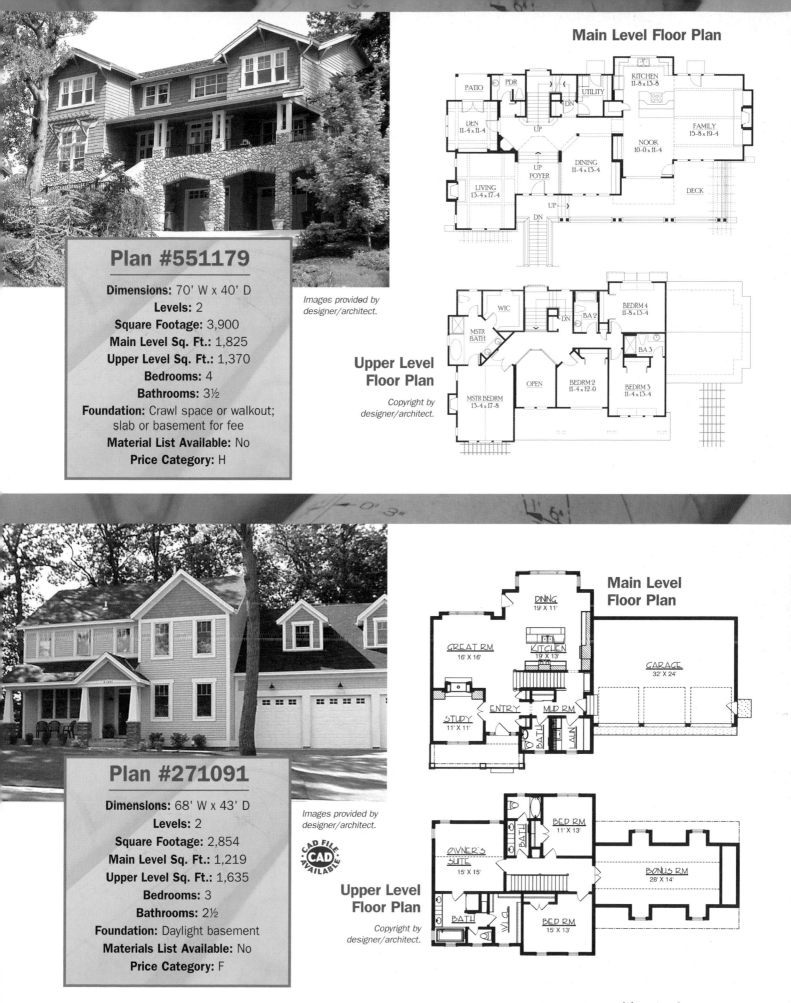

Main Level Floor Plan

PATIO

PDR

DEN
11-4 x 11-4

UP

DN

UTILITY

KITCHEN
11-8 x 13-8

DN

UP

LIVING
13-4 x 17-4

UP
FOYER

DINING
11-4 x 13-4

NOOK
10-0 x 11-4

FAMILY
15-8 x 19-4

DECK

UP

DN

Images provided by designer/architect.

WIC

DN

BA 2

BEDRM 4
11-8 x 13-4

MSTR
BATH

BA 3

Upper Level Floor Plan

MSTR BEDRM
13-4 x 17-8

OPEN

BEDRM 2
11-4 x 12-0

BEDRM 3
11-4 x 13-4

Copyright by designer/architect.

Plan #551179

Dimensions: 70' W x 40' D

Levels: 2

Square Footage: 3,900

Main Level Sq. Ft.: 1,825

Upper Level Sq. Ft.: 1,370

Bedrooms: 4

Bathrooms: 3½

Foundation: Crawl space or walkout; slab or basement for fee

Material List Available: No

Price Category: H

DINING
19' X 11'

Main Level Floor Plan

GREAT RM
16' X 16'

KITCHEN
19' X 13'

GARAGE
32' X 24'

STUDY
11' X 11'

ENTRY

BATH

MUD RM

LAUN

Images provided by designer/architect.

CAD FILE AVAILABLE

BED RM
11' X 13'

OWNER'S SUITE
15' X 15'

BATH

BONUS RM
28' X 14'

Upper Level Floor Plan

BATH

W.I.C.

BED RM
15' X 13'

Copyright by designer/architect.

Plan #271091

Dimensions: 68' W x 43' D

Levels: 2

Square Footage: 2,854

Main Level Sq. Ft.: 1,219

Upper Level Sq. Ft.: 1,635

Bedrooms: 3

Bathrooms: 2½

Foundation: Daylight basement

Materials List Available: No

Price Category: F

Plan #551074

Dimensions: 55' W x 44' D
Levels: 2
Square Footage: 2,475
Main Level Sq. Ft.: 1,324
Upper Level Sq. Ft.: 1,023
Lower Level Sq. Ft.: 128
Bedrooms: 4
Bathrooms: 2½
Foundation: Crawl space; slab or walkout for fee
Material List Available: No
Price Category: E

Main Level Floor Plan

Copyright by designer/architect.

PATIO

NOOK 9-4 x 13-4

DINING 11-4 x 12-0

FAMILY 13-8 x 17-4

KITCHEN 10-0 x 10-4

LIVING 12-0 x 13-4

UP

FOYER

UTILITY

BA 3

DN

COVD ENTRY

DN

DEN 9-8 x 12-0

Lower Level Floor Plan

CRAWL SPACE

3-CAR GARAGE 23-2 x 32-4

UP

UP

Upper Level Floor Plan

BEDRM 3 9-8 x 13-8

BEDRM 2 9-8 x 11-4

WIC

MSTR BATH

DN

BEDRM 4 9-8 x 11-4

BA 2

OPEN

MSTR BEDRM 12-0 x 17-4

Images provided by designer/architect.

Plan #281009

Dimensions: 46' W x 52' D
Levels: 1
Square Footage: 1,423
Bedrooms: 3
Bathrooms: 2
Foundation: Walkout basement
Materials List Available: Yes
Price Category: B

Images provided by designer/architect.

SUNDECK

down

NOOK 11-0 x 16-0

MBR 12-0 x 14-0

DINING 10-0 x 11-4

LR 13-0 x 17-0

KITCHEN

dw

Pan.

down

railing

ENS.
skylite

BATH

BR2 10-0 x 10-0

Foyer vaulted

STUDY/BR3 10-0 x 11-0

DOUBLE GARAGE

Porch

©Wesplan

Copyright by designer/architect.

Rear Elevation

Main Level Floor Plan

Lower Level Floor Plan

Images provided by designer/architect.

Copyright by designer/architect.

Plan #451217

Dimensions: 103'6" W x 53'11" D

Levels: 1

Square Footage: 4,711

Main Level Sq. Ft.: 2,470

Lower Level Sq. Ft.: 2,241

Bedrooms: 4

Bathrooms: 3

Foundation: Walkout basement

Materials List Available: No

Price Category: I

Plan #481012

Dimensions: 69' W x 58' D

Levels: 2

Square Footage: 2,740

Main Level Sq. Ft.: 1,512

Upper Level Sq. Ft.: 1,228

Bedrooms: 3

Bathrooms: 2½

Foundation: Walkout

Material List Available: No

Price Category: F

Images provided by designer/architect.

Main Level Floor Plan

Upper Level Floor Plan

Copyright by designer/architect.

Plan #481025

Dimensions: 84' W x 62'6" D
Levels: 1
Square Footage: 3,772
Main Level Sq. Ft.: 2,227
Lower Level Sq. Ft.: 1,545
Bedrooms: 3
Bathrooms: 2½
Foundation: Walkout basement
Material List Available: No
Price Category: H

Traditional in style, this gorgeous home is sure to be a perfect accent to any neighborhood.

Images provided by designer/architect.

Features:

• Entry: Ideal for enjoying a quiet summer night outdoors, this porch is a quaint retreat.

• Great Room: With soaring 11-ft.-high ceiling and a sizzling built-in fireplace, this great room is amazing for entertaining guests or snuggling up on snowy days.

• Master Suite: Also including 11-ft.-high ceiling, this master suite has everything a busy couple needs to get ready in the morning. A whirl-pool tub, a dual-sink vanity, and a generously sized walk-in closet are all included in this luxurious haven.

• Outdoor Living Space: This two-car garage gives way to a mudroom complete with built-in benches and lockers-an ideal setup for kids who enjoy outdoor sports, and even better for moms and dads who store their gear.

Rear Elevation

Main Level Floor Plan

Copyright by designer/architect.

Lower Level Floor Plan

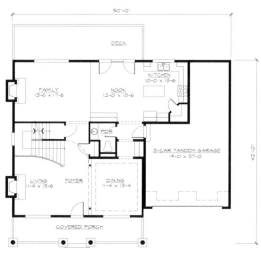

Plan #551103

Dimensions: 46' W x 71' D
Levels: 2
Square Footage: 2,668
Main Level Sq. Ft.: 1,409
Upper Level Sq. Ft.: 1,259
Bedrooms: 4
Bathrooms: 2½
Foundation: Crawl space or walkout; slab or basement for fee
Material List Available: No
Price Category: F

Images provided by designer/architect.

Features:

- **Foyer:** A front porch opens into this two-story foyer, which leads visitors to the formal dining room.
- **Kitchen:** A functional island kitchen will be useful to the family chef when he or she is creating culinary delights. A walk-in pantry can hold all the supplies a family needs.

- **Master Suite:** The location on the upper level near the secondary bedrooms puts this retreat in the center of things. The master bath features dual vanities, a stall shower, and a toilet room.
- **Garage:** A three-car tandem garage can hold cars or be a workshop.

A Craftsman-style home that contains a great floor plan is just what you have been looking for.

Copyright by designer/architect.

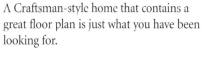

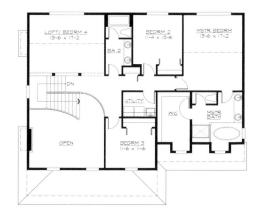

Main Level Floor Plan

Upper Level Floor Plan

Plan #551093

Dimensions: 42' W x 40' D
Levels: 2
Square Footage: 2,590
Main Level Sq. Ft.: 1,171
Upper Level Sq. Ft.: 1,419
Bedrooms: 4
Bathrooms: 3
Foundation: Crawl space or walkout; slab or basement for fee
Material List Available: No
Price Category: E

Images provided by designer/architect.

The myriad textures featured on the exterior of this Craftsman-style home add interest to the design.

Features:

- **Living Room:** This quaint room is great for throwing an intimate gathering or for an afternoon nap on the couch.

- **Kitchen:** This U-shaped kitchen has plenty of room for cooking or baking bundles of homemade pastries.

- **Master Suite:** Included in this luxurious design are two vanity sinks, a whirlpool tub, and a large walk-in closet. Enjoy a generous amount of space in this master bedroom.

- **Additional Bedrooms:** Two additional bedrooms are great for your growing family or for guests to stay in over the holidays.

Main Level Floor Plan

Upper Level Floor Plan

Copyright by designer/architect.

Plan #271092

Dimensions: 68' W x 47' D
Levels: 2
Square Footage: 2,636
Main Level Sq. Ft.: 1,596
Upper Level Sq. Ft.: 1,040
Bedrooms: 3
Bathrooms: 2½
Foundation: Walkout
Materials List Available: No
Price Category: F

Images provided by designer/architect.

Natural stone and craftsman-style columns dress up this traditional exterior.

CAD FILE AVAILABLE

Features:

• **Great Room:** The first thing your guests will see upon entering the house in the evening is glowing light from the fireplace competing with streaming moonlight from the flanking windows. Look deeply into the flames, and you'll see the study opposite you.

• **Kitchen:** There is plenty of space for helpers in this kitchen, and more for spectators on the other side of the snack bar. Enjoy your meals in either of two adjacent dining areas or have a relaxing meal on the deck.

• **Owner's Suite:** This spacious master bedroom adjoins a large walk-in closet and a compartmentalized master bath with dual vanities, a glass-block shower, and a large whirlpool tub.

• **Secondary Bedrooms:** Both of these rooms enjoy spacious closets and access to a compartmentalized bathroom with dual sinks, which makes it easier for two people to get ready in the morning.

Copyright by designer/architect.

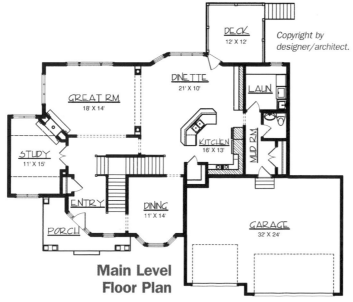

Main Level Floor Plan

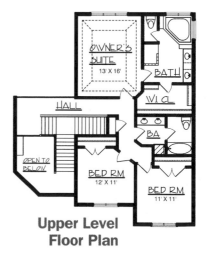

Upper Level Floor Plan

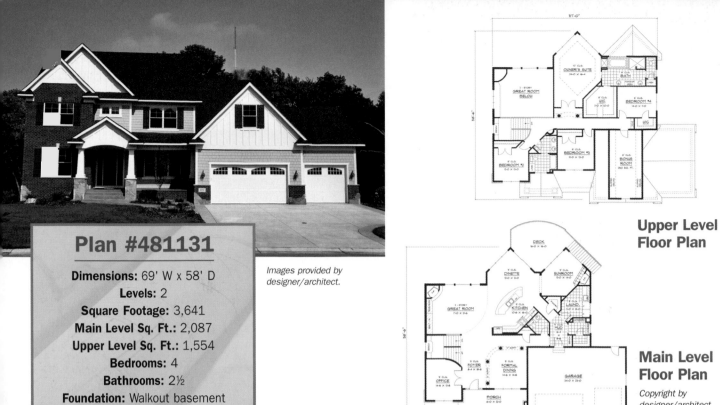

Upper Level Floor Plan

Main Level Floor Plan

Copyright by designer/architect.

Plan #481131

Dimensions: 69' W x 58' D
Levels: 2
Square Footage: 3,641
Main Level Sq. Ft.: 2,087
Upper Level Sq. Ft.: 1,554
Bedrooms: 4
Bathrooms: 2½
Foundation: Walkout basement
Materials List Available: No
Price Category: H

Images provided by designer/architect.

Garage Level Floor Plan

Main Level Floor Plan

Plan #271125

Dimensions: 45' W x 34'8" D
Levels: 1
Square Footage: 1,776
Main Level Sq. Ft.: 1,329
Lower Level Sq. Ft.: 447
Bedrooms: 3
Bathrooms: 2½
Foundation: Walkout
Material List Available: No
Price Category: C

Images provided by designer/architect.

Copyright by designer/architect.

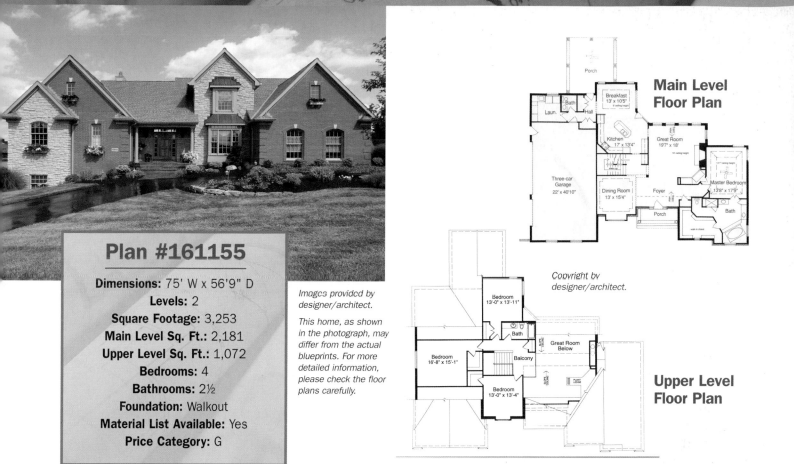

Main Level Floor Plan

Plan #161155

Dimensions: 75' W x 56'9" D
Levels: 2
Square Footage: 3,253
Main Level Sq. Ft.: 2,181
Upper Level Sq. Ft.: 1,072
Bedrooms: 4
Bathrooms: 2½
Foundation: Walkout
Material List Available: Yes
Price Category: G

Images provided by designer/architect.

This home, as shown in the photograph, may differ from the actual blueprints. For more detailed information, please check the floor plans carefully.

Copyright by designer/architect.

Upper Level Floor Plan

Main Level Floor Plan

Copyright by designer/architect.

Plan #161100

Dimensions: 89' W x 59'2" D
Levels: 1
Square Footage: 5,377
Main Level Sq. Ft.: 2,961
Lower Level Sq. Ft.: 2,416
Bedrooms: 3
Bathrooms: 2 full, 2 half
Foundation: Walkout; basement for fee
Material List Available: No
Price Category: J

CAD FILE AVAILABLE

Images provided by designer/architect.

Rear View

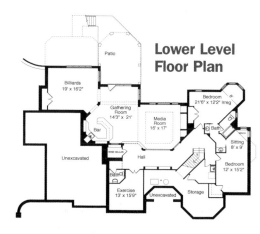

Lower Level Floor Plan

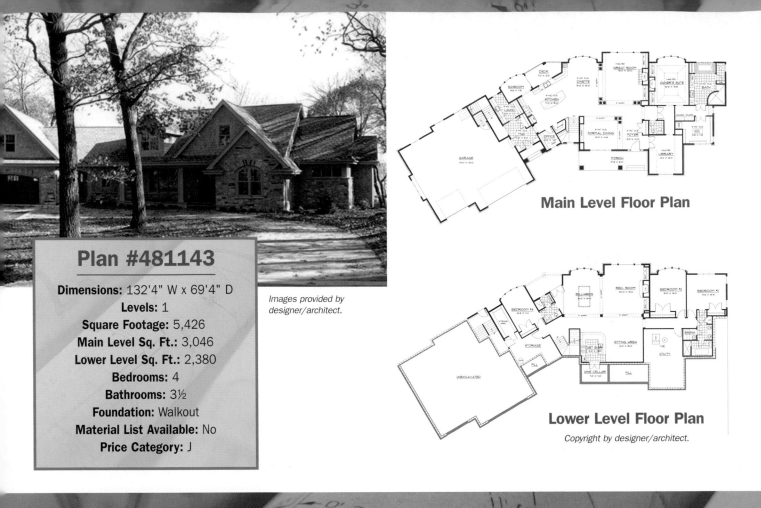

Main Level Floor Plan

Lower Level Floor Plan

Images provided by designer/architect.

Copyright by designer/architect.

Plan #481143

Dimensions: 132'4" W x 69'4" D
Levels: 1
Square Footage: 5,426
Main Level Sq. Ft.: 3,046
Lower Level Sq. Ft.: 2,380
Bedrooms: 4
Bathrooms: 3½
Foundation: Walkout
Material List Available: No
Price Category: J

Main Level Floor Plan

Lower Level Floor Plan

Images provided by designer/architect.

Copyright by designer/architect.

CAD FILE AVAILABLE

Plan #451392

Dimensions: 63'8" W x 64'6" D
Levels: 1
Square Footage: 3,773
Main Level Sq. Ft.: 1,976
Lower Level Sq. Ft.: 1,797
Bedrooms: 2
Bathrooms: 2½
Foundation: Walkout – insulated concrete form
Material List Available: No
Price Category: H

Plan #481034

Dimensions: 97' W x 78' D

Levels: 2

Square Footage: 2,830

Main Level Sq. Ft.: 1,673

Upper Level Sq. Ft.: 1,157

Bedrooms: 3

Bathrooms: 2½

Foundation: Walkout

Materials List Available: No

Price Category: F

Images provided by designer/architect.

Rear View

Main Level Floor Plan

Upper Level Floor Plan

Copyright by designer/architect.

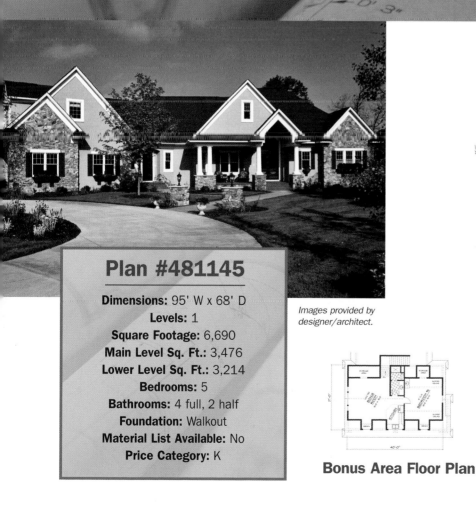

Plan #481145

Dimensions: 95' W x 68' D

Levels: 1

Square Footage: 6,690

Main Level Sq. Ft.: 3,476

Lower Level Sq. Ft.: 3,214

Bedrooms: 5

Bathrooms: 4 full, 2 half

Foundation: Walkout

Material List Available: No

Price Category: K

Images provided by designer/architect.

Copyright by designer/architect.

Main Level Floor Plan

Bonus Area Floor Plan

Lower Level Floor Plan

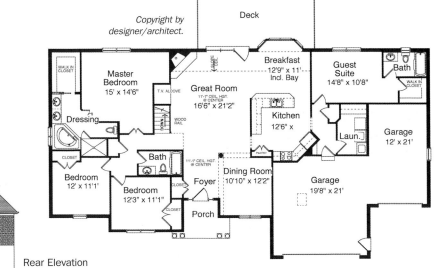

Plan #161115

Dimensions: 79'8" W x 44'2" D
Levels: 1
Square Footage: 2,253
Bedrooms: 4
Bathrooms: 3
Foundation: Walkout basement
Material List Available: Yes
Price Category: E

Images provided by designer/architect.

This one-level home offers a beautiful exterior of brick and stone with shake siding.

Features:

- **Great Room:** This open gathering area features an 11-foot-high ceiling and access to the rear yard. Turn on the corner gas fireplace, and fill the room with warmth and charm.

- **Kitchen:** This peninsula kitchen with built-in pantry and counter seating offers easy access to both formal and informal dining. The laundry facilities and the garage are just a few steps away. A magnificent bay window decorates the breakfast room and brings natural light into the area.

- **Master Suite:** This retreat offers a furniture alcove in the sleeping area and a walk-in closet. The private bath features a double-bowl vanity and a whirlpool tub.

- **Guest Suite:** This private bedroom suite is located behind the three-car garage and offers a welcoming environment for your overnight guests.

- **Basement:** This full walkout basement expands the living space of the delightful home.

Left Side Elevation

Right Side Elevation

Rear Elevation

Plan #481132

Dimensions: 109' W x 52' D
Levels: 1
Square Footage: 4,056
Main Level Sq. Ft.: 2,222
Lower Level Sq. Ft.: 1,834
Bedrooms: 4
Bathrooms: 4½
Foundation: Walkout
Material List Available: No
Price Category: I

Designed for a large family that loves to entertain, this home is a dream come true.

Features:

• **Great Room:** This welcoming space is perfect for relaxing and entertaining. Whether experienced in the bright sun or the warm glow of the fireplace, it will be everyone's favorite place to gather.

• **Kitchen:** Great for the busy family, this kitchen has all the workspace and storage that the family chef needs, as well as a snack bar that acts as a transition to the large dinette area.

• **Master Suite:** Located away from the busy areas of the home, this master suite is ideal for shedding your daily cares and relaxing in a romantic atmosphere. It includes a full master bath with his and her sinks, a stall shower, and a whirlpool tub.

• **Lower Level:** This is the ideal space for entertaining. The huge recreation room contains a wet bar, a billiards nook, and a fireplace flanked by built-in shelves. The space also contains an exercise area, two bathrooms, and two bedrooms.

Main Level Floor Plan

Lower Level Floor Plan

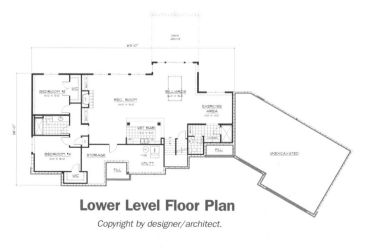

Copyright by designer/architect.

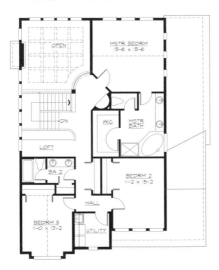

Plan #551085

Dimensions: 40' W x 52' D
Levels: 2
Square Footage: 2,630
Main Level Sq. Ft.: 1,380
Upper Level Sq. Ft.: 1,250
Bedrooms: 3
Bathrooms: 2½
Foundation: Crawl space or walkout; slab or basement for fee
Material List Available: No
Price Category: F

Images provided by designer/architect.

This house with its Tudor-style facade and European detailing has a compact footprint, making it the perfect starter home.

Features:

- **Elegant Details:** Coffered ceilings and cased openings add elegance to the formal living and dining areas.

- **Master Suite:** Escape to this luxury master suite with full bath and walk-in closet. The suite is secluded from the secondary bedrooms for added privacy.

- **Balcony:** This charming Juliet balcony over looks the two-story family room.

- **Loft:** This open loft with a built-in desk is the perfect place for homework, crafts, or an out-of-the-way place for the computer.

- **Garage:** This tandem-style garage fills the bill for recreational vehicles and extra storage; it can also function as a shop area.

Copyright by designer/architect.

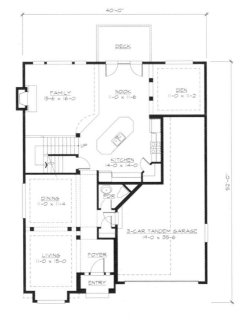

Main Level Floor Plan

Upper Level Floor Plan

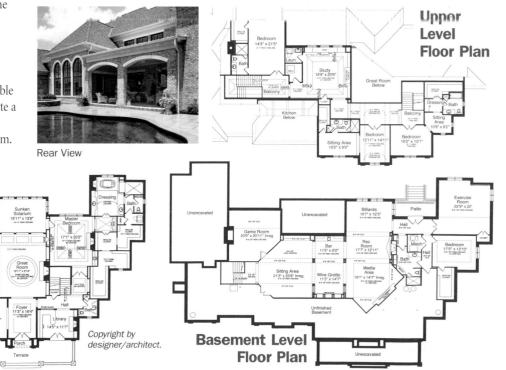

Plan #161104

Dimensions: 130' W x 84'6" D
Levels: 2
Square Footage: 8,088
Main Level Sq. Ft.: 5,418
Upper Level Sq. Ft.: 2,670
Bedrooms: 4
Bathrooms: 4 full, 2 half
Foundation: Basement
Material List Available: No
Price Category: L

Images provided by designer/architect.

Spectacular exterior with solid brick, limestone trim, and custom wood door reflects an authentic European manor.

Features:

- Kitchen: A 17-ft. high ceiling with arched timber beams, wall oven, island with vegetable sink, and second island with seating all create a true gourmet working space that overlooks the breakfast room and the cozy hearth room.

- Master Suite: This palatial suite with curved ceilings, fireplace-side whirlpool tub, large shower, sunken solarium, dressing room with two vanities and dressing table will pamper you. Four closets, including a compartmented double-entry master and secondary laundry area provide unmatched convenience.

- Bedrooms: Two sets of stairs lead to the second floor bedrooms—two with private sitting areas. Each bedroom enjoys a private bath and walk in closet.

- Additional Space: A sunken covered porch, enhances the rear-yard enjoyment, while a finished lower level creates additional rooms for fun and entertainment.

Rear View

Upper Level Floor Plan

Main Level Floor Plan

Copyright by designer/architect.

Basement Level Floor Plan

Plan #481036

Dimensions: 84'8" W x 82'4" D
Levels: 1
Square Footage: 4,258
Main Level Sq. Ft.: 2,440
Lower Level Sq. Ft.: 1,818
Bedrooms: 4
Bathrooms: 3½
Foundation: Walkout
Material List Available: No
Price Category: I

Old-world style with a modern floor plan makes this home perfect for you.

Rear Elevation

Images provided by designer/architect.

Features:

- Great Room: With a 12-ft.-high ceiling and a glowing fireplace, this room welcomes you home. Relax with your family, or entertain your friends.

- Study: Located off the foyer, this room would make a perfect home office; clients can come and go without disturbing the family.

- Master Suite: Unwind in this private space, and enjoy its many conveniences. The full master bath includes a standing shower, his and her sinks, a large tub, and a spacious walk-in closet.

- Garage: This large storage space has room for three full-size cars and includes a convenient sink. The stairs to the storage area in the basement will help keep things organized.

Front View

Main Level
Floor Plan

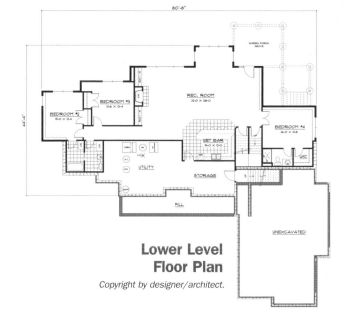

Lower Level
Floor Plan

Copyright by designer/architect.

Breakfast Room/Kitchen

Master Bath

Study

Great Room

Main Level Floor Plan

Upper Level Floor Plan

Images provided by designer/architect.

CAD FILE AVAILABLE

Copyright by designer/architect.

Plan #221121

Dimensions: 102'4" W x 89' D

Levels: 1.5

Square Footage: 5,140

Main Level Sq. Ft.: 3,989

Upper Level Sq. Ft.: 1,151

Bedrooms: 4

Bathrooms: 4½

Foundation: Walkout

Material List Available: No

Price Category: J

Rear View

Plan #271362

Dimensions: 74'6" W x 68' D

Levels: 2

Square Footage: 2,645

Main Level Sq. Ft.: 1,402

Upper Level Sq. Ft.: 1,243

Bedrooms: 4

Bathrooms: 2½

Foundation: Walkout

Material List Available: No

Price Category: F

Images provided by designer/architect.

Main Level Floor Plan

Upper Level Floor Plan

Copyright by designer/architect.

Plan #481024

Dimensions: 87'2" W x 59'8" D

Levels: 1

Square Footage: 3,458

Main Level Sq. Ft.: 2,016

Lower Level Sq. Ft.: 1,442

Bedrooms: 4

Bathrooms: 3

Foundation: Walkout basement

Material List Available: No

Price Category: G

Images provided by designer/architect.

Lower Level Floor Plan

Copyright by designer/architect.

Plan #161086

Dimensions: 65'8" W x 52'8" D

Levels: 2

Square Footage: 3,610

Main Level Sq. Ft.: 1,838

Upper Level Sq. Ft.: 1,772

Bedrooms: 4

Bathrooms: 3½

Foundation: Walkout; crawl space, slab or basement for fee

Materials List Available: Yes

Price Category: H

Images provided by designer/architect.

Main Level Floor Plan

Upper Level Floor Plan

Optional Basement Level Floor Plan

Copyright by designer/architect.

Plan #481137

Dimensions: 77' W x 66' D

Levels: 1

Square Footage: 4,425

Main Level Sq. Ft.: 2,482

Lower Level Sq. Ft.: 1,943

Bedrooms: 3

Bathrooms: 2½

Foundation: Walkout

Material List Available: No

Price Category: I

Images provided by designer/architect.

Lower Level Floor Plan

Copyright by designer/architect.

Plan #451395

Dimensions: 56' W x 46' D

Levels: 1

Square Footage: 3,231

Main Level Sq. Ft.: 1,327

Lower Level Sq. Ft.: 1,904

Bedrooms: 3

Bathrooms: 2½

Foundation: Walkout – insulated concrete form

Material List Available: No

Price Category: G

Images provided by designer/architect.

Main Level Floor Plan

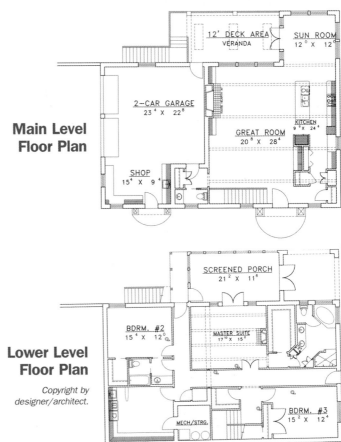

Lower Level Floor Plan

Copyright by designer/architect.

Plan #451187

Dimensions: 75'10" W x 85' D

Levels: 1

Square Footage: 4,638

Main Level Sq. Ft.: 2,305

Lower Level Sq. Ft.: 2,333

Bedrooms: 4

Bathrooms: 5

Foundation: Walkout

Materials List Available: No

Price Category: I

Images provided by designer/architect.

CAD FILE AVAILABLE

Lower Level Floor Plan

Main Level Floor Plan

Bonus Room

Copyright by designer/architect.

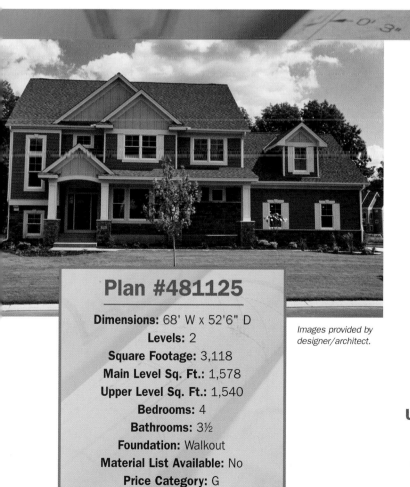

Plan #481125

Dimensions: 68' W x 52'6" D

Levels: 2

Square Footage: 3,118

Main Level Sq. Ft.: 1,578

Upper Level Sq. Ft.: 1,540

Bedrooms: 4

Bathrooms: 3½

Foundation: Walkout

Material List Available: No

Price Category: G

Images provided by designer/architect.

Main Level Floor Plan

Upper Level Floor Plan

Copyright by designer/architect.

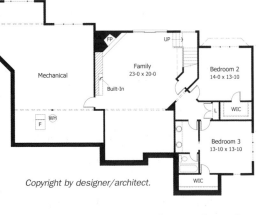

Plan #481026

Dimensions: 72' W x 66' D

Levels: 1

Square Footage: 3,837

Main Level Sq. Ft.: 2,374

Lower Level Sq. Ft.: 1,463

Bedrooms: 3

Bathrooms: 2½

Foundation: Walkout basement

Material List Available: No

Price Category: H

Elegant looks with a great floor plan make this home perfect for your family.

Images provided by designer/architect.

Features:

- **Great Room:** This large gathering area boasts a 12-ft.-high ceiling and a built-in cabinet. The fireplace is open to the kitchen.

- **Dining Room:** Columns separate this eating area from the foyer and the great room. The accented ceiling work adds to the formal appeal of this area.

- **Master Suite:** Located just off the great room, this retreat contains a tray ceiling and a bay window. The large walk-in closet and elegant private bath make this space special.

- **Lower Level:** A family room with a large fireplace and a built-in cabinet occupy most of this level. Also two oversize bedrooms, both with walk-in closets, are sectioned off for privacy.

Rear Elevation

Main Level Floor Plan

Lower Level Floor Plan

Copyright by designer/architect.

Plan #541049

Dimensions: 67'6" W x 55'6" D
Levels: 2
Square Footage: 2,740
Main Level Sq. Ft.: 2,069
Upper Level Sq. Ft.: 671
Bedrooms: 3
Bathrooms: 2½
Foundation: Walkout
Material List Available: No
Price Category: F

Images provided by designer/architect.

Varying textures and gable sizes add enticing appeal to the exterior of this mod contemporary-style house.

CAD FILE AVAILABLE

Features:

• Dining: This elegant dining room features space to display treasured china and antiques.

• Kitchen: An eating bar in the center of the kitchen provides the perfect space for baking or eating a quick meal. Appliances are spread out throughout the kitchen – a valuable setup for families who enjoy cooking together.

• Master Suite: This master suite features a large walk-in closet, dual vanities, and access to a covered deck.

• Additional Bedrooms: Your growing family will appreciate the amount of space and privacy the upstairs offers, especially in these bedrooms. Featuring a beautiful loft outside the doors, both bedrooms have walk-in closets and easy access to a full bathroom

Rear Elevation

Main Level Floor Plan

Upper Level Floor Plan

Copyright by designer/architect.

Plan #481104

Dimensions: 77' W x 46' D

Levels: 2

Square Footage: 3,149

Main Level Sq. Ft.: 1,665

Upper Level Sq. Ft.: 1,484

Bedrooms: 4

Bathrooms: 3½

Foundation: Walkout

Material List Available: No

Price Category: G

Practicality and luxury come in one beautifully cozy package in the form of this European-style home.

Images provided by designer/architect.

Features:

- **Great Room:** Enjoy an evening by the fire in this gorgeous great room with its fireplace that radiates from the corner.

- **Office:** Working parents will fall in love with this office with its 10-ft. ceilings. Located near the main living areas, it is an ideal retreat for at-home work.

- **Mudroom:** This mudroom, combined with the laundry room, makes laundry an easy task, with the added perk of no more over flowing hampers in the bathroom or hallway.

- **Bedrooms:** Two bedrooms and a sumptuous owner's suite are located on the second level. The suite boasts a full bath and large walk-in closet.

- **Garage:** This garage has three-bays, ideal for housing that prized car or for setting up a workshop with your tools.

Rear Elevation

Main Level Floor Plan

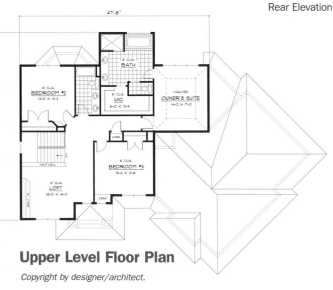

Upper Level Floor Plan

Copyright by designer/architect.

Plan #551091

Dimensions: 52' W x 38' D
Levels: 2
Square Footage: 2,565
Main Level Sq. Ft.: 1,281
Upper Level Sq. Ft.: 1,284
Bedrooms: 3
Bathrooms: 2½
Foundation: Crawl space or walkout; slab or basement for fee
Material List Available: No
Price Category: F

Images provided by designer/architect.

Gable brackets, flared columns, and bold trim give this Craftsman home its curb appeal.

Features:

- **Foyer:** This cozy entry porch invites you in to a spacious two-story foyer that leads to the vaulted living room.

- **Spacious Layout:** This design has an open floor plan for informal living, using columns, cased openings, and half-walls to define and differentiate spaces.

- **Kitchen:** This gourmet island kitchen is open to family room, creating the perfect place to entertain friends and family.

- **Master Suite:** Double doors invite you into the private luxury of the master suite. Complete with a luxurious bath and oversize walk-in closet.

- **Bonus Room:** This bonus room, which has its own closet, makes a great place for family movie night or, if needed, can easily be converted to a fourth bedroom.

Main Level Floor Plan

Upper Level Floor Plan

Copyright by designer/architect.

Plan #451389

Dimensions: 84' W x 67' D
Levels: 1
Square Footage: 6,246
Main Level Sq. Ft.: 3,082
Lower Level Sq. Ft.: 3,164
Bedrooms: 6
Bathrooms: 5½
Foundation: Walkout – insulated concrete form
Material List Available: No
Price Category: K

A hint of Craftsman style on the outside and attention to detail on the inside make this home a true treasure.

CAD FILE AVAILABLE

Images provided by designer/architect.

Features:

- **Living Room:** A coffered ceiling adds to the elegance in this formal gathering area. The fireplace, which it shares with the great room, adds a warm glow to the room.

- **Kitchen:** The large island in this kitchen helps at mealtime. The room is open to the breakfast nook and the great room, providing an open and airy feeling.

- **Lower Level:** This area is home to five bedrooms and a family room. There is also a guest apartment located on this level.

Rear Elevation

Copyright by designer/architect.

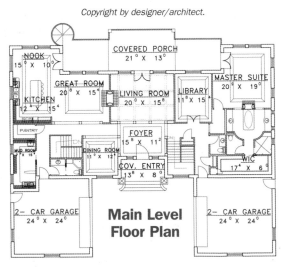

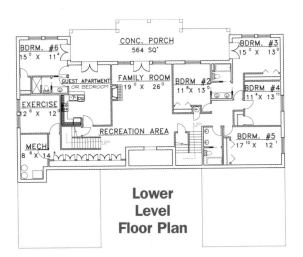

Plan #481090

Dimensions: 72'6" W x 65'8" D
Levels: 2
Square Footage: 2,896
Main Level Sq. Ft.: 1,713
Upper Level Sq. Ft.: 1,183
Bedrooms: 3
Bathrooms: 2½
Foundation: Walkout
Material List Available: No
Price Category: F

Images provided by designer/architect.

Turn this European style house into a home. With an ample amount of space, your family will have plenty of room to grow.

Features:

- **Porch:** This front porch welcomes visitors and provides a sanctuary for an afternoon nap in the warm weather.

- **Dining Room:** This formal dining room is a luxurious center for entertaining with class.

- **Kitchen:** This large kitchen with its central island is an ideal setup for the master chef. Enjoy a relaxed meal in the kitchen or in the adjoining dinette, which features 9-ft. ceilings.

- **Master Suite:** An impressive second level features this master suite with vaulted ceilings and a gorgeous full bath, which includes a whirlpool tub, his and her sinks, and large walk-in closet.

- **Garage:** This garage offers you the option of storage for your cars or other home accessories.

Main Level Floor Plan

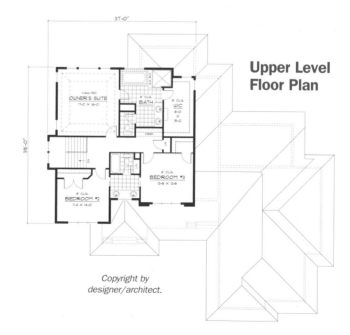

Upper Level Floor Plan

Copyright by designer/architect.

Plan #541048

Dimensions: 95' W x 65' D
Levels: 1
Square Footage: 4,923
Main Level Sq. Ft.: 2,754
Lower Level Sq. Ft.: 2,199
Bedrooms: 4
Bathrooms: 3½
Foundation: Walkout
Material List Available: No
Price Category: I

Images provided by designer/architect.

The dreamy exterior of this gorgeous European-style house features round pillars and beaming bay windows.

CAD FILE AVAILABLE

Features:

- **Entry:** Enter through a porch into an impressive foyer featuring 12-ft.-high ceilings and a view of the dining room.

- **Kitchen:** Everything you need and more is wrapped up in this U-shaped kitchen. The room offers a large pantry, a desk for helping with homework while you cook dinner, an eating bar, and a breakfast nook overlooking the backyard.

- **Library:** Enter this vaulted library through an ornate arch and get lost in your favorite book.

- **Master Suite:** This master bedroom and bath is ideal for a busy couple. The bath features a make-up counter, dual sinks, and a deep tub where you can melt away stress. The bedroom features his and her closets and access to the deck outside.

Lower Level Floor Plan

Main Level Floor Plan

Copyright by designer/architect.

Rear Elevation

Plan #481035

Dimensions: 99' W x 64' D
Levels: 2
Square Footage: 3,204
Main Level Sq. Ft.: 1,701
Upper Level Sq. Ft.: 1,503
Bedrooms: 3
Bathrooms: 2½
Foundation: Walkout
Material List Available: No
Price Category: G

Images provided by designer/architect.

Distinctive design details set this home apart from others in the neighborhood.

Features:

- **Foyer:** This large foyer welcomes you home and provides a view through the home and into the family room. The adjoining study can double as a home office.

- **Family Room:** This two-story gathering space features a fireplace flanked by built-in cabinets. The full-height windows on the rear wall allow natural light to flood the space.

- **Kitchen:** This island kitchen flows into the nearby family room, allowing mingling between both spaces when friends or family are visiting. The adjacent dinette is available for daily meals.

- **Master Suite:** This private retreat waits for you to arrive home. The tray ceiling in the sleeping area adds elegant style to the area.

Rear Elevation

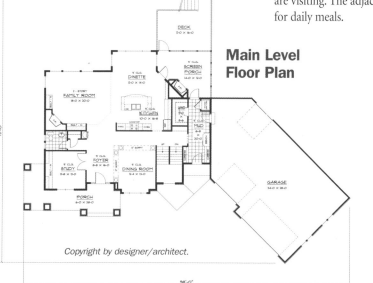

Main Level Floor Plan

Copyright by designer/architect.

Upper Level Floor Plan

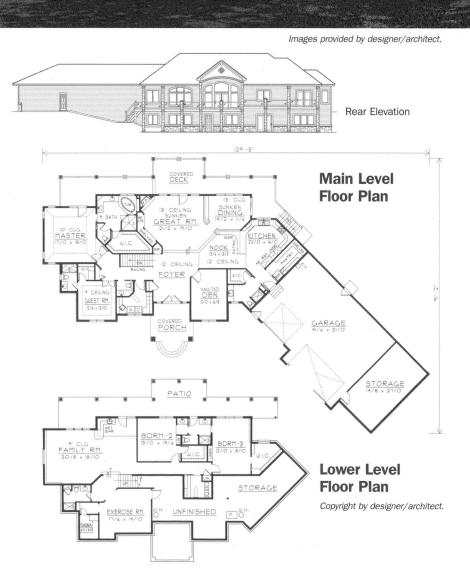

Plan #541050

Dimensions: 129'5" W x 91'2" D
Levels: 1
Square Footage: 5,022
Main Level Sq. Ft.: 2,907
Lower Level Sq. Ft.: 2,115
Bedrooms: 5
Bathrooms: 5½
Foundation: Walkout; basement for fee
Material List Available: No
Price Category: J

Rear Elevation

Main Level Floor Plan

Lower Level Floor Plan

The sleek exterior of this European-style home is charming and unique.

Features:

- **Entry:** Welcome guests with this impressive entry. A porch opens to a foyer with 12-ft.-high ceilings.

- **Great Room:** Relax in style in this sunken great room. Featured in the room are 13-ft.-high ceilings, a fireplace, and built-in shelves to display books or photos of loved ones.

- **Master Suite:** This master suite is something to brag about. Featuring 10-ft.-high ceilings, the bedroom has an airy feel and a view of the backyard. The bath offers a luxurious tub, a walk-in closet, and two vanity sinks.

- **Outdoor Living Space:** This two-car garage is the ideal space for storing your prized cars or even setting up a workshop for your tools. This storage space is great for stashing off-season decorations or for use as a weight room for the fitness enthusiast.

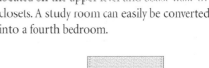

Plan #481105

Dimensions: 77' W x 46' D
Levels: 2
Square Footage: 3,103
Main Level Sq. Ft.: 1,953
Upper Level Sq. Ft.: 1,150
Bedrooms: 4
Bathrooms: 3½
Foundation: Walkout
Material List Available: No
Price Category: G

Excellent curb appeal and an efficient floor plan make this home perfect.

Features:

• Living Room: Located just off the foyer, this formal gathering area features a large bay window and a 9-ft.-high ceiling.

• Great Room: This entertaining area feels open due to the two-story-high ceiling and a wall of windows, which affords a view of the backyard. Because it is open to the kitchen and the dinette area all three spaces work as one large room.

• Master Suite: This conveniently located main-level retreat is just what you have been searching for. The oversize walk-in closet and

master bath will either help you get to work on time or pamper you after a long day.

• Bedrooms: Two secondary bedrooms are located on the upper level and boast walk-in closets. A study room can easily be converted into a fourth bedroom.

Rear Elevation

Main Level Floor Plan

Upper Level Floor Plan

Easy-Care Surfaces

Building a new home means you will be making a number of decisions on the many materials that will be visible throughout your house. Your builder won't ask you which brand of drywall to buy, but he or she will ask what color to paint the walls, what material to use on the kitchen counters, and what type of finish you want on the faucets in the master bathroom. It is a lot to think about, but the following will help you make decisions on some of the major materials.

Countertop Materials

The market offers lots of countertop materials, all of which are worth consideration for your kitchen and bathroom surfaces. Pick the materials and designs that best suit your needs and the look of the room. You can also enhance a basic design by combining it with an eye-catching edge treatment. Another option is to combine different materials on the same surface.

Plastic Laminate. This thin, durable surface comes in hundreds of colors, textures, and patterns. The material is relatively easy to install; its smooth surface washes easily and can stand up well to everyday wear and tear. It is heat-resistant, although very hot pots can discolor or even burn it, and it will show scratches from knives and other sharp utensils; surface damage is difficult to repair.

Home centers and kitchen supply dealers sell post-formed counters. These are the types that come in 8- or 10-foot lengths that you or your builder will trim to fit. Both the laminate sheets and the post-form counters are available in a limited number of colors and patterns. Another option is to order a laminate counter from a counter fabricator—some home centers and kitchen dealers offer this service as well. The counter will be

built to your measurements, and you will get a wide variety of colors and patterns from which to choose. Most fabricators also offer a variety of edge treatments.

Ceramic Tile. Glazed tile can be magnificently decorative for counters, backsplashes, and walls, or as a display inset in another material. Tile is smooth and easy to wipe off, and it can't be burned by hot pots. In addition to the standard square tiles, ceramic tiles are available in a number of specialty shapes and sizes, allowing you to create a truly custom look. Ceramic tile costs more than laminate, but you can save money by doing the installation yourself.

When shopping, you should also consider the finish. There are two kinds: unglazed and glazed. Unglazed tiles are not sealed and always come in a matte look. They are not practical for use near water unless you apply a sealant. On the

other hand, glazed tiles are coated with a material that makes them impervious to water—or spills and stains from other liquids, too. This glaze on the tile can be matte or highly polished. The upkeep of tile is fairly easy, but you must regrout and reseal periodically. White grout shows dirt easily, but a dark-color mix can camouflage stains. Still, unless it is sealed, grout will harbor bacteria. So clean the countertop regularly with a nonabrasive antibacterial cleanser. Tile that is well-maintained will last a lifetime.

Ceramic tile provides a clean, nonporous surface for countertops, opposite.

Colorful tiles make a strong design statement in the bath shown bottom left.

Solid surfacing, right, resists burns and scratches.

Plastic laminates, below, are available in a variety of colors and patterns.

Solid-Surfacing Material. Made of acrylics and composite materials, solid surfacing comes in ½ inch and ¾ inch thicknesses. This is a premium material that resists moisture, heat, stains, and cracks.

There is almost no limit to the colors and patterns of solid surfacing. It can be fabricated to resemble marble and granite, or it can be a block of solid color. Either way, the material can be carved or beveled for decorative effects just like wood. Manufacturers recommend professional installation.

The surface becomes scratched fairly easily, but the scratches are not readily apparent. Because the material is a solid color, serious blemishes can be removed by sanding or buffing.

Natural Stone. Marble, slate, and granite can be formed into beautiful but expensive counters. Of the three, granite is probably the most popular because it cannot be hurt by moisture or heat, nor does it stain if finished properly. Installers polish granite to produce a high-gloss finish.

Marble scratches, cracks, and stains easily, even if waxed. Slate can be easily scratched and cracked and cannot take a high polish.

These are heavy materials that should be installed by a professional. However, you can get the look of granite and marble by installing granite or marble tiles. Cut from the natural stones, these products are available in 12 x 12-inch tiles and are installed and cut in much the same way as ceramic tiles.

Wood. Butcher block consists of hardwood laminated under pressure and sealed with oil or a polymer finish. Because it's thicker than other materials, butcher block will raise the counter level about ¾ inch above standard height. Also, wood is sub-

Natural stone, left, can be used on counters and backsplashes.

Counter fabricators can create decorative edge treatments such as the one above.

A bathroom vanity, above right, benefits from a polished quartz counter.

Strong countertop color, right, can set off neutral-color cabinets.

ject to damage by standing water or hot pans. Butcher-block tops are moderately expensive but can be installed by amateurs.

Other kinds of wood counters may be used, especially in serving areas. Any wood used near water must be resistant to moisture or well sealed to prevent water from penetrating below the surface.

Concrete. There aren't a great number of concrete counters, but the material is catching on with some in the kitchen design community. If your goal is to install a cutting-edge material that can still have a traditional look, concrete is it. Thanks to new

staining techniques, concrete can be saturated with color all the way through, and it can be preformed to any shape and finished to any texture. Set stone or ceramic tile chips into the surface for a decorative effect. Form it to drain off water at the sink. Be cautious, however, as a concrete countertop must be sealed, and it may crack. Installation is best left to a professional.

Stainless Steel. Stainless steel used for a countertop, whether it is for the entire counter or just a section of it, can look quite sophisticated, especially with a wood trim. What's practical about it is its capaci-

ty to take high heat without scorching, which makes it suitable as a landing strip for pots and pans straight from the cooktop. It is also impervious to water, so it's practical at the sink. On the negative side, stainless steel can be noisy to work on, and it will show smudges. Depending on the grade of the material, it may also be vulnerable to scrapes, stains, and corrosion. The higher the chromium and nickel content (and therefore the grade), the better. Also, look for a thick-gauge stainless steel that won't dent easily. If you prefer not to have a stainless-steel counter but like the look, consider a stainless-steel sink.

Selecting colors for walls can be intimidating. Fortunately, kitchens, above, usually have small unused wall areas so you can experiment more freely than you would in other rooms.

Wall Treatments

It's hard to beat the ease of a coat of paint for decorating a room. But there are other ways to finish off the walls, too, such as vinyl wallcovering and paneling. You can go with one, two, or all three of these options in several combinations to achieve the decor that will complement your new house.

Paint. Basically, there are two kinds of paint: latex, which is a water-based formulation, and oil-based products. You can buy latex and oil paint in at least four finishes: flat, eggshell, semigloss, and gloss. In general, stay away from flat paint in the kitchen because it is difficult to keep clean. The other finishes, or sheens, resist dirt better than flat paint and are easier to clean.

Latex is a term used to describe a variety of water-based paints. They are recommended for most interior surfaces, including walls, woodwork, and cabinets. Latex paints come in a huge assortment of colors,

clean up with soap and water, and dry quickly.

Oil-based paint refers to products that use alkyd resins as the solvent. Manufacturers once used linseed or some other type of oil as the solvent and the name stuck. They provide tough, long-lasting finishes. However, the convenience of latex products, along with government regulations limiting the amount of volatile organic compounds oil-based products produce, has forced their use to decline. This kind of paint is especially good for use over bare wood and surfaces that have been

previously painted. If you plan to use it (or latex, for that matter) on new wallboard, you'll have to apply a primer first.

Wallcoverings. Vinyl wallcoverings and coordinated borders offer an easy, low-cost way to put style into your new kitchen. Practical because they are nonporous, stain resistant, and washable, vinyl coatings are available in a great variety of colors, textures, and patterns. Prepasted, pretrimmed rolls are the easiest for a novice to install. Just remember to remove any old wallpaper before applying new covering to walls.

Paneling. If you're looking for a simple way to create a "cottage" feel, paneling is it. Today's paneling options include prefinished softwood- or hardwood-veneered plywood, simulated wood grain on plywood or hardboard, prehung wallpaper on plywood, simulated wood grain or decorative finish panel board, tile board, or other decorative hardboard paneling, and solid pine or cedar plank paneling. For a versatile look, apply wainscoting, which is paneling that goes halfway or three-quarters of the way up the wall. Top it off with chair rail molding; paint or wallpaper the rest of the wall. Depending on how you install it, you can create horizontal, diagonal, or herringbone patterns.

Wallpaper and borders are an easy, inexpensive way to enliven a room's design, above. Pick colors and patterns to set off your cabinet finishes.

Ceramic tile is a popular choice for bathroom walls. Note how the tiles below contain decorative inlays to add sparkle to what would otherwise be a white wall.

Flooring

Floor coverings fall into two broad categories: resilient flooring, which has some resiliency, or bounce, and hard flooring, with no flex whatsoever. Resilient floors are less tiring to stand on than hard-surface floors and less likely to produce instant disaster for dropped glasses or chinaware. But the flooring you select plays more than a practical role in your kitchen.

Resilient Vinyl Tile and Sheet Flooring.
Vinyl flooring wears fairly well to very well, needs only occasional waxing or polishing (in some cases none at all), and is easy to clean. It comes in a wide variety of colors and patterns suitable to the cottage style, and is an economical alternative among flooring choices.

These products are available in individual tiles or in large sheets. (The sheets can look like individual tiles as well as a wide range of designs.) Installing vinyl tile is a

popular do-it-yourself project. Installing sheet goods is a bit more complex but well within the skills of an experienced do-it-yourselfer.

Laminate.
This type of flooring consists of laminate material, a tougher version of the material used on counters, bonded to fiberboard core. The decorative top layer of material can be made to look like just about anything. Currently, wood-grain patterns are the most popular, but laminates are available in many colors and patterns, including tile and natural stone designs.

Vinyl flooring, left, comes in a variety of patterns.

Carpeting, below, adds warmth to most rooms.

Available in both plank and tile form, they are easy to install, hold up well to normal traffic, and are easy to clean.

Wood.
Thanks largely to polyurethane coatings that are impervious to water, wood flooring continues to be a popular choice for just about any room of the home, except bathrooms. Wood can be finished any way you like, though much of the wood flooring available today comes prefinished in an assortment of shades.

Hardwoods like oak and maple are popular and stand up to a lot of abuse. Softwoods like pine give a more distressed, countrified look. Flooring comes in 2¼-inch strips as well as variable-width planks. Parquet flooring, another good option, consists of wood pieces glued together into a geometric pattern. These prefinished

Stone flooring imparts a feeling of solidity to an area, such as the foyer above. Inlay designs such as this one are the mark of a true stone craftsman.

squares can be installed in a way similar to that used for vinyl tiles.

Hard-Surface Flooring. Ceramic tile, stone, and slate floors are hard, durable, and easy to clean, especially when you use grout sealers. Because these floors are so inflexible, anything fragile dropped on them is likely to break. Also, they are tiring to stand on and noisy, and they conduct extremes of temperature. For those who love the look of this kind of flooring, however, the drawbacks can be mitigated with accent and area rugs that add a cushion.

Ceramic tile makes an excellent kitchen or bathroom floor when installed with proper grout and sealants. The tiles range from the earth tones of unglazed, solid-color quarry tile to the great array of colors, patterns, and finishes in surface-glazed tiles. Grout comes color-keyed, so

it can be either inconspicuous or a design element. Ceramic and quarry tiles are best suited to a concrete subfloor, though you can lay them over any firm base. Cost ranges from moderate to expensive.

Stone and slate are cut into small slabs and can be laid in a regular or random pattern. Materials are inexpensive or costly, depending on quality and local availability. Even if you find these materials more expensive than other floor coverings, don't dismiss them because of price. They will never need to be replaced, making your initial investment your final one. Because stone and slate are laid in mortar and are themselves weighty materials, a concrete slab makes the ideal subfloor. In other situations, the subfloor must be able to carry a significantly heavy load. Installation is a complex job that should be left to contractors with experience in this type of stone work.

Carpeting and Rugs. The terms carpet and rug are often used interchangeably, but they're not the same. Carpeting is manufactured in rolls ranging from just over 2 feet wide to broadlooms that measure as much as 18 feet wide. Carpeting is usually laid wall-to-wall and can be installed over raw subflooring. Rugs are soft floor coverings that don't extend wall-to-wall and are used over another finished flooring surface. A mat is a small rug.

Differences in fiber composition, construction, color, texture, and cost make choosing a carpet or rug a complex job. Carpeting can be made of natural wool, synthetic fibers, or blends of wool and synthetics. Other natural fibers commonly used in area rugs, scatter rugs, and mats are cotton or plant materials known as cellulosics—hemp, jute, sisal, or grasses. Synthetic fibers are acrylics, nylon, olefin, and polyester.

Plan #131030

Dimensions: 51' W x 41'10" D

Levels: 2

Square Footage: 2,470

Main Level Sq. Ft.: 1,290

Upper Level Sq. Ft.: 1,180

Bedrooms: 4

Bathrooms: 2½

Foundation: Crawl space, slab, basement, or walkout

Materials List Available: Yes

Price Category: F

This home, as shown in the photograph, may differ from the actual blueprints. For more detailed information, please check the floor plans carefully.

Images provided by designer/architect.

Master Bedroom

Master Bathroom

Entry

If high ceilings and spacious rooms make you happy, you'll love this gorgeous home.

Features:

- **Family Room:** An 18-ft. vaulted ceiling that's open to the balcony above, a corner fireplace, and a wall of windows make this room feel special.

- **Dining Room:** This formal room, which flows into the living room, also opens to the front porch and optional backyard deck.

- **Kitchen:** A bright breakfast room joins with this kitchen and opens to the backyard deck.

- **Master Suite:** You'll smile when you see the 11-ft. vaulted ceiling, stunning arched window, and two walk-in closets in the bedroom. A skylight lets natural light into the private bath, with its spa tub, separate shower, and dual-sink vanity.

- **Bedrooms:** To reach these three charming bedrooms, you'll admire the view into the family room below as you walk along the balcony hall.

Main Level Floor Plan

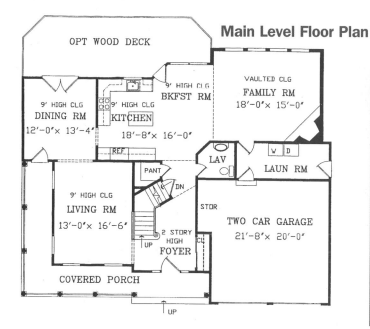

OPT WOOD DECK

9' HIGH CLG
BKFST RM

VAULTED CLG
FAMILY RM
18'-0" x 15'-0"

9' HIGH CLG
DINING RM
12'-0" x 13'-4"

9' HIGH CLG
KITCHEN
18'-8" x 16'-0"

REF

PANT

LAV

W   D
LAUN RM

9' HIGH CLG
LIVING RM
13'-0" x 16'-6"

DN

UP

2 STORY
HIGH
FOYER

STOR

CL

TWO CAR GARAGE
21'-8" x 20'-0"

COVERED PORCH

UP

Upper Level Floor Plan

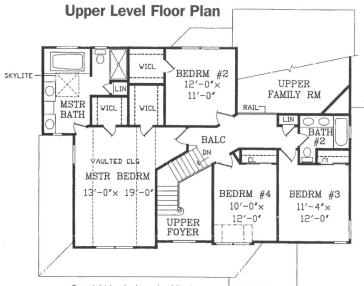

SKYLITE

WICL

BEDRM #2
12'-0" x
11'-0"

UPPER
FAMILY RM

LIN

RAIL

MSTR
BATH

WICL   WICL

LIN

BATH
#2

BALC

DN

CL

VAULTED CLG
MSTR BEDRM
13'-0" x 19'-0"

UPPER
FOYER

BEDRM #4
10'-0" x
12'-0"

BEDRM #3
11'-4" x
12'-0"

CL

Copyright by designer/architect.

Kitchen/Breakfast Area

Dining Room

Living Room

Kitchen/Breakfast Area

Plan #451239

Dimensions: 71'6" W x 87'6" D
Levels: 2
Square Footage: 4,772
Main Level Sq. Ft.: 2,241
Upper Level Sq. Ft.: 290
Lower Level Sq. Ft.: 2,241
Bedrooms: 3
Bathrooms: 3½
Foundation: Walkout
Material List Available: No
Price Category: I

Images provided by designer/architect.

Main Level Floor Plan

Lower Level Floor Plan

Upper Level Floor Plan

Copyright by designer/architect.

Plan #451143

Dimensions: 58'6" W x 58'8" D
Levels: 2
Square Footage: 4,125
Main Level Sq. Ft.: 1,754
Upper Level Sq. Ft.: 1,590
Lower Level Sq. Ft.: 781
Bedrooms: 3
Bathrooms: 4
Foundation: Walkout
Material List Available: No
Price Category: G

Images provided by designer/architect.

Main Level Floor Plan

Copyright by designer/architect.

Lower Level Floor Plan

Upper Level Floor Plan

Plan #181232

Dimensions: 33' W x 26' D

Levels: 2

Square Footage: 1,325

Main Level Sq. Ft.: 741

Upper Level Sq. Ft.: 584

Bedrooms: 2

Bathrooms: 1½

Foundation: Basement or walkout

Materials List Available: Yes

Price Category: B

Images provided by designer/architect.

CAD FILE AVAILABLE
CAD

Main Level Floor Plan

Upper Level Floor Plan

Copyright by designer/architect.

Optional Upper Level Floor Plan

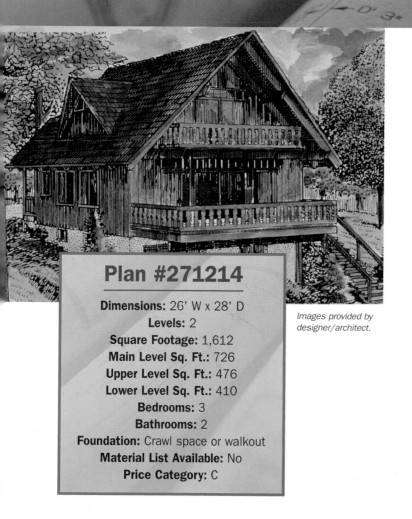

Plan #271214

Dimensions: 26' W x 28' D

Levels: 2

Square Footage: 1,612

Main Level Sq. Ft.: 726

Upper Level Sq. Ft.: 476

Lower Level Sq. Ft.: 410

Bedrooms: 3

Bathrooms: 2

Foundation: Crawl space or walkout

Material List Available: No

Price Category: C

Images provided by designer/architect.

Main Level Floor Plan

Copyright by designer/architect.

Lower Level Floor Plan

Upper Level Floor Plan

Main Level Floor Plan

VEST 20'2" X 6'6"

FOYER

GARAGE 33'0" X 24'8"

M. BATH 11'0" X 12'8"

MASTER BDRM 15'0" X 19'0"

OFFICE 13'0" X 16'0"

GREAT ROOM 20'6" X 20'6"

KITCHEN 22'0" X 16'0"

HEARTH ROOM

OPEN DECK

OPEN DECK

COVERED DECK 21'0" X 16'0"

Copyright by designer/architect.

Lower Level Floor Plan

FOYER

MECH. & STORAGE

BDRM. #2 13'0" X 13'8"

RECREATION ROOM 35'10" X 20'6"

EXERCISE 10'8" X 12'8"

BDRM. #3 11'0" X 13'0"

OPEN DECK

OPEN DECK

COVERED DECK 21'0" X 16'0"

Plan #451390

Dimensions: 83'10" W x 43' D

Levels: 1

Square Footage: 4,320

Main Level Sq. Ft.: 2,160

Lower Level Sq. Ft.: 2,160

Bedrooms: 3

Bathrooms: 2½

Foundation: Walkout – insulated concrete form

Material List Available: No

Price Category: I

Images provided by designer/architect.

Rear Elevation

Main Level Floor Plan

Upper Level Floor Plan

Lower Level Floor Plan

Copyright by designer/architect.

Plan #151716

Dimensions: 113' W x 72' D

Levels: 2

Square Footage: 7,870

Main Level Sq. Ft.: 2,181

Upper Level Sq. Ft.: 2,663

Lower Level Sq. Ft.: 3,026

Bedrooms: 6

Bathrooms: 5

Foundation: Walkout

CompleteCost List Available: Yes

Price Category: L

Images provided by designer/architect.

Plan #111025

Dimensions: 45'10" W x 48'5" D

Levels: 2

Square Footage: 2,428

Main Level Sq. Ft.: 1,533

Upper Level Sq. Ft.: 895

Bedrooms: 4

Bathrooms: 2½

Foundation: Basement or walkout

Materials List Available: No

Price Category: F

Images provided by designer/architect.

Main Level Floor Plan

Porch 24'x 8'

Utility

Breakfast 9'2"x 9'11"

Living 18'8"x 15'

Kitchen 11'6"x 12'

Dining 12'8"x 11'6"

Foyer 8'8"x 6'6"

Master Bedroom 14'10"x 13'

Porch 35'10"x 5'

Optional Basement Level Floor Plan

Two-Car Garage 26'5"x 24'10"

Upper Level Floor Plan

Bedroom 13'7"x 11'9"

Open to Below

Bedroom 11'11"x 11'4"

Bedroom 15'x 11'11"

Copyright by designer/architect.

Plan #341206

Dimensions: 23'4" W x 30'8" D

Levels: 2

Square Footage: 1,348

Main Level Sq. Ft.: 674

Upper Level Sq. Ft.: 674

Bedrooms: 2

Bathrooms: 2½

Foundation: Crawl space, slab, basement or walkout

Material List Available: No

Price Category: B

Images provided by designer/architect.

CAD FILE AVAILABLE

DECK

KITCHEN 10'-0" X 8'-0"

RANGE

REF. PAN.

DINING ROOM 12'-2" X 12'-4"

COATS

BATH 3

FOYER

GATE

PORCH

STOOP

LIVING ROOM 12'-2" X 18'-4"

23'-4"

Main Level Floor Plan

Copyright by designer/architect.

BATH 1

BEDROOM 1 14'-2" X 11'-5"

LIN

W. D. CLOS.

BATH 2

BEDROOM 2 14'-2" X 12'-0"

CLOS.

30'-8"

Upper Level Floor Plan

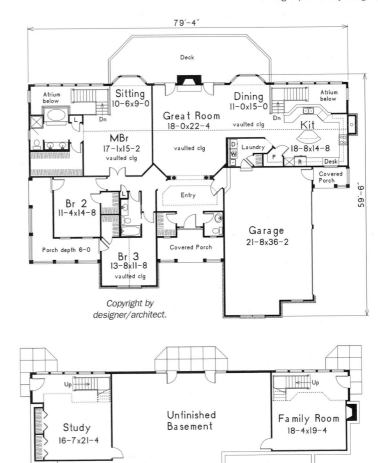

Plan #321031

Dimensions: 79'4" W x 59'6' D
Levels: 1
Square Footage: 3,200
Bedrooms: 3
Bathrooms: 2½
Foundation: Daylight basement
Materials List Available: Yes
Price Category: G

The stone exterior and the multiple roof peaks give this home an elegant look.

Features:

- **Great Room:** This large gathering area features a vaulted ceiling and a beautiful fireplace. The area is open to the dining room, allowing convenient flow between the two spaces.

- **Kitchen:** This grand-scale kitchen features bay-shaped cabinetry built over an atrium that overlooks the two-story window wall. The walk-in pantry will hold all items needed for the family.

- **Master Suite:** A second atrium dominates this master suite, which boasts a sitting area with bay window as well as a luxurious master bath, which has a whirlpool tub open to the garden atrium and lower-level study.

- **Secondary Bedrooms:** Two large bedrooms with walk-in closets share the second full bathroom. Each room has access to its own covered porch.

79'-4"

Deck

Atrium below · Sitting 10-6x9-0 · Great Room 18-0x22-4 vaulted clg · Dining 11-0x15-0 vaulted clg · Atrium below

MBr 17-1x15-2 vaulted clg

Kit 18-8x14-8

Laundry · Desk · Covered Porch

Br 2 11-4x14-8

Entry

Garage 21-8x36-2

Porch depth 6-0

Covered Porch

Br 3 13-8x11-8 vaulted clg

59'-6"

Copyright by designer/architect.

Up · Study 16-7x21-4 · Unfinished Basement · Family Room 18-4x19-4 · Up

Optional Basement Level Floor Plan

Plan #181708

Dimensions: 53' W x 40' D
Levels: 1
Square Footage: 2,800
Main Level Sq. Ft.: 1,400
Lower Level Sq. Ft.: 1,400
Bedrooms: 3
Bathrooms: 2
Foundation: Basement or walkout
Material List Available: Yes
Price Category: F

This gorgeous hillside home is designed for comfort and convenience.

CAD FILE AVAILABLE

Images provided by designer/architect.

Features:

- Great Room: No matter the time of day, this room will be filled with natural light from a sunlit wall of windows or a glowing fireplace.

- Dining Area: Not only does this dining room feature a beautiful bay of windows, but it also adjoins a deck where you might place a small table and chairs for picnic lunches with an elevated view.

- Kitchen: A unique element of this kitchen is the divided snack bar, which flanks the entry to the dining area and curves to provide more open space.

- Bedrooms: Each of these two nicely sized bedrooms has access to a bathroom. The front bedroom opens onto a small private deck.

Main Level Floor Plan

Lower Level Floor Plan

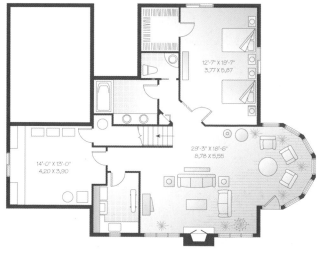

Copyright by designer/architect.

Plan #541042

Dimensions: 85'6" W x 57'6" D
Levels: 1
Square Footage: 4,012
Main Level Sq. Ft.: 2,302
Lower Level Sq. Ft.: 1,710
Bedrooms: 4
Bathrooms: 3 full. 2 half
Foundation: Walkout
Material List Available: No
Price Category: I

All of the attractive elements of Country styling are wrapped up in the decorative tastes of this beautiful home.

Features:

- Great Room: It's the little charms, such as a plant ledge that is perfect for displaying your favorite floral arrangements and the crackling fireplace, that make this vaulted room great.

- Kitchen: Cook like a pro in this smartly designed kitchen, complete with double sinks and a sweet, cozy breakfast nook that's ideal for enjoying morning coffee and the paper

- Master Suite: Heighten your comforts in this swanky master suite. A built-in fireplace

keeps inhabitants warm. A bubbling hot tub is located just off of the master suite; relax in the cool night air just outside your bedroom.

- Additional Bedrooms: On the main level, a second bedroom and bathroom is the perfect combination of rooms to make guests comfortable. Additional bedrooms are located on the lower level.

Rear Elevation

Main Level Floor Plan

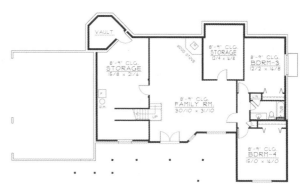

Lower Level Floor Plan

Plan #151369

Dimensions: 39'4" W x 70' D
Levels: 2
Square Footage: 2,260
Main Level Sq. Ft.: 1,419
Upper Level Sq. Ft.: 841
Bedrooms: 4
Bathrooms: 2½
Foundation: Crawl space, slab, basement or walkout
CompleteCost List Available: Yes
Price Category: E

Images provided by designer/architect.

The classic design of this home makes it the perfect choice for a growing family.

Features:

- **Great Room:** Friends and family will love to gather in this large space, complete with fireplace, media center, and built-in shelves. The triple window will allow an abundance of natural light, making this space warm and bright.

- **Dining Room:** As the sun begins to fade, leave the hustle and bustle of your day behind as you relax in this dining room. Cleverly designed swinging doors connect the room to the kitchen.

- **Kitchen:** The chef in the family will love the layout of this kitchen, which is open to the breakfast nook. Adjacent to a bright breakfast nook is a marvelous grilling porch-perfect for the aspiring grill master.

- **Master Suite:** Unwind in this private space, and enjoy its many conveniences. The master bath includes a glass shower, his and her sinks, a large tub, and a spacious walk-in closet.

Main Level Floor Plan

Upper Level Floor Plan

Images provided by designer/architect.

Plan #341234

Dimensions: 32' W x 42' D
Levels: 1.5
Square Footage: 1,476
Main Level Sq. Ft.: 1,049
Upper Level Sq. Ft.: 427
Bedrooms: 4
Bathrooms: 2
Foundation: Crawl space, slab, basement or walkout
Material List Available: No
Price Category: B

Get away from it all in this charming recreational home.

Features:

- Porch: Climb the staircase up this great front porch, perfectly suited for outdoor chatting and relaxing.

- Living Area: This capacious living area is a beautiful element of this home designed with comfort in mind.

- Kitchen: This kitchen is located two steps down from the living area. For added convenience, the appliances are located along one wall, making meal preparation a breeze.

- Bedrooms: The home offers four bedrooms that can be converted into guest rooms or a home office. If you're planning on building this home as a vacation retreat, consider using an extra bedroom for storage for your favorite outdoor equipment, such as water skis.

**Main Level
Floor Plan**

**Upper Level
Floor Plan**

Copyright by designer/architect.

Plan #341251

Dimensions: 64' W x 38'8" D

Levels: 2

Square Footage: 2,254

Main Level Sq. Ft.: 1,127

Upper Level Sq. Ft.: 1,127

Bedrooms: 4

Bathrooms: 3

Foundation: Crawl space, slab, basement or walkout

Material List Available: Yes

Price Category: E

Features:

- Kitchen: This spacious kitchen offers an island useful for food prep or enjoying a cup of coffee while doing your paperwork. Attached to the kitchen is a morning room, a place to soak in the sunshine and start the day off right.

- Master Suite: Located near an open loft, this suite offers a huge walk-in closet, dual vanities, and a whirlpool tub.

- Unfinished Bonus Room: Tap into your creative side to create a unique use for this unfinished bonus room offered in the upper level. Fashion a music room with plenty of space to store equipment or even a dancer's studio for the ballerina in your family.

The gorgeous columns, symmetrical gable, and generous amount of windows are the exterior elements that make this Southern-style home irresistible.

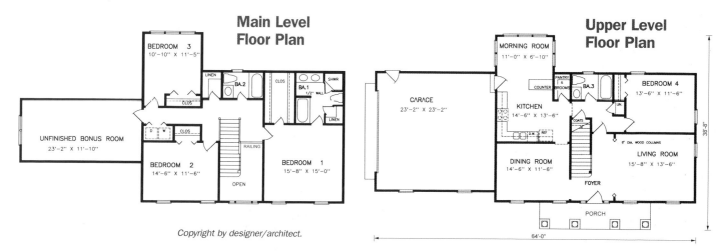

Main Level Floor Plan

Upper Level Floor Plan

Plan #151295

Dimensions: 122'10" W x 75'5" D
Levels: 1.5
Square Footage: 3,659
Main Level Sq. Ft.: 2,711
Lower Level Sq. Ft.: 948
Bedrooms: 4
Bathrooms: 3½
Foundation: Basement or walkout
CompleteCost List Available: Yes
Price Category: H

Images provided by designer/architect.

This stately 3,600-square-foot brick home is elegantly designed inside and out and is perfect for entertaining friends and family.

CAD FILE AVAILABLE

Features:

- **Sitting Areas:** Two sitting areas provide plenty of entertaining options. One sitting room has access to a grilling deck, while the sitting area in the great room opens onto a covered deck. Both areas overlook the downward slope of the hill.

- **Kitchen:** This efficiently designed kitchen has plenty of workspace and storage for a cook of any skill level and is conveniently located adjacent to both the sunny breakfast area and the formal dining room.

- **Master Suite:** This master bedroom is nestled between a private deck and a full bath, which includes a whirlpool tub, a standing shower, and his and her walk-in closets.

- **Secondary Bedrooms:** This plan includes three additional bedrooms, one of which has the lower level all to itself in a small apartment-style setup. This is perfect for guests, both occasional and extended, and includes a full bathroom, small kitchen, and large media room.

Rear View

Main Level Floor Plan

Copyright by designer/architect.

Lower Level Floor Plan

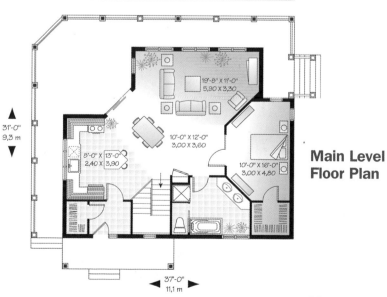

Plan #181159

Dimensions: 37' W x 31' D
Levels: 2
Square Footage: 1,992
Main Level Sq. Ft.: 996
Lower Level Sq. Ft.: 996
Bedrooms: 3
Bathrooms: 2
Foundation: Walkout basement
Materials List Available: Yes
Price Category: D

Ideal for the family who loves the outdoors, this charmer features a wraparound porch that creates a covered pavilion and roofed terrace.

Features:

- **Ceiling Height:** 9-ft. ceilings enhance the airy feeling given by the many windows here.

- **Family Rooms:** These family rooms (one on each floor) allow a busy family adequate space for entertaining a crowd.

- **Kitchen:** Designed for efficient work patterns, this kitchen features ample work and storage space, as well as an island that can double as a

- **Bedrooms:** Each bedroom features a large, walk-in closet and easy access to a large, amenity-filled bathroom with a double vanity, tub, enclosed shower, and a private toilet.

- **Porch:** Enjoy the panoramic view from this spacious covered porch at any time of day.

Images provided by designer/architect.

Lower Level Floor Plan

19'-4" X 15'-0"
5,80 X 4,50

10'-0" X 15'-0"
3,00 X 4,50

10'-0" X 15'-8"
3,00 X 4,70

Copyright by designer/architect.

Main Level Floor Plan

19'-8" X 11'-0"
5,90 X 3,30

10'-0" X 12'-0"
3,00 X 3,60

8'-0" X 13'-0"
2,40 X 3,90

10'-0" X 16'-0"
3,00 X 4,80

31'-0"
9,3 m

37'-0"
11,1 m

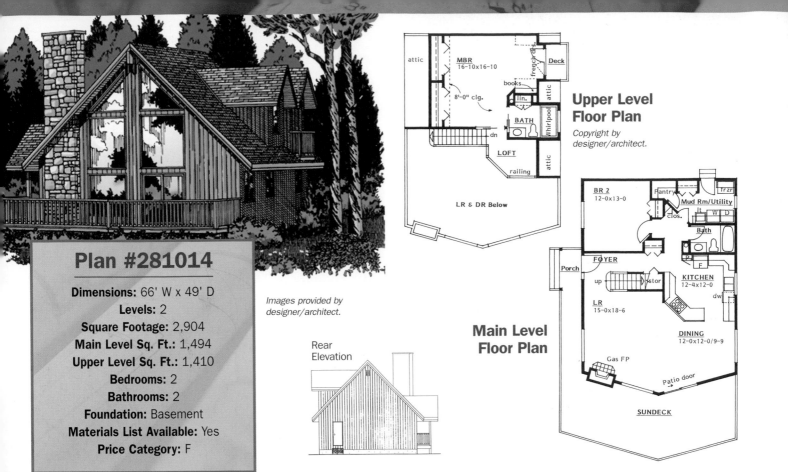

Plan #281014

Dimensions: 66' W x 49' D

Levels: 2

Square Footage: 2,904

Main Level Sq. Ft.: 1,494

Upper Level Sq. Ft.: 1,410

Bedrooms: 2

Bathrooms: 2

Foundation: Basement

Materials List Available: Yes

Price Category: F

Images provided by designer/architect.

Rear Elevation

Upper Level Floor Plan

Copyright by designer/architect.

attic

MBR 16-10x16-10

8'-0" clg.

books

lin.

BATH

Whirlpool

Deck

french drs

attic

attic

LOFT

dn

railing

attic

LR & DR Below

Main Level Floor Plan

BR 2 12-0x13-0

Pantry

frzr

Mud Rm/Utility

clos.

W D

Bath

FOYER

Porch

up

stor

KITCHEN 12-4x12-0

dw

LR 15-0x18-6

DINING 12-0x12-0/9-9

Gas FP

Patio door

SUNDECK

Plan #151099

Dimensions: 39' W x 52' D

Levels: 1.5

Square Footage: 1,897

Main Level Sq. Ft.: 1,299

Upper Level Sq. Ft.: 598

Bedrooms: 3

Bathrooms: 2½

Foundation: Crawl space, slab, basement or walkout

CompleteCost List Available: Yes

Price Category: D

Images provided by designer/architect.

Main Level Floor Plan

39'-0"

GREAT ROOM 14'-10" X 16'-6"

MASTER SUITE 12'-6" X 16'-6"

M. BATH 10'-4" X 6'-6"

DINING ROOM 12'-2" X 9'-4"

LAU. 9'-4" X 6'-10"

KITCHEN 12'-8" X 9'-9"

FOYER

STORAGE 8'-0" X 4'-4"

BREAKFAST ROOM 12'-8" X 8'-6"

GARAGE 19'-4" X 21'-2"

COVERED PORCH 19'-0" X 13'-6"

Upper Level Floor Plan

Copyright by designer/architect.

ATTIC STORAGE

BATH

BEDROOM 3 11'-8" X 14'-6"

OPTIONAL BONUS ROOM / OFFICE 10'-6" X 10'-0"

BEDROOM 2 13'-6" X 14'-6"

Main Level Floor Plan

Images provided by designer/architect.

Upper Level Floor Plan

Copyright by designer/architect.

Plan #641001

Dimensions: 61'6" W x 56' D

Levels: 2

Square Footage: 3,034

Main Level Sq. Ft.: 1,323

Upper Level Sq. Ft.: 1,711

Bedrooms: 4

Bathrooms: 2½

Foundation: Basement or walkout; crawl space or slab for fee

Material List Available: No

Price Category: G

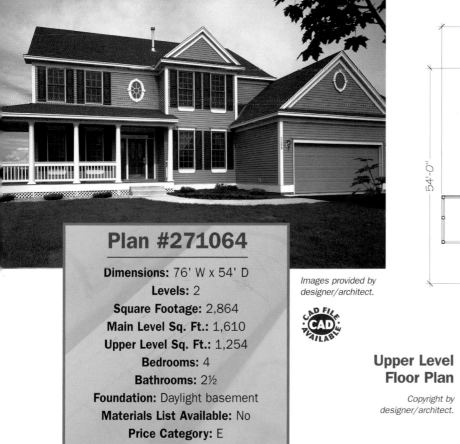

Plan #271064

Dimensions: 76' W x 54' D

Levels: 2

Square Footage: 2,864

Main Level Sq. Ft.: 1,610

Upper Level Sq. Ft.: 1,254

Bedrooms: 4

Bathrooms: 2½

Foundation: Daylight basement

Materials List Available: No

Price Category: E

Images provided by designer/architect.

Main Level Floor Plan

Upper Level Floor Plan

Copyright by designer/architect.

Plan #341064

Dimensions: 58'6" W x 36'9" D
Levels: 1
Square Footage: 1,418
Bedrooms: 3
Bathrooms: 2
Foundation: Crawl space, slab, basement, or walkout
Materials List Available: Yes
Price Category: B

Images provided by designer/architect.

CAD FILE AVAILABLE

Copyright by designer/architect.

BEDROOM 3
10'-0" X 11'-5"

BATH 2

KITCHEN
10'-4" X 11'-5"

DINING
11'-1" X 11'-5"

DECK

GARAGE
13'-7" X 23'-3"

BEDROOM 2
10'-0" X 10'-1"

FAMILY ROOM
17'-3" X 15'-5"

PREFAB GAS LOG FIREPLACE

BEDROOM 1
14'-9" X 13'-8"

BATH 1

PORCH

GARDEN TUB

36'-9"

58'-6"

Plan #451124

Dimensions: 90' W x 52' D
Levels: 2
Square Footage: 4,016
Main Level Sq. Ft.: 2,008
Lower Level Sq. Ft.: 2,088
Bedrooms: 4
Bathrooms: 3
Foundation: Walkout – insulated concrete form
Material List Available: No
Price Category: I

Images provided by designer/architect.

CAD FILE AVAILABLE

8' COVERED PORCH

8' COVERED PORCH

DINING
14'8" X 13'1"
VAULTED

KITCHEN
11'1" X 15'5"

MASTER SUITE
15'8" X 15'2"

W-I-C
10'X6'-2"

LIVING ROOM
21'8" X 17'0"
VAULTED

OFFICE
12'0" X 12'0"

BDRM. #2
15'8" X 15'1"

2-CAR GARAGE
29'8" X 27'4"

8' COVERED PORCH

Main Level Floor Plan

8' COVERED PORCH

BDRM. #3
12'0" X 11'0"

BDRM. #4
12'0" X 11'0"

RECREATION ROOM
19'10" X 23'0"

SHOP/STORAGE
21'8" X 13'0"

WET BAR
8'5" X 9'0"

WEIGHT ROOM
19'4" X 11'10"

WINE
8'5" X 7'0"

Lower Level Floor Plan

Copyright by designer/architect.

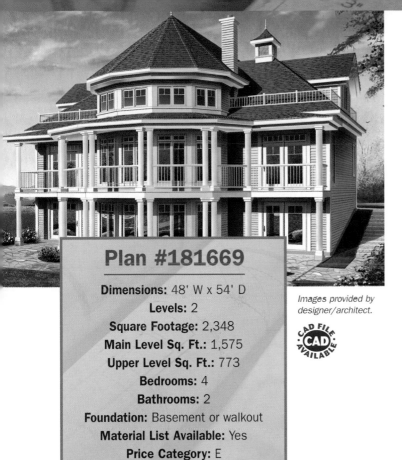

Plan #181669

Dimensions: 48' W x 54' D

Levels: 2

Square Footage: 2,348

Main Level Sq. Ft.: 1,575

Upper Level Sq. Ft.: 773

Bedrooms: 4

Bathrooms: 2

Foundation: Basement or walkout

Material List Available: Yes

Price Category: E

Images provided by designer/architect.

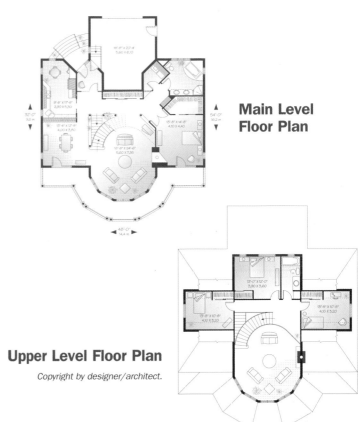

Main Level Floor Plan

Upper Level Floor Plan

Copyright by designer/architect.

Plan #151282

Dimensions: 72'10" W x 67' D

Levels: 1

Square Footage: 2,502

Bedrooms: 4

Bathrooms: 2

Foundation: Crawl space, slab, basement or walkout

CompleteCost List Available: Yes

Price Category: E

Images provided by designer/architect.

Copyright by designer/architect.

Plan #131013

Dimensions: 50' W x 41'8" D
Levels: 1
Square Footage: 1,489
Bedrooms: 3
Bathrooms: 2
Foundation: Crawl space, slab or basement
Materials List Available: Yes
Price Category: C

You'll love the Victorian details on the exterior of this charming ranch-style home.

Features:

- **Front Porch:** This porch is large enough so that you can sit out on warm summer nights to catch a breeze or create a garden of potted ornamentals.

- **Great Room:** Running from the front of the house to the rear, this great room is bathed in natural light from both directions. The volume ceiling adds a luxurious feeling to it, and the fireplace creates a cozy place on chilly afternoons.

- **Kitchen:** Cooking will be a pleasure in this kitchen, thanks to the thoughtful layout and well-designed work areas.

- **Master Suite:** Enjoy the quiet in this room, where it will be easy to relax and unwind, no matter what the time of day. The walk-in closet gives you plenty of storage space, and you're sure to appreciate both the privacy and large size of the master bath.

Images provided by designer/architect.

Copyright by designer/architect.

Rear Elevation

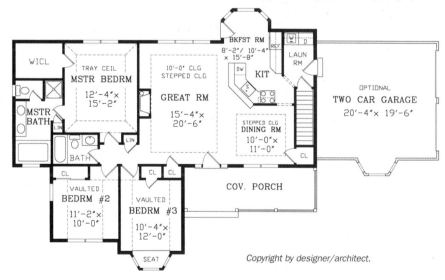

Plan #441012

Dimensions: 65' W x 55' D
Levels: 1
Square Footage: 3,682
Main Level Sq. Ft.: 2,192
Basement Level Sq. Ft.: 1,490
Bedrooms: 4
Bathrooms: 4
Foundation: Slab
Materials List Available: No
Price Category: H

Images provided by designer/architect.

Accommodating a site that slopes to the rear, this home is not only good-looking but practical.

Features:

- **Den:** Just off the foyer is this cozy space, complete with built-ins.
- **Great Room:** This vaulted gathering area features a lovely fireplace, a built-in media center, and a view of the back yard.

- **Kitchen:** This island kitchen is ready to handle the daily needs of your family or aid in entertaining your guests.
- **Lower Level:** Adding even more livability to the home, this floor contains the games room with media center and corner fireplace, two more bedrooms (each with a full bathroom), and the wide covered patio.

Rear Elevation

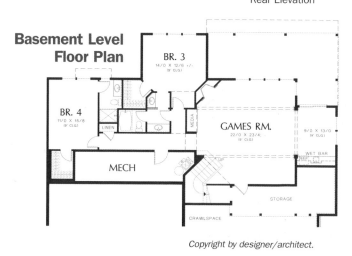

Copyright by designer/architect.

Plan #141009

Dimensions: 44' W x 34'5" D

Levels: 2

Square Footage: 1,683

Main Level Sq. Ft.: 797

Upper Level Sq. Ft.: 886

Bedrooms: 3

Bathrooms: 2½

Foundation: Crawl space, slab, or basement

Materials List Available: No

Price Category: C

A full front porch combined with brick, wood siding, and metal roofing create a visually interesting facade.

Features:

• Ceiling Height: 8 ft. unless otherwise noted.

• Foyer: Guests will be greeted with a sense of spaciousness in this two-story entrance, with its dramatic angled staircase.

• Living Area: This large area is designed to accommodate formal gatherings as well as more intimate family get-togethers.

• Kitchen: You'll love the corner window above the sink. It's perfect for an indoor kitchen herb garden.

• Breakfast Area: Just off the kitchen, this breakfast area is the perfect spot for informal family dining. There's a private bathroom just off this area.

• Master Bath: This luxurious bath boasts a garden tub, his and her vanities, and a commode closet, features usually associated with larger homes.

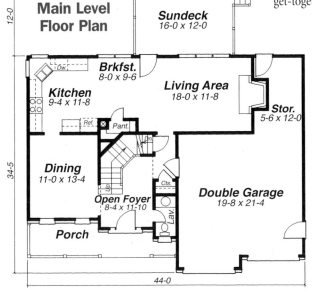

Main Level Floor Plan

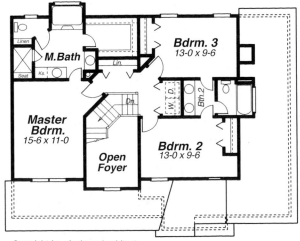

Upper Level Floor Plan

Copyright by designer/architect.

Plan #161061

Dimensions: 90' W x 69'10" D
Levels: 2
Square Footage: 3,816
Main Level Sq. Ft.: 2,725
Upper Level Sq. Ft.: 1,091
Bedrooms: 4
Bathrooms: 3½
Foundation: Basement, walkout basement
Materials List Available: No
Price Category: H

Luxurious amenities make living in this spacious home a true pleasure for the whole family.

Features:

- Great Room: A fireplace, flanking built-in shelves, a balcony above, and three lovely windows create a luxurious room that's always comfortable.

- Hearth Room: Another fireplace with surrounding built-ins and double doors to the outside deck (with its own fireplace) highlight this room.

- Kitchen: A butler's pantry, laundry room, and mudroom with a window seat and two walk-in closets complement this large kitchen.

- Library: Situated for privacy and quiet, this spacious room with a large window area may be reached from the master bedroom as well as the foyer.

- Master Suite: A sloped ceiling and windows on three walls create a lovely bedroom, and the huge walk-in closet, dressing room, and luxurious bath add up to total comfort.

Main Level Floor Plan

Upper Level Floor Plan

Copyright by designer/architect.

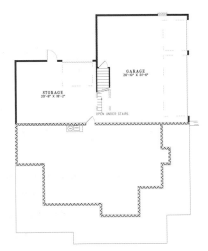

Plan #151309

Dimensions: 52' W x 62'2" D
Levels: 2
Square Footage: 3,435
Main Level Sq. Ft.: 2,343
Upper Level Sq. Ft.: 1,092
Bedrooms: 3
Bathrooms: 3½
Foundation: Walkout
CompleteCost List Available: Yes
Price Category: G

Images provided by designer/architect.

Life will be grand in this country home with its wraparound porch and large rooms.

Features:

• **Porch:** A long covered porch, with 10-in. columns, shelters guests from the elements or gives you outdoor living space where you can sit and greet the neighbors.

• **Great Room:** This area is the interior high light of the home. The large exciting space features a fireplace flanked by a pair of magnificent windows to capture the view.

• **Kitchen:** This spacious gourmet kitchen features a large island with additional seating. The adjoining breakfast room with its vaulted ceiling adds a warm and comfortable feeling to this area.

• **Master Suite:** This main level retreat features a 10-ft.-high boxed ceiling and French doors that lead to the master bath. The bath houses a large walk-in closet, corner whirlpool tub, and corner glass shower.

Main Level Floor Plan

Upper Level Floor Plan

Copyright by designer/architect.

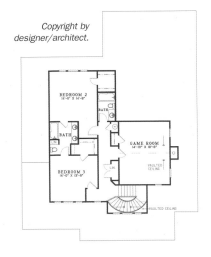

Basement Level Floor Plan

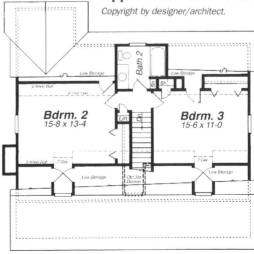

Plan #141038

Dimensions: 40'4" W x 38' D

Levels: 2

Square Footage: 1,668

Main Level Sq. Ft.: 1,057

Upper Level Sq. Ft.: 611

Bedrooms: 3

Bathrooms: 2½

Foundation: Basement with drive-under garage

Materials List Available: Yes

Price Category: C

Images provided by designer/architect.

If you're looking for the ideal plan for a sloping site, this could be the home of your dreams.

Features:

- Porch: Set a couple of rockers on this large porch so you can enjoy the evening views.

- Living Room: A handsome fireplace makes a lovely focal point in this large room.

- Dining Room: Three large windows over looking the sundeck flood this room with natural light.

- Kitchen: The U-shaped, step-saving layout makes this kitchen a cook's dream.

- Breakfast Room: With an expansive window area and a door to the sundeck, this room is sure to be a family favorite in any season of the year.

- Master Suite: A large walk-in closet and a private bath with tub, shower, and double vanity complement this suite's spacious bedroom.

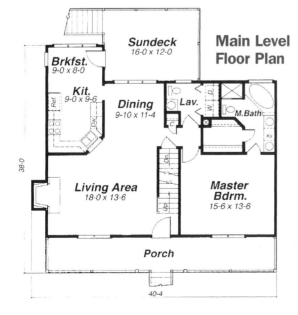

Main Level Floor Plan

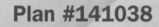

Upper Level Floor Plan

Copyright by designer/architect.

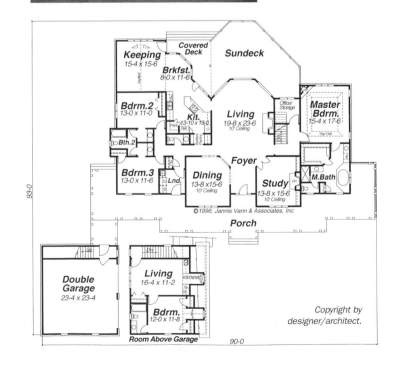

Plan #141022

Dimensions: 90' W x 93' D
Levels: 1
Square Footage: 2,911
Bedrooms: 3
Bathrooms: 2½
Foundation: Basement
Materials List Available: No
Price Category: F

Rear View

Second-floor dormers accent this charming country ranch, which features a gracious porch that spans its entire front. A detached garage, connected by a covered extension, creates an impressive, expansive effect.

Features:

- Living Room: As you enter the foyer, you are immediately drawn to this dramatic, bayed living room.

- Study: Flanking the foyer, this cozy study features built-in shelving and a direct-vent fireplace.

- Kitchen: From a massive, partially covered deck, a wall of glass floods this spacious kitchen, breakfast bay, and keeping room with light.

- Master Suite: Enjoy the complete privacy provided by this strategically located master suite.

- Guest Quarters: You can convert the bonus room, above the garage, into a guest apartment.

Plan #141051

Dimensions: 44' W x 50' D
Levels: 2
Square Footage: 3,011
Main Level Sq. Ft.: 1,285
Upper Level Sq. Ft.: 1,726
Bedrooms: 4
Bathrooms: 3½
Foundation: Basement
Material List Available: No
Price Category: G

This country home has a hint of craftsman styling to make it a neighborhood standout.

Features:

- Family Room: Exposed beams and a fireplace flanked by built-in shelves add to the charm of this gathering area. French doors lead to the backyard patio.

- Kitchen: This large, open kitchen features additional seating at the island. The layout allows guests in the family room to overflow into the kitchen during parties. The generously sized pantry is available to hold all of the supplies needed for your family.

- Master Suite: This retreat features a tray ceiling in the sleeping area plus an additional sitting area. The master bath boasts a stall shower and a large walk-in closet.

- Secondary Bedrooms: Bedrooms 2 and 3 share a Jack-and-Jill bathroom. Bedroom 4 has a private bathroom.

Images provided by designer/architect.

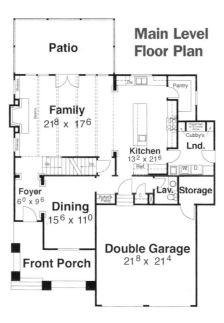

Main Level Floor Plan

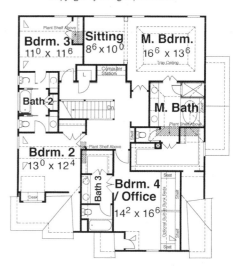

Upper Level Floor Plan

Copyright by designer/architect.

Kitchen

Kitchen/Family Room

COMES WITH DETACHED GARAGE PLAN

LAUNDRY 8-0 X 9-4

COVERED PORCH 17-10 X 6-0

BATH

MASTER BEDROOM 14-0 X 13-8

KITCHEN 12-0 X 13-8

GREAT ROOM 21-8 X 17-0

CLOSET

BATH

BREAKFAST AREA 12-0 X 9-0

DINING ROOM 13-0 X 12-0

FOYER

BEDROOM #3 12-0 X 12-0

BEDROOM #2 10-0 X 13-0

COVERED PORCH 32-4 X 7-0

42'-0"

56'-0"

Images provided by designer/architect.

Copyright by designer/architect.

Plan #191023

Dimensions: 56' W x 42' D

Levels: 1

Square Footage: 1,785

Bedrooms: 3

Bathrooms: 3

Foundation: Crawl space, slab, basement or walkout

Materials List Available: No

Price Category: C

Plan #341214

Dimensions: 56'4" W x 36' D

Levels: 2

Square Footage: 1,806

Main Level Sq. Ft.: 828

Upper Level Sq. Ft.: 978

Bedrooms: 3

Bathrooms: 2½

Foundation: Crawl space, slab, basement or walkout

Material List Available: Yes

Price Category: D

Images provided by designer/architect.

CAD FILE AVAILABLE

BEDROOM 2 11'-5"X12'-0"

CLOSET

BEDROOM 3 10'-10"X12'-0"

LINENS

CLOSET

WASH DRY

UNFINISHED BONUS SPACE 14'-10"X12'-10"

BATH 2

CLOSET

COMPUTER CORNER

BEDROOM 1 15'-0"X12'-0"

BATH 1

SHWR

PEDESTAL TUB

Upper Level Floor Plan

DECK

DINING ROOM 15'-0"X10'-0"

KITCHEN 10'-10"X 12'-0"

REF.

LIVING ROOM 15'-0"X19'-5"

BATH 3

FOYER

PORCH

GARAGE 24'-0"X24'-0"

36'-0"

56'-4"

Main Level Floor Plan

Copyright by designer/architect.

Plan #551101

Dimensions: 50' W x 40' D

Levels: 2

Square Footage: 2,700

Main Level Sq. Ft.: 1,360

Upper Level Sq. Ft.: 1,340

Bedrooms: 4

Bathrooms: 2½

Foundation: Crawl space or walkout; slab or basement for fee

Material List Available: No

Price Category: F

Images provided by designer/architect.

Main Level Floor Plan

Upper Level Floor Plan

Copyright by designer/architect.

Plan #341284

Dimensions: 57'7" W x 26' D

Levels: 2

Square Footage: 2,384

Main Level Sq. Ft.: 960

Lower Level Sq. Ft: 1,424

Bedrooms: 3

Bathrooms: 2½

Foundation: Crawl space, slab, basement, or walkout

Materials List Available: Yes

Price Category: E

Images provided by designer/architect.

CAD FILE AVAILABLE

Main Level Floor Plan

Copyright by designer/architect.

Upper Level Floor Plan

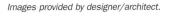
Images provided by designer/architect.

Plan #161037

Dimensions: 46' W x 59'4" D
Levels: 1
Square Footage: 2,469
Main Level Sq. Ft.: 1,462
Basement Level Sq. Ft.: 1,007
Bedrooms: 2
Bathrooms: 2½
Foundation: Walkout; basement for fee
Materials List Available: Yes
Price Category: E

Kitchen

A brick-and-stone facade welcomes you into this lovely home, which is designed to fit into a narrow lot.

Features:

- Foyer: This entrance, with vaulted ceiling, introduces the graciousness of this home.

- Great Room: A vaulted center ceiling creates the impression that this large great room and dining room are one space, making entertaining a natural in this area.

- Kitchen: Designed for efficiency with ample storage and counter space, this kitchen also allows casual dining at the counter.

- Master Suite: A tray ceiling sets this room off from the rest of the house, and the lavishly equipped bathroom lets you pamper yourself.

- Lower Level: Put extra bedrooms or a library in this finished area, and use the wet bar in a game room or recreation room.

Main Level Floor Plan

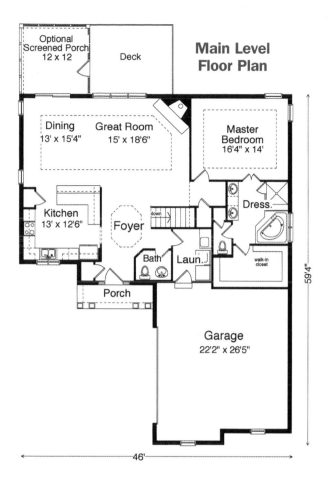

Optional Screened Porch
12 x 12

Deck

Dining
13' x 15'4"

Great Room
15' x 18'6"

Master Bedroom
16'4" x 14'

Kitchen
13' x 12'6"

Foyer

down

Dress.

walk-in closet

Bath

Laun.

Porch

Garage
22'2" x 26'5"

59'4"

46'

Basement Level Floor Plan

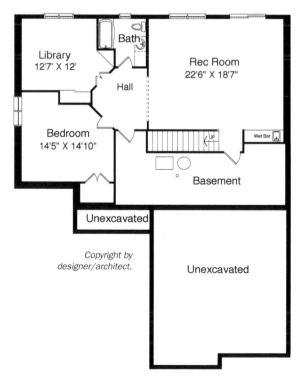

Library
12'7" X 12'

Bath

Rec Room
22'6" X 18'7"

Hall

Bedroom
14'5" X 14'10"

Basement

Wet Bar

UP

Unexcavated

Unexcavated

Copyright by designer/architect.

Rear Elevation

Great Room

Dining Room

Plan #181673

Dimensions: 72' W x 42' D
Levels: 2
Square Footage: 3,392
Main Level Sq. Ft.: 1,434
Upper Level Sq. Ft.: 524
Lower Level Sq. Ft.: 1,434
Bedrooms: 4
Bathrooms: 3½
Foundation: Basement or walkout
Material List Available: Yes
Price Category: G

Images provided by designer/architect.

CAD FILE AVAILABLE

Main Level Floor Plan

Lower Level Floor Plan

Upper Level Floor Plan

Copyright by designer/architect.

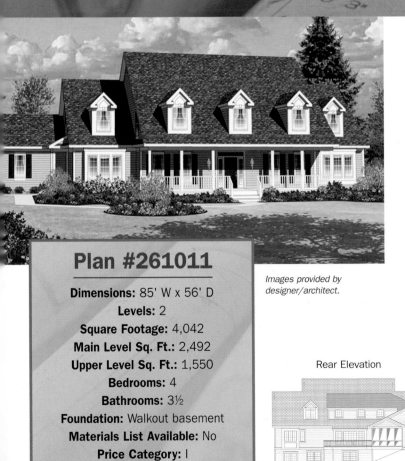

Plan #261011

Dimensions: 85' W x 56' D
Levels: 2
Square Footage: 4,042
Main Level Sq. Ft.: 2,492
Upper Level Sq. Ft.: 1,550
Bedrooms: 4
Bathrooms: 3½
Foundation: Walkout basement
Materials List Available: No
Price Category: I

Images provided by designer/architect.

Rear Elevation

Main Level Floor Plan

Upper Level Floor Plan

Copyright by designer/architect.

**Main Level
Floor Plan**

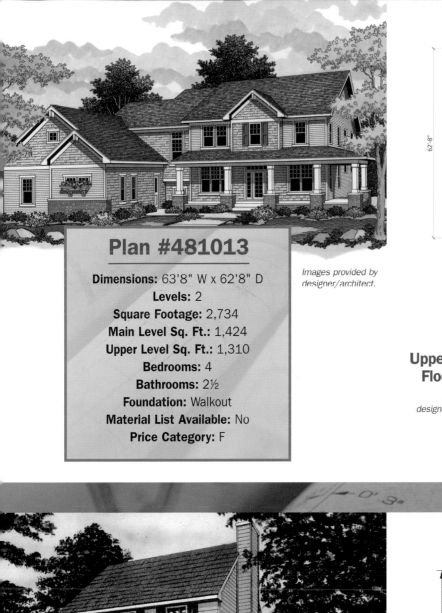

Plan #481013

Dimensions: 63'8" W x 62'8" D
Levels: 2
Square Footage: 2,734
Main Level Sq. Ft.: 1,424
Upper Level Sq. Ft.: 1,310
Bedrooms: 4
Bathrooms: 2½
Foundation: Walkout
Material List Available: No
Price Category: F

*Images provided by
designer/architect.*

**Upper Level
Floor Plan**

*Copyright by
designer/architect.*

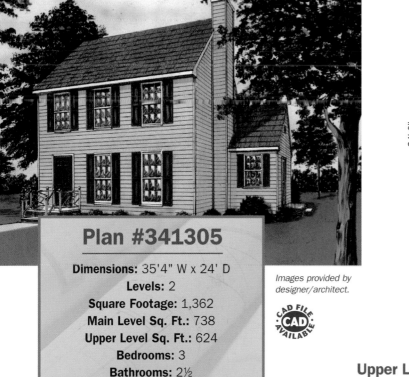

Plan #341305

Dimensions: 35'4" W x 24' D
Levels: 2
Square Footage: 1,362
Main Level Sq. Ft.: 738
Upper Level Sq. Ft.: 624
Bedrooms: 3
Bathrooms: 2½
Foundation: Crawl space, slab,
basement or walkout
Material List Available: No
Price Category: B

*Images provided by
designer/architect.*

**CAD FILE
AVAILABLE**

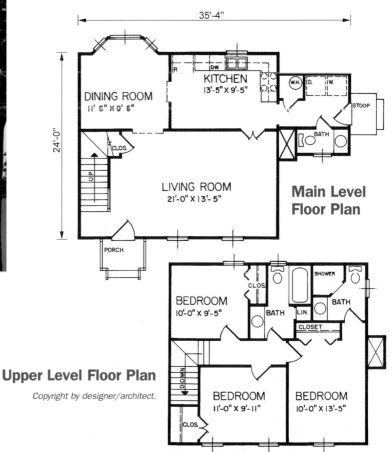

**Main Level
Floor Plan**

Upper Level Floor Plan

Copyright by designer/architect.

Plan #151290

Dimensions: 34'8" W x 61'10" D
Levels: 1.5
Square Footage: 1,541
Main Level Sq. Ft.: 990
Upper Level Sq. Ft.: 551
Bedrooms: 3
Bathrooms: 2
Foundation: Crawl space, slab, basement or walkout
CompleteCost List Available: Yes
Price Category: C

Images provided by designer/architect.

CAD FILE AVAILABLE

GARAGE
18'-4" X 20'-0"

STRG

KITCHEN
16'-9" X 11'-6"

PATIO

WHIRL TUB

M.BATH
16'-10" X 11'-6"

GREAT RM.
14'-6" X 15'-0"

MASTER SUITE
13'-0" X 15'-0"

COVERED PORCH
32'-0" X 8'-0"

Upper Level Floor Plan

BATH

BED RM 2
12'-2" X 11'-0"

BED RM 3
10'-4" X 11'-0"

Main Level Floor Plan

Copyright by designer/architect.

Plan #291023

Dimensions: 34'3" W x 60'8" D
Levels: 1
Square Footage: 2,047
Main Level Sq. Ft.: 1,284
Lower Level Sq. Ft.: 763
Bedrooms: 2
Bathrooms: 2½
Foundation: Walkout basement
Material List Available: No
Price Category: D

Images provided by designer/architect.

34'-3"

BEDROOM #2
14'-4"x12'-0"

SLOPED CEILING

BEDROOM #1
11'-8"x13'-4"

SLOPED CEILING

BATH #2

PR

B#1

LIN

Copyright by designer/architect.

PORCH

KITCHEN

DN

60'-8"

GREAT ROOM
26'-0"x24'-6"

DECK
13'-0"x9'-8"

DN

SCREENED PORCH
12'-8"x9'-8"

SLOPED CEILING

Side View

Plan #151142

Dimensions: 75'10" W x 126'6" D
Levels: 2
Square Footage: 6,239
Main Level Sq. Ft.: 3,173
Upper Level Sq. Ft.: 2,120
Lower Level Sq. Ft.: 946
Bedrooms: 3
Bathrooms: 2 full, 2 half
Foundation: Basement or walkout
CompleteCost List Available: Yes
Price Category: K

Images provided by designer/architect.

CAD FILE AVAILABLE

Main Level Floor Plan

Copyright by designer/architect.

Upper Level Floor Plan

Lower Level Floor Plan

Plan #481003

Dimensions: 63'8" W x 48' D
Levels: 2
Square Footage: 2,278
Main Level Sq. Ft.: 1,231
Upper Level Sq. Ft.: 1,047
Bedrooms: 3
Bathrooms: 2½
Foundation: Walkout
Material List Available: No
Price Category: E

Images provided by designer/architect.

Main Level Floor Plan

Upper Level Floor Plan

Copyright by designer/architect.

Plan #481022

Dimensions: 85'8" W x 48' D

Levels: 2

Square Footage: 3,217

Main Level Sq. Ft.: 1,667

Upper Level Sq. Ft.: 1,550

Bedrooms: 3

Bathrooms: 2½

Foundation: Walkout

Material List Available: No

Price Category: G

This elegant house has an open interior design that is made for family living.

Images provided by designer/architect.

Features:

- **Family Room:** An 18-ft.-high ceiling and an angled fireplace flanked with built-ins add to the great atmosphere in this gathering area. The large windows allow for a view of the backyard.

- **Dining Room:** This formal dining area features columns, which define its boundaries. The stepped ceiling adds an elegant feature to the area.

- **Kitchen:** This island kitchen features a built-in pantry and large center island. The dinette area has access to the rear screened porch.

- **Bedrooms:** The master suite and two secondary bedrooms are located on the upper level. Bedrooms 2 and 3 share a "Jack-and-Jill" bathroom.

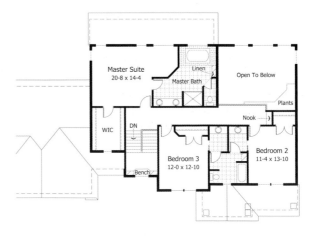

Rear Elevation

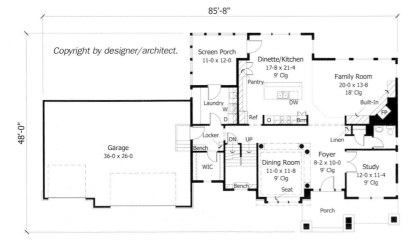

Main Level Floor Plan

Upper Level Floor Plan

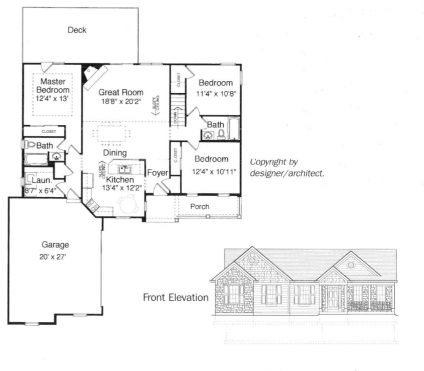

Plan #161081

Dimensions: 50' W x 55'8" D
Levels: 1
Square Footage: 1,390
Bedrooms: 3
Bathrooms: 2
Foundation: Walk-out Basement
Materials List Available: Yes
Price Category: B

Images provided by designer/architect.

The stone-and-siding facade, front porch, and multiple gables decorate the exterior of this charming one-floor plan.

Features:

- **Great Room:** The standard 8–ft. ceiling height vaults to an 11-ft. height through this room.

- **Kitchen:** This kitchen can accommodate a small dining area or can be designed to offer more cabinets and allow for a larger great room.

- **Master Suite:** This suite enjoys a raised center ceiling and a private bath.

- **Basement:** The home is designed with this unfinished walk-out basement, which can be finished to provide additional living space.

Copyright by designer/architect.

Front Elevation

Rear Elevation

Plan #441011

Dimensions: 67' W x 46' D
Levels: 1
Square Footage: 2,898
Main Level Sq. Ft.: 1,744
Basement Level Sq. Ft.: 1,154
Bedrooms: 3
Bathrooms: 2½
Foundation: Walkout basement
Materials List Available: No
Price Category: F

Images provided by designer/architect.

Think one-story, then think again—it's a hillside home designed to make the best use of a sloping lot. Elegant in exterior appeal, this home uses high arches and a hipped room to promote a sense of style.

CAD FILE AVAILABLE

Features:

- Dining Room: Box beams and columns define this formal space, which is just off the foyer.

- Kitchen: This fully equipped kitchen has everything the chef in the family could want. Nearby is the breakfast nook with sliding glass doors to the deck, which acts as the roof for the patio below.

- Master Suite: This suite is located on the right side of the main level. The master bath is

replete with a spa tub, compartmented toilet, separate shower, and dual lavatories.

- Lower Level: The two extra bedrooms, full bathroom, and games room are on this lower floor, which adds to the great livability of the home. The wet bar in the games room is a bonus.

Rear Elevation

Main Level Floor Plan

Basement Level Floor Plan

Copyright by designer/architect.

Plan #161087

Dimensions: 48'10" W x 53'4" D

Levels: 1

Square Footage: 1,664

Bedrooms: 3

Bathrooms: 2

Foundation: Walkout basement

Materials List Available: Yes

Price Category: C

Images provided by designer/architect.

A brick-and-stone facade with cedar shakes, a large front porch, arches, and a double gable decorate the exterior of this charming cottage-style home.

Features:

- **Great Room:** This area has plenty of space for entertaining or just relaxing. It features a gas fireplace and access to the rear deck.

- **Kitchen:** This well equipped cooking center has everything the chef in the family could want. It is open to the dining room and great room.

- **Master Suite:** This private space boasts a large sleeping area with a bath that has two vanities.

- **Expansion:** The lower level can be finished to add an additional bedroom, bathroom, and recreation room.

Copyright by designer/architect.

Deck

Master Bedroom
15'4" x 15'6"

Great Room
15'6" x 17'2"

Dining
10'1" x 13'
Incl. Bay

WALK IN CLOSET

Kitchen
9'7" x 13'7"

Bath

LINEN

Hall

Bedroom
11'6" x 11'1"

Library/ Bedroom
10'1" x 12'1"

OPTIONAL DOORS

CLOSET

Foyer

Laun.

PANTRY

Porch

Garage
20' x 21'

Main Level Floor Plan

Bedroom
14'6" x 14'6"

Rec. Room
31'8" x 17'3"

Bath

Basement

Unexcavated

Unexcavated

Basement Level Floor Plan

Left Side Elevation

Right Side Elevation

Rear Elevation

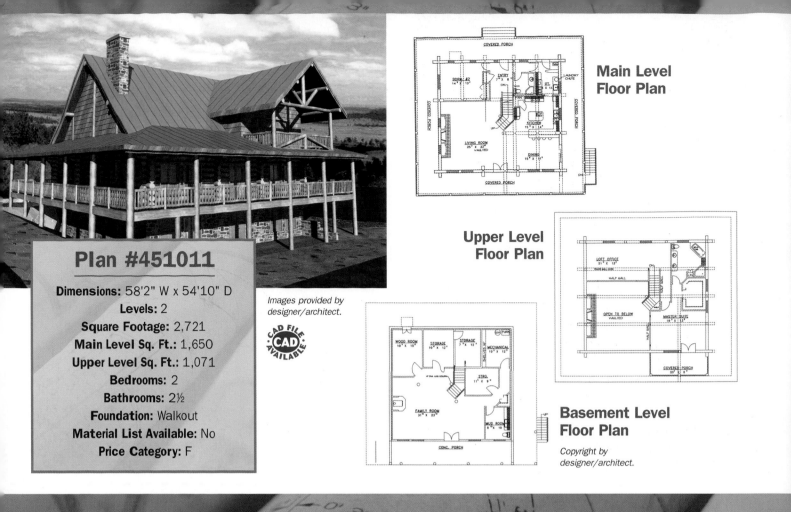

Main Level Floor Plan

Upper Level Floor Plan

Basement Level Floor Plan

Images provided by designer/architect.

Copyright by designer/architect.

Plan #451011

Dimensions: 58'2" W x 54'10" D
Levels: 2
Square Footage: 2,721
Main Level Sq. Ft.: 1,650
Upper Level Sq. Ft.: 1,071
Bedrooms: 2
Bathrooms: 2½
Foundation: Walkout
Material List Available: No
Price Category: F

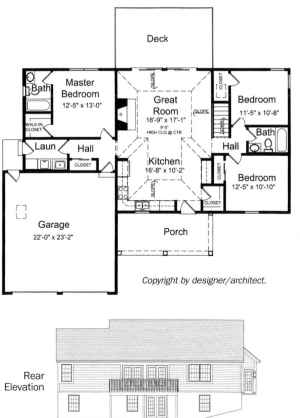

Images provided by designer/architect.

Copyright by designer/architect.

Rear Elevation

Plan #161162

Dimensions: 56'10" W x 43'7" D
Levels: 1
Square Footage: 1,321
Bedrooms: 3
Bathrooms: 2
Foundation: Walkout; crawl space, slab or basement for fee
Material List Available: Yes
Price Category: B

Main Level Floor Plan

Images provided by designer/architect.

Copyright by designer/architect.

Upper Level Floor Plan

Plan #181243

Dimensions: 67' W x 40' D

Levels: 2

Square Footage: 2,219

Main Level Sq. Ft.: 1,232

Upper Level Sq. Ft.: 987

Bedrooms: 3

Bathrooms: 3½

Foundation: Basement

Materials List Available: Yes

Price Category: E

CAD FILE AVAILABLE

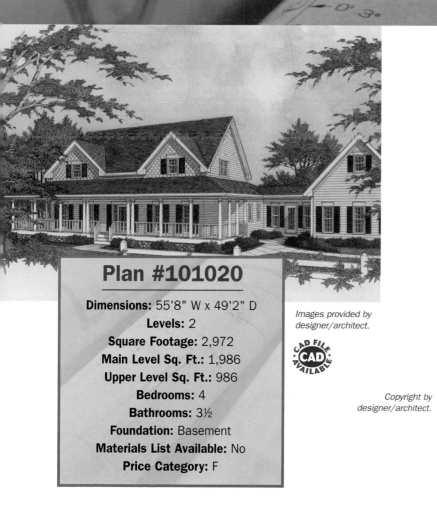

Plan #101020

Dimensions: 55'8" W x 49'2" D

Levels: 2

Square Footage: 2,972

Main Level Sq. Ft.: 1,986

Upper Level Sq. Ft.: 986

Bedrooms: 4

Bathrooms: 3½

Foundation: Basement

Materials List Available: No

Price Category: F

CAD FILE AVAILABLE

Images provided by designer/architect.

DECK 40'0" x 11'7"

SCREENED PORCH 11'10" x 11'7"

BREAKFAST 10'11" x 10'0"

GARAGE 21'4" x 32'1"

MASTER BDRM 14'9" x 18'5"

FAMILY 19'0" x 17'0"

KITCHEN 13'10" x 13'2"

LIVING 14'9" x 11'11"

ENTRY 11'7" x 14'5"

DINING 14'9" x 11'11"

49'2"-36'-4"

22'-0"

55'-8"

Main Level Floor Plan

BEDROOM 4 14'9" x 13'0"

OPEN BELOW

MECHANICAL STORAGE 7'5" x 8'9"

BONUS ROOM 11'9" x 32'1"

BEDROOM 3 14'9" x 13'0"

OPEN BELOW

BEDROOM 2 14'9" x 15'5"

Copyright by designer/architect.

Upper Level Floor Plan

Lower Level
Floor Plan

Copyright by designer/architect.

COVERED PATIO
16'-0" X 6'-0"

BEDROOM 2
15'-8" X 10'-0"

BONUS ROOM
16'-0" X 16'-4"

BATH

BEDROOM 3
14'-8" X 12'-2"

STORM / SAFE ROOM
10'-0" X 6'-0"

MECH

UP

Plan #151508

Dimensions: 54' W x 54'8" D
Levels: 1
Square Footage: 2,447
Main Level Sq. Ft.: 1,484
Lower Level Sq. Ft.: 963
Bedrooms: 3
Bathrooms: 2½
Foundation: Walkout
CompleteCost List Available: Yes
Price Category: E

Images provided by designer/architect.

54'-0"

DINING
15'-0" X 10'-8"
9' BOXED CEILING

COVERED DECK
16'-0" X 6'-0"

MASTER SUITE
15'-8" X 13'-6"
12' TRAY CEILING

GREAT ROOM
16'-0" X 18'-4"
16' BEADED CEILING

8" COLUMNS

KITCHEN
15'-8" X 11'-7"

PASS-THRU
GAS FIREPLACE

8" BOX BEAM

8" BOX BEAM

MASTER BATH
14'-8" X 11'-0"

FOYER
16'-0" X 6'-0"

DW

REF

PAN

LIN

LAU.
8'-8" X 6'-2"

DN

TV CAB

SHWR

WHP TUB

P.R.

COVERED PORCH
20'-7" X 6'-0"

8" BOXED COLUMNS

GARAGE
21'-6" x 22'-0"

BRICK STEPS

54'-8"

Main Level
Floor Plan

Plan #141001

Dimensions: 48' W x 29' D
Levels: 1
Square Footage: 1,208
Bedrooms: 3
Bathrooms: 2
Foundation: Basement
Materials List Available: Yes
Price Category: B

Images provided by designer/architect.

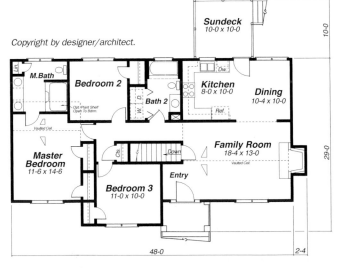

Copyright by designer/architect.

Sundeck
10-0 x 10-0

10-0

M.Bath

Bedroom 2

Bath 2

W / D

Kitchen
8-0 x 10-0

Dw

Ref.

Dining
10-4 x 10-0

Opt. Plant Shelf Open To Bdrm

Vaulted Ceil.

Master Bedroom
11-6 x 14-6

Clts

Down

Family Room
18-4 x 13-0

Vaulted Ceil.

Entry

Bedroom 3
11-0 x 10-0

29-0

48-0

2-4

SMARTtip
Hydro-seeding

An alternative to traditional seeding is hydro-seeding. In this process, a slurry of grass seed, wood fibers, and fertilizer is spray-applied in one step. Hydro-seeding is relatively inexpensive. Compared with seeding by hand, hydro-seeding is also very fast.

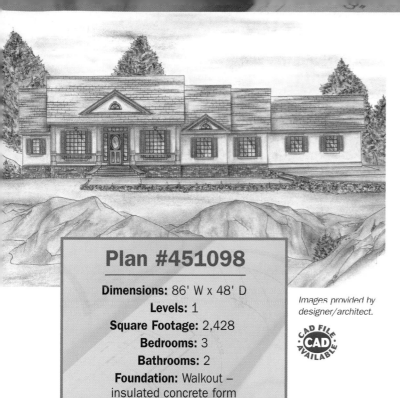

Plan #451098

Dimensions: 86' W x 48' D

Levels: 1

Square Footage: 2,428

Bedrooms: 3

Bathrooms: 2

Foundation: Walkout – insulated concrete form

Material List Available: No

Price Category: E

Images provided by designer/architect.

CAD FILE AVAILABLE

Copyright by designer/architect.

Plan #161124

Dimensions: 30' W x 58' D

Levels: 2

Square Footage: 1,728

Main Level Sq. Ft.: 1,092

Upper Level Sq. Ft.: 636

Bedrooms: 3

Bathrooms: 2

Foundation: Walkout

Material List Available: Yes

Price Category: C

Images provided by designer/architect.

Main Level Floor Plan

Copyright by designer/architect.

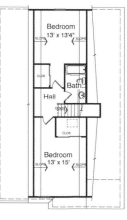

Upper Level Floor Plan

Rear Elevation

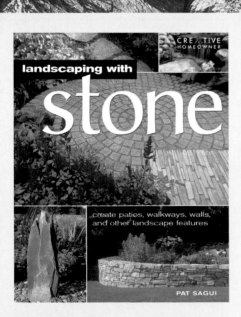

landscaping with
stone
create patios, walkways, walls,
and other landscape features

PAT SAGUI

The following article was reprinted from
Landscaping with Stone (Creative Homeowner
2005).

Retaining Wall

Retaining walls let you alter the grade or slope of the land to create level areas that you can use for planting, adding a patio, or any one of a number of uses. They also protect the slope from eroding or collapsing. As with freestanding stone walls, you can build a dry-laid wall or a mortared version. Dry-laid walls are informal and do not require a concrete footing, so they are easier to build than mortared retaining walls. Mortared walls offer more stability, but they tend to be more difficult to build.

The walls in the sunken garden, shown below, are a good example of retaining wall construction. With thoughtful, creative planning you can build a dry-laid retaining wall that is handsome, durable, and an asset to your landscape.

An evergreen shrub, opposite, softens the transition between the lawn area and the wall.

Retaining walls create a sunken garden room, below, that extends the normal growing season.

Preparing the Site

Begin by calculating the height of the wall. Usually, the angle of the slope determines the height of the wall—the steeper the slope the taller the wall. There are exceptions to this rule. For example, privacy walls are usually tall no matter how steep the slope against which they are built. You may want a wall at a specific height so that you can get access to a garden bed.

Tall walls are more difficult and more costly to build. Structural and drainage issues are more critical for walls more than 3 feet tall and, if you have no prior experience, should not be attempted without professional advice or assistance. The visual mass of a tall wall can also present problems. Rather than build one tall wall, consider adding terraces and building a series of shorter walls.

Walls and Permits

Before you start digging, find out whether you need a permit to build a dry-laid stone retaining wall.

Terracing a Slope. Farmers have been terracing hillsides for thousands of years. For a homeowner, the incentive usually comes from a desire to turn an otherwise uninspiring or difficult-to-maintain hillside into accessible and attractive gardens.

The shorter walls typical of terraces require less skill to fabricate, and you can construct them in stages. Terraces are also less expensive to construct than one tall wall, and they create an inviting destination. All the steps that apply to retaining walls apply to terracing a natural hillside or constructed berm. If the slope is steep and you want wide terraces, then you will have extra fill to remove from the site.

Excavation. Once you know the location and height of the wall, you are ready to begin excavating the site. Short walls with little slope behind them may require nothing more than removing the sod and excavating down 4 to 6 inches. On sloped ground, excavation is usually a cut-and-fill process. As you cut into the slope, you use the soil to level off another area.

Plan on excavating more soil than may appear necessary. You will need space for the wall, space to work, room for gravel backfill, and space for additional backfill to minimize pressure on the wall—an important consideration for walls that front steep, tall slopes.

In many cases, you will end up with more soil than you can use on the current project. Try to find some other landscaping use for the removed soil.

The Base of the Wall. Because they can shift with the movement of the earth, dry-laid retaining walls do not require a concrete footing. In gravelly soil that drains well, re-

move the sod and 4 to 6 inches of topsoil. Slope the grade in the trench ¼ to ½ inch per foot into the hill. In sandy or wet soils, excavate an additional 4 to 12 inches; lay down landscape fabric; and backfill the trench with gravel that compacts and drains.

The height of the wall will determine the width of your trench. Use this guide: for walls under 3 feet tall, make the width of the wall at its base equal to one-half the finished height of the wall; for taller walls, the width of the base should be closer to two-thirds the height of the wall. A 3-foot-tall wall should have a 2-foot-wide base. Consult a professional mason or landscape contractor when planning on a wall that is taller than 3 feet.

Mortared walls require a concrete footing. Local building codes determine the depth and width of the footing.

Drainage. Runoff from the slope will seep out between the stones of a dry-laid retaining wall. Typically, these types of walls do not require an additional drainage system. But if the

Building with rounded stone is challenging and best suited for short walls, opposite.

Rather than build one tall wall, consider building a series of shorter walls with terraces that you can plant, left.

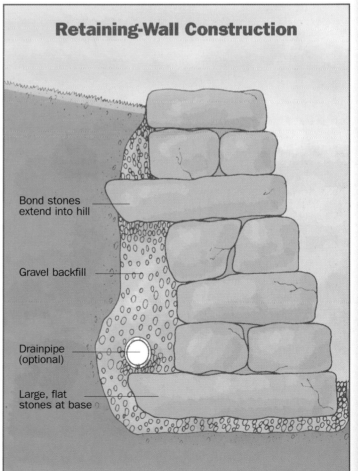

Retaining-Wall Construction

Bond stones extend into hill

Gravel backfill

Drainpipe (optional)

Large, flat stones at base

site is wet and you want to minimize seepage through the wall, add a drainpipe that can move the water away from the wall. Backfilling with a few inches of coarse gravel minimizes erosion and loss of soil through the wall. For greater stability, particularly with steep slopes, lay landscape fabric between the soil and the backfill gravel.

If you are planning a mortared wall, you must provide a drainage system. Without weep holes or some other drainage system, runoff from the slope will exert tremendous pressure against the wall, resulting in buckling of the wall.

Building the Wall

When the stone is delivered to the site, sort it as you would for a freestanding wall: larger stones for the base, bond stones to span between wythes, rubble for fill between the wythes, and cap stones or coping for the top of the wall. Unlike freestanding walls, retaining walls need only one good face. If your wall is short and there isn't a lot of pressure on it, you can build the wall one stone wide provided your stones are large and good building stone, that is, they fit together well.

Calculate the Batter. Retaining walls lean back into the slope they support. This lean is called the batter. Retaining walls typically have about a 2-inch batter for every foot of height. If a wall is short and the stone is at least semidressed, you can reduce or eliminate the batter.

Lay the Base Course. Use your largest and flattest stones for the base course. Place bond stones at each end of the wall and at 4- to 6-foot intervals along the wall. Ideally, the bond stones should be long enough to extend into the slope. Between the bond stones, lay wall stones, one in front of the other, to create a double-wythe wall. Fill any gaps between these stones with smaller stones or rubble.

Tilt all the main wall stones into the hill. After laying the first course, you can backfill along the front of the wall and firmly tamp the soil in 2-inch layers. If you are going to install perforated drainpipe, now is the time to lay it along the backside of the wall. Slope the pipe to facilitate drainage.

Add the Remaining Courses. Place the next course, setting it back slightly from the first. Stagger the location of the bond stones, offsetting them from the bond stones in the first course. Lay stones so that all joints between courses are staggered.

After the second course is laid, backfill with gravel and fill almost to the top of the second course. Firmly tamp the gravel in 2-inch layers. Continue laying up courses in the same manner, checking the angle of the face with your batter gauge periodically and backfilling after every two courses.

Cap the Wall. Cap stones usually span the width of the wall and protrude slightly over it. Because water can move through a dry-laid wall, the water-shedding function of the cap stones isn't as crucial. For stability, especially if the wall is located

somewhere where it will be used as seating, you may want to mortar the capstones.

Finish Backfilling and Grading. After laying the capstones, backfill with gravel up to within 4 inches or so of the top of the wall. Lay landscape fabric over the top of the gravel, and finish backfilling with soil or mulch.

As with freestanding walls, flat, square-cut stone, opposite, is the easiest with which to work.

Retaining walls lean back into the slope, left. Plan on a 2-in. batter for every foot of height.

Bond stones, bottom left, should extend from the face of the wall into the slope that the wall supports.

To facilitate drainage as you set the stones, backfill with gravel behind the wall, bottom right.

order direct: 1-800-523-6789

Mortared retaining walls require the installation of drainage pipe, above.

Cap stones span the width of the wall and overhang its edges slightly, right.

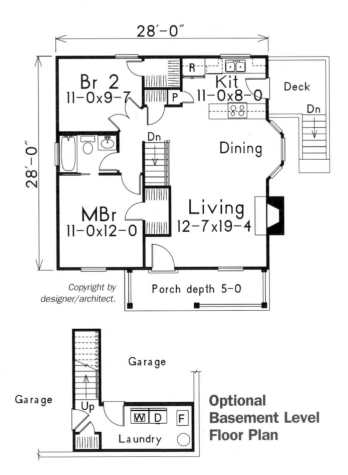

Plan #321025

Dimensions: 28' W x 28' D

Levels: 1

Square Footage: 914

Bedrooms: 2

Bathrooms: 1

Foundation: Basement, walkout

Materials List Available: Yes

Price Category: A

This cute little home's great layout packs in an abundance of features.

Features:

• Living Room: The cozy fireplace in this open, welcoming room invites you to relax awhile.

• Dining Room: This area has a bay window and is open to the kitchen and the living room.

• Kitchen: This compact kitchen has everything you'll need, including a built-in pantry.

• Master Bedroom: Generously sized, with a large closet, this room has a private door into the common bathroom.

• Bedroom: This secondary bedroom can also be used as a home office.

Images provided by designer/architect.

Copyright by designer/architect.

Optional Basement Level Floor Plan

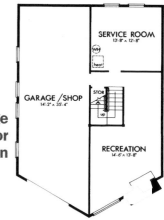

Plan #271051

Dimensions: 30' W x 44'8" D
Levels: 2
Square Footage: 1,920
Main Level Sq. Ft.: 1,210
Upper Level Sq. Ft.: 710
Bedrooms: 3
Bathrooms: 2
Foundation: Crawl space or walkout
Materials List Available: Yes
Price Category: D

Dramatic windows soar to the peak of this vacation home, offering unlimited views of the outdoor scenery.

CAD FILE AVAILABLE

Features:

- **Living Room:** This spacious living room, with its 26-ft. vaulted ceiling, boasts a cozy fireplace. The sliding glass doors open to the wraparound deck, while the wall of windows fill the space with natural light.

- **Secluded Bedroom:** This main-floor bedroom has convenient access to the full bathroom and two large closets.

- **Upper Level:** Going up the U-shaped stairs brings you to this level, where you are greeted by an open loft, a full bathroom and two bedrooms. Each bedroom has two large closets and a window with a view of the backyard.

- **Lower Level:** The daylight basement provides a versatile recreation room that has another fireplace, a garage and shop area, and a service room for lots of storage.

Images provided by designer/architect.

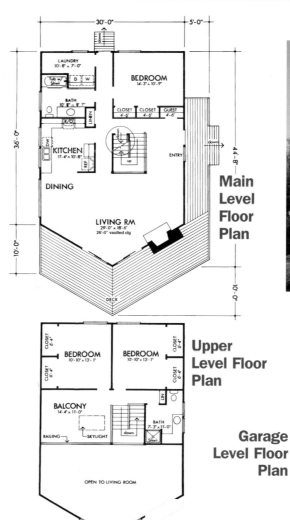

Main Level Floor Plan

Copyright by designer/architect.

Upper Level Floor Plan

Garage Level Floor Plan

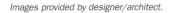

Plan #181128

Dimensions: 36' W x 36' D

Levels: 2

Square Footage: 1,634

Main Level Sq. Ft.: 1,087

Second Level Sq. Ft.: 547

Bedrooms: 3

Bathrooms: 2

Foundation: Basement

Materials List Available: Yes

Price Category: C

This stone-accented rustic vacation home offers the perfect antidote to busy daily life.

CAD FILE AVAILABLE

Images provided by designer/architect.

Features:

- Ceiling Height: 8 ft. unless otherwise noted.

- Family Room: Family and friends will be unable to resist relaxing in this airy two-story family room, with its own handsome fireplace. French doors lead to the front deck.

- Kitchen: This eat-in kitchen features double sinks, ample counter space, and a pantry. It offers plenty of space for the family to gather for informal vacation meals.

- Master Suite: This first-floor master retreat occupies almost the entire length of the home. It includes a walk-in closet and a lavish bath.

- Secondary Bedrooms: On the second floor, two family bedrooms share a full bath.

- Mezzanine: This lovely balcony overlooks the family room.

- Basement: This full unfinished basement offers plenty of space for expansion.

Main Level Floor Plan

36'-0"
10,8 m

36'-0"
10,8 m

14'-0" X 12'-0"
4,20 X 3,60

20'-0" X 14'-0"
6,00 X 4,20

13'-0" X 17'-0"
3,90 X 5,10

Upper Level Floor Plan

10'-0" X 11'-8"
3,00 X 3,50

12'-0" X 11'-8"
3,60 X 3,50

Copyright by designer/architect.

Plan #271086

Dimensions: 56'6" W x 67'6" D

Levels: 2

Square Footage: 1,910

Main Level Sq. Ft.: 1,324

Upper Level Sq. Ft.: 586

Bedrooms: 3

Bathrooms: 2

Foundation: Crawl space, daylight basement

Materials List Available: Yes

Price Category: D

A passive-solar sunroom is the highlight of this popular home and helps to minimize heating costs.

Features:

- Living/Dining Area: This expansive space is brightened by numerous windows and offers panoramic views of the outdoor scenery. A handsome woodstove gives the area a delightful ambiance, especially when the weather outside is frightful. Your dining table goes in the corner by the sun room.

- Kitchen: This room's efficient design keeps all of the chef's supplies at the ready. A snack bar could be used to help serve guests during parties.

- Bedrooms: With three bedrooms to choose from, all of your family members will be able to find secluded spots of their very own.

- Lower Level: This optional space includes a recreation room with a second woodstove. Let the kids gather here and make as much noise as they want.

Optional Basement Level Floor Plan

Main Level Floor Plan

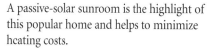

Upper Level Floor Plan

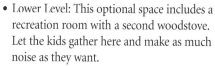

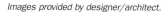

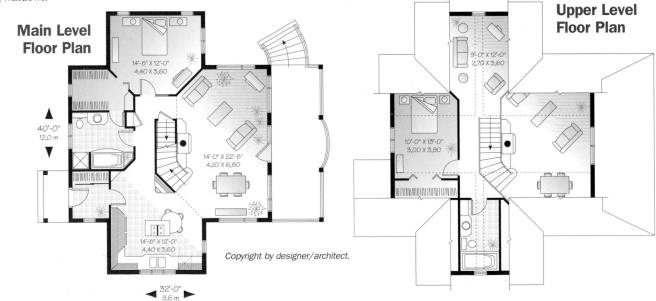

Plan #181120

Dimensions: 32' W x 40' D
Levels: 2
Square Footage: 1,480
Main Level Sq. Ft.: 1,024
Second Level Sq. Ft.: 456
Bedrooms: 2
Bathrooms: 2
Foundation: Basement
Materials List Available: Yes
Price Category: B

Escape to this charming all-season vacation home with lots of view-capturing windows.

Images provided by designer/architect.

Features:

- Ceiling Height: 8 ft. unless otherwise noted.
- Living/Dining Area: The covered back porch opens into this large, inviting combined area. Its high ceiling adds to the sense of spaciousness.
- Family Room: After relaxing in front of the fireplace that warms this family room, family and guests can move outside onto the porch to watch the sun set.
- Kitchen: Light streams through a triple window in this well-designed kitchen. It's conveniently located next to the dining area and features a center island with a breakfast bar and double sinks.
- Master Suite: This first floor suite is located in the front of the house and is enhanced by its large walk-through closet and the adjoining private bath.

Main Level Floor Plan

14'-8" X 12'-0"
4,40 X 3,60

40'-0"
12,0 m

14'-0" X 22'-8"
4,20 X 6,80

14'-8" X 12'-0"
4,40 X 3,60

32'-0"
9,6 m

Upper Level Floor Plan

9'-0" X 12'-0"
2,70 X 3,60

10'-0" X 13'-0"
3,00 X 3,90

Copyright by designer/architect.

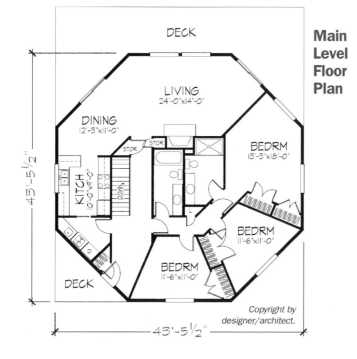

Plan #271087

Dimensions: 43'5½" W x 43'5½" D

Levels: 2

Square Footage: 2,734

Main Level Sq. Ft.: 1,564

Lower Level Sq. Ft.: 1,170

Bedrooms: 4

Bathrooms: 3

Foundation: Crawl space or walkout basement

Materials List Available: No

Price Category: F

Images provided by designer/architect.

This octagonal home offers a choice of exterior finish: wood or stucco.

Features:

- Entry: A seemingly endless deck leads to the main entry, which includes a coat closet.
- Living Room: A fireplace enhances this spacious room, which offers great outdoor views, plus deck access via sliding glass doors.
- Master Suite: At the end of a hallway, the quiet master bedroom boasts a private bath.
- Lower Level: The basement includes a versatile general area, which could be a nice playroom. A handy den, an extra bedroom and a two-car garage round out this level.

Main Level Floor Plan

Lower Level Floor Plan

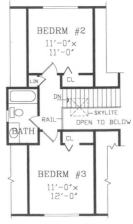

Plan #131058

Dimensions: 53' W x 36' D
Levels: 1.5
Square Footage: 1,648
Main Level Sq. Ft.: 1,191
Upper Level Sq. Ft.: 457
Bedrooms: 3
Bathrooms: 2
Foundation: Walkout basement
Material List Available: Yes
Price Category: D

Images provided by designer/architect.

Great Room

This rustic multilevel cabin offers an impressive wraparound deck.

Features:

- **Great Room:** The vaulted ceiling in this gathering area gives the space an open and airy feeling. The fireplace, flanked by sliding glass doors, adds a focal point to the room.

- **Kitchen:** This massive country kitchen, with its peninsula and fireplace, adds a cozy feeling to the home. The snack bar adds additional seating space for overflow from the main table.

- **Master Bedroom:** Located on the main level for convenience, this bedroom has access to the main bathroom. The large closet is a welcome feature.

- **Upper Level:** This area holds two bedrooms and the second full bathroom. The skylight above the stairwell floods the area with natural light.

Copyright by designer/architect.

Main Level Floor Plan

Upper Level Floor Plan

Plan #181133

Dimensions: 38' W x 40' D
Levels: 2
Square Footage: 1,832
Main Level Sq. Ft.: 1,212
Second Level Sq. Ft. 620
Bedrooms: 3
Bathrooms: 2
Foundation: Walkout; crawl space, slab, or basement for fee
Materials List Available: Yes
Price Category: D

Images provided by designer/architect.

You'll enjoy sunshine indoors and out with a wraparound deck and windows all around.

CAD FILE AVAILABLE

Features:

- Ceiling Height: 8 ft.
- Family Room: Family and friends will be drawn to this large sunny room. Curl up with a good book before the beautiful see-through fireplace.
- Screened Porch: This porch shares the see-through fireplace with the family room so you can enjoy an outside fire on cool summer nights.

- Master Suite: This romantic first-floor master suite offers a large walk-in closet and a luxurious private bathroom enhanced by dual vanities.
- Secondary Bedrooms: Upstairs you'll find two generous bedrooms with ample closet space. These bedrooms share a full bathroom.
- Basement: This large walkout basement with large glass door is perfectly suited for future expansion.

Main Level Floor Plan

40' 0"
12,0 m

15'-0" X 14'-8"
4,50 X 4,40

13'-8" X 11'-4"
4,10 X 3,40

12'-0" X 16'-0"
3,60 X 4,80

13'-8" X 14'-8"
4,10 X 4,40

11'-0" X 16'-0"
3,30 X 4,80

38'-0"
11,4 m

Upper Level Floor Plan

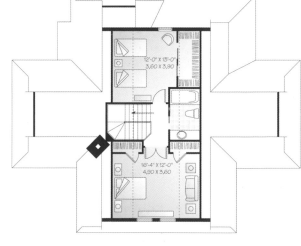

12'-0" X 13'-0"
3,60 X 3,90

16'-4" X 12'-0"
4,90 X 3,80

Copyright by designer/architect.

Images provided by designer/architect.

Plan #271050

Dimensions: 40' W x 40' D
Levels: 2
Square Footage: 1,188
Main Level Sq. Ft.: 936
Upper Level Sq. Ft.: 252
Bedrooms: 3
Bathrooms: 2
Foundation: Daylight basement
Materials List Available: Yes
Price Category: B

This open and attractive design features multi-level construction and efficient use of living space.

CAD FILE AVAILABLE

Features:

- Living Room: A fireplace and a dramatic 15-ft. vaulted ceiling make family and friends gravitate to this area.

- Kitchen/Dining: A U-shaped counter with a snack bar facilitates meals and entertaining. A stacked washer/dryer unit makes weekend chores a breeze.

- Secondary Bedrooms: Five steps up, two sizable bedrooms with vaulted ceilings share

a nice hall bath. One of the bedrooms could serve as a den and features sliding glass doors to a deck.

- Master Suite: On a level of its own, this private space includes a personal bathroom and a romantic deck for stargazing.

- Basement/Garage: The home's lower level offers plenty of space for expansion or storage, plus a tandem, tuck-under garage.

Basement Level Floor Plan

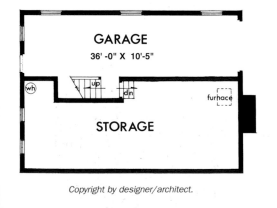

Copyright by designer/architect.

Main Level Floor Plan

Upper Level Floor Plan

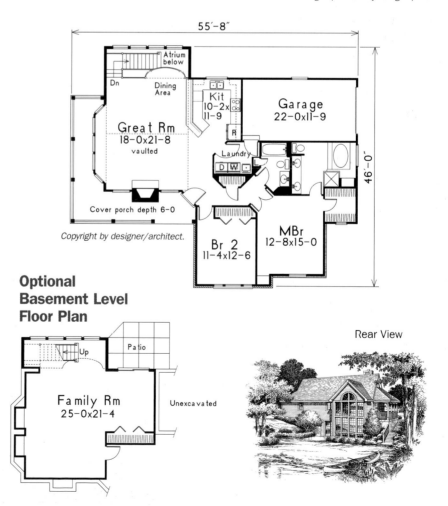

Plan #321035

Dimensions: 55'8" W x 46' D
Levels: 1
Square Footage: 1,384
Bedrooms: 2
Bathrooms: 2
Foundation: Walkout
Materials List Available: Yes
Price Category: B

Images provided by designer/architect.

You'll love the way the two-story atrium windows meld this home with your sloped site.

Features:

- Great Room: A masonry fireplace, vaulted ceiling, huge bayed area, and stairs to the atrium below make this room a natural gathering spot.

- Dining Area: You'll love sitting here and admiring the view by sunlight or starlight.

- Kitchen: An angled bar is both a snack bar and work space in this well-designed kitchen with an attached laundry room.

- Master Suite: Double doors open into the spacious bedroom with a huge walk-in closet. The bath has a garden tub, separate shower, and double vanity.

- Optional Basement Plan: Take advantage of this space to build a family room, media room, or home studio that's lit by the huge atrium windows and opens to the patio.

Copyright by designer/architect.

Optional Basement Level Floor Plan

Rear View

Plan #451321

Dimensions: 65' W x 56'6" D

Levels: 1

Square Footage: 3,304

Main Level Sq. Ft.: 1,652

Lower Level Sq. Ft.: 1,652

Bedrooms: 2

Bathrooms: 3

Foundation: Slab or walkout

Material List Available: No

Price Category: G

Features:

- Outdoor Living Space: With a covered porch and large open deck, sunbathers and barbecuers alike will enjoy relaxing outdoors.

- Kitchen: This room is perfect for relaxing or enjoying a home-cooked meal.

- Den: This den doubles as an office, or can be converted into an entertainment center for a movie night.

- Master Suite: This luxurious master suite features one of the three large bathrooms in the home.

- Garage: This two-car garage is ideal for multi-car families or those with a lot of sports equipment to store.

If you're searching for an ideal vacation home that's inviting and spacious enough to accommodate loved ones, this is it.

CAD FILE AVAILABLE

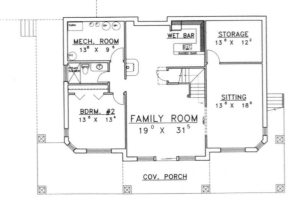

Rear Elevation

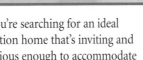

Main Level Floor Plan

2-CAR GARAGE
23⁴ X 21⁴

MUD

COV. ENTRY PORCH

DEN/OFFICE
10⁰ X 11⁷

FOYER
8⁸ X 13⁰

KITCHEN
15⁰ X 13¹⁰

DINING
13⁸ X 9⁸

GREAT ROOM
19⁰ X 18¹⁰

MASTER SUITE
13⁸ X 16⁰

OPEN DECK

COV. PORCH

OPEN DECK

Lower Level Floor Plan

MECH. ROOM
13⁸ X 9⁶

WET BAR

STORAGE
13⁸ X 12²

BDRM. #2
13⁸ X 13⁴

FAMILY ROOM
19⁰ X 31⁵

SITTING
13⁸ X 18⁶

COV. PORCH

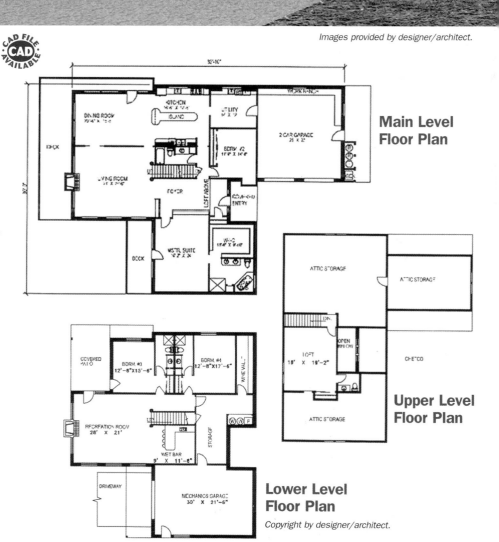

Plan #451075

Dimensions: 110'4" W x 65' D
Levels: 2
Square Footage: 4,910
Main Level Sq. Ft.: 2,913
Lower Level Sq. Ft.: 1,997
Bedrooms: 4
Bathrooms: 4½
Foundation: Walkout insulated concrete form
Material List Available: No
Price Category: I

Images provided by designer/architect.

Perfect for a quiet neighborhood or as a lakefront residence, this home has many desirable elements.

Features:

• **Living Room:** This welcoming space is perfect for relaxing and entertaining. Whether experienced in the bright sun or the warm glow of the fireplace, it will be everyone's favorite place to gather.

• **Kitchen:** The family chef will love this kitchen. The room contains extra seating at the island and is open to the dining area. A large adjacent utility room can work as a walk-in pantry.

• **Master Suite:** This private oasis boasts an oversize sleeping area, large windows, and a private balcony. The master bath features dual vanities, a large shower, and a walk-in closet.

• **Lower Level:** Two bedrooms, each with a private full bathroom, and a large recreation room are located on this level. A wine vault, storage, and garage are also nearby.

Main Level Floor Plan

Upper Level Floor Plan

Lower Level Floor Plan

Copyright by designer/architect.

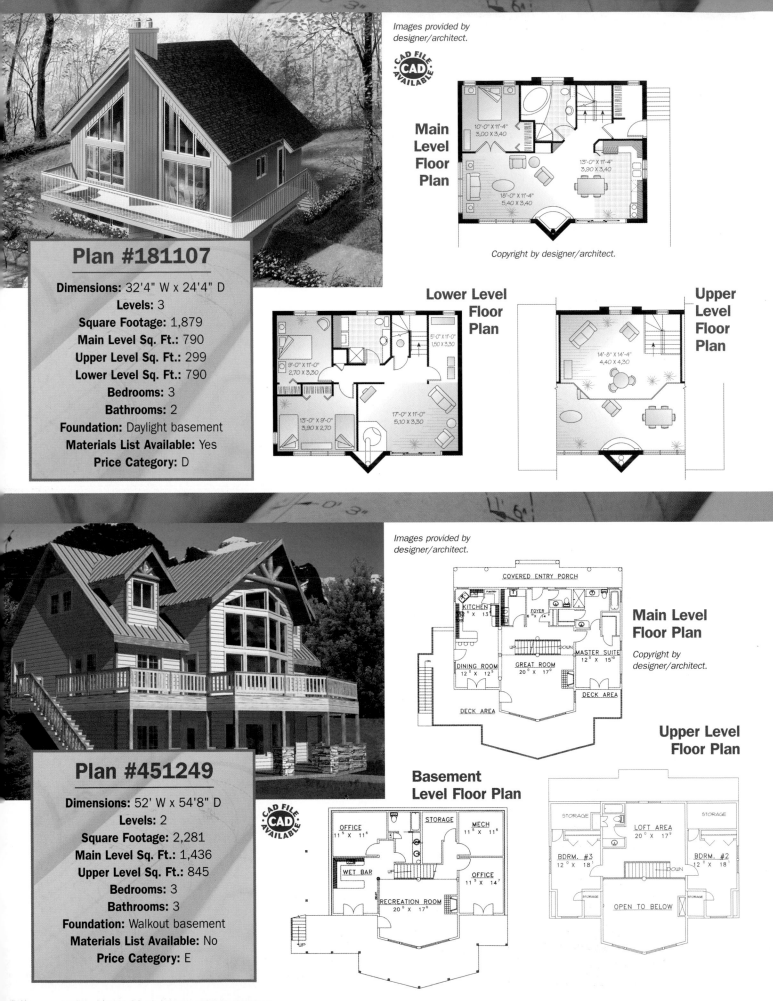

CAD FILE AVAILABLE

Main Level Floor Plan

10'-0" X 11'-4"
3,00 X 3,40

13'-0" X 11'-4"
3,90 X 3,40

18'-0" X 11'-4"
5,40 X 3,40

Copyright by designer/architect.

Plan #181107

Dimensions: 32'4" W x 24'4" D

Levels: 3

Square Footage: 1,879

Main Level Sq. Ft.: 790

Upper Level Sq. Ft.: 299

Lower Level Sq. Ft.: 790

Bedrooms: 3

Bathrooms: 2

Foundation: Daylight basement

Materials List Available: Yes

Price Category: D

Lower Level Floor Plan

9'-0" X 11'-0"
2,70 X 3,30

5'-0" X 11'-0"
1,50 X 3,30

13'-0" X 9'-0"
3,90 X 2,70

17'-0" X 11'-0"
5,10 X 3,30

Upper Level Floor Plan

14'-8" X 14'-4"
4,40 X 4,30

Main Level Floor Plan

Copyright by designer/architect.

COVERED ENTRY PORCH

KITCHEN
X 13

FOYER
X 14

MASTER SUITE
12' X 15'

DINING ROOM
12' X 12'5

GREAT ROOM
20' X 17'

DECK AREA

DECK AREA

Plan #451249

Dimensions: 52' W x 54'8" D

Levels: 2

Square Footage: 2,281

Main Level Sq. Ft.: 1,436

Upper Level Sq. Ft.: 845

Bedrooms: 3

Bathrooms: 3

Foundation: Walkout basement

Materials List Available: No

Price Category: E

Basement Level Floor Plan

CAD FILE AVAILABLE

OFFICE
11'5 X 11'6

STORAGE

MECH
11'5 X 11'6

WET BAR

OFFICE
11'5 X 14'7

RECREATION ROOM
20' X 17'

Upper Level Floor Plan

STORAGE

LOFT AREA
20' X 17'

STORAGE

BDRM. #3
12' X 18'

BDRM. #2
12' X 18'

STORAGE

OPEN TO BELOW

STORAGE

Main Level Floor Plan

Images provided by designer/architect.

Upper Level Floor Plan

Copyright by designer/architect.

Plan #181123

Dimensions: 38' W x 36' D

Levels: 2

Square Footage: 1,482

Main Level Sq. Ft.: 895

Upper Level Sq. Ft.: 587

Bedrooms: 2

Bathrooms: 1½

Foundation: Full basement with walkout

Materials List Available: Yes

Price Category: B

Upper Level Floor Plan

Copyright by designer/architect.

Main Level Floor Plan

Plan #151316

Dimensions: 47' W x 63' D

Levels: 2

Square Footage: 2,054

Main Level Sq. Ft.: 1,413

Upper Level Sq. Ft.: 641

Bedrooms: 3

Bathrooms: 2½

Foundation: Crawl space, slab, basement or walkout

CompleteCost List Available: Yes

Price Category: D

Images provided by designer/architect.

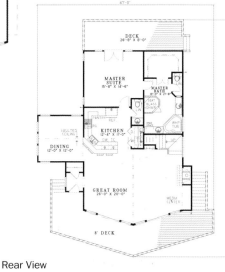

Rear View

Main Level Floor Plan

26'-0"
7,8 m

44'-0"
13,2 m

Upper Level Floor Plan

Images provided by designer/architect.

CAD FILE AVAILABLE

Copyright by designer/architect.

Plan #181132

Dimensions: 44' W x 26' D

Levels: 2

Square Footage: 1,437

Main Level Sq. Ft.: 856

Upper Level Sq. Ft.: 581

Bedrooms: 3

Bathrooms: 1½

Foundation: Walkout basement

Materials List Available: Yes

Price Category: B

Main Level Floor Plan

41'-0"
12,3 m

60'-0"
18,0 m

Lower Level Floor Plan

Copyright by designer/architect.

Images provided by designer/architect.

CAD FILE AVAILABLE

Plan #181038

Dimensions: 66' W x 41' D

Levels: 1

Square Footage: 1,932

Main Level Sq. Ft.: 1,110

Lower Level Sq. Ft.: 822

Bedrooms: 3

Bathrooms: 4

Foundation: Basement or walkout

Material List Available: Yes

Price Category: D

Plan #181106

Dimensions: 32'4" W x 25'6" D
Levels: 1
Square Footage: 1,648
Main Level Sq. Ft.: 824
Lower Level Sq. Ft.: 824
Bedrooms: 3
Bathrooms: 2
Foundation: Basement or walkout
Materials List Available: Yes
Price Category: C

Images provided by designer/architect.

Lower Level Floor Plan

9'-0" X 11'-0"
2,70 X 3,30

7'-8" X 11'-0"
2,30 X 3,30

17'-0" X 11'-0"
5,10 X 3,30

13'-0" X 9'-0"
3,90 X 2,70

Main Level Floor Plan

10'-0" X 11'-4"
3,00 X 3,40

18'-0" X 11'-4"
5,40 X 3,40

13'-0" X 11'-4"
3,90 X 3,40

Copyright by designer/architect.

Plan #451256

Dimensions: 86' W x 43'10" D
Levels: 2
Square Footage: 3,837
Main Level Sq. Ft.: 1,819
Upper Level Sq. Ft.: 385
Lower Level Sq. Ft.: 1,633
Bedrooms: 3
Bathrooms: 2½
Foundation: Walkout
Material List Available: No
Price Category: H

Images provided by designer/architect.

Main Level Floor Plan

COV. ENTRY
11' x 8'

KITCHEN
12' x 13'

FOYER
10' x 8'

DINING ROOM
14' x 12'

GREAT ROOM
22' x 21'

MASTER SUITE
20' x 16'

Upper Level Floor Plan

LOFT
13' x 17'

OPEN TO BELOW

Lower Level Floor Plan

GARAGE
24' x 29'

MECH
16' x 7'

STRG
8' x 6'

MECH
10' x 8'

STORAGE
12' x 8'

REC ROOM
21' x 22'

BDRM. #3

BDRM. #2
10' x 12'

CONC PATIO

CONC PATIO

Copyright by designer/architect.

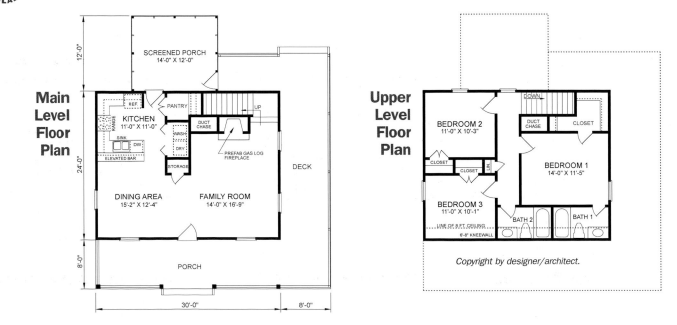

Plan #341190

Dimensions: 38' W x 34' D

Levels: 1.5

Square Footage: 1,440

Main Level Sq. Ft.: 720

Upper Level Sq. Ft.: 720

Bedrooms: 3

Bathrooms: 2

Foundation: Crawl space, slab, basement or walkout

Material List Available: No

Price Category: B

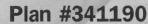

Images provided by designer/architect.

Have you dreamed of a mountain cabin retreat or a peaceful countryside residence? Imagine snow outside, a well-stocked pantry, a fire in your gas-log fireplace, no deadlines, and no obligations. This home is designed with you in mind.

Features:

- Family Room: Welcome guests in from the cold to relax by a warm fire, sip hot chocolate, and get caught up.

- Kitchen: Efficiently set up, this kitchen includes a raised snack bar as a transition between the kitchen and dining areas, as well as a walk-in pantry for additional storage.

- Master Suite: Situated away from the bustle of everyday life, this relaxing space includes a spacious walk-in closet and a full bath.

- Secondary Bedrooms: Comparably sized to prevent sibling squabbles, both additional bedrooms feature wide closets and access to a full bathroom.

Main Level Floor Plan

SCREENED PORCH
14'-0" X 12'-0"

REF.
PANTRY
KITCHEN
11'-0" X 11'-0"
RANGE
SINK
DW
ELEVATED BAR
WASH
DRY
STORAGE
DUCT CHASE
UP
PREFAB GAS LOG FIREPLACE

DINING AREA
15'-2" X 12'-4"

FAMILY ROOM
14'-0" X 16'-9"

DECK

PORCH

12'-0" 24'-0" 8'-0"

30'-0" 8'-0"

Upper Level Floor Plan

DOWN

BEDROOM 2
11'-0" X 10'-3"
DUCT CHASE
CLOSET

CLOSET CLOSET LIN.

BEDROOM 1
14'-0" X 11'-5"

BEDROOM 3
11'-0" X 10'-1"

LINE OF 8-FT CEILING
6'-8" KNEEWALL

BATH 2 BATH 1

Copyright by designer/architect.

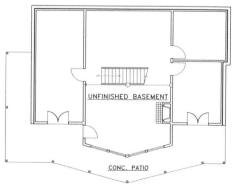

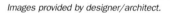
Images provided by designer/architect.

Plan #451231

Dimensions: 53' W x 42' D
Levels: 2
Square Footage: 2,281
Main Level Sq. Ft.: 1,436
Upper Level Sq. Ft.: 845
Bedrooms: 3
Bathrooms: 2½
Foundation: Walkout basement
Materials List Available: No
Price Category: F

Boasting a craftsman-accent look, this home will be the talk of the neighborhood.

Features:

- **Great Room:** As you enter this large gathering area from the foyer, the warmth of the fireplace welcomes you home. The two-story-high ceiling gives the area an open feeling.

- **Kitchen:** An efficient space, this kitchen features a snack bar and walk-in pantry, and it is located near the laundry room, the great room, and the dining room. The glass doors in the dining room function to extend and open the kitchen area.

- **Master Suite:** This main-level suite contains a large sleeping area and access to the rear deck. The master bath has a marvelous whirlpool tub, dual vanities, and a stall shower.

- **Upper Level:** Two bedrooms, with large closets, share a common bathroom. The loft has a view down into the great room.

Images provided by designer/architect.

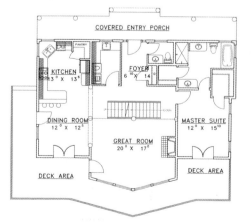

Main Level Floor Plan

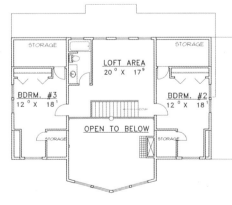

Upper Level Floor Plan

Basement Level Floor Plan

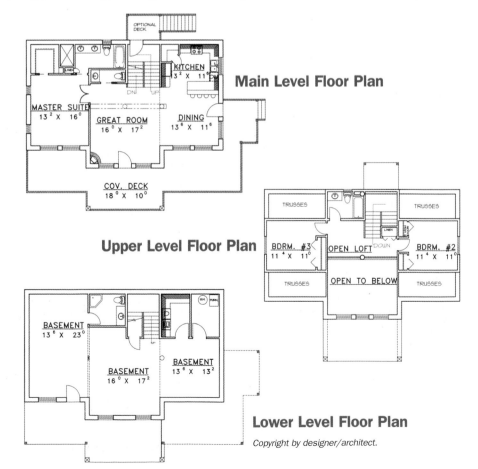

Plan #451334

Dimensions: 54'8" W x 29' D
Levels: 2
Square Footage: 2,999
Main Level Sq. Ft.: 1,197
Upper Level Sq. Ft.: 605
Lower Level Sq. Ft.: 1,197
Bedrooms: 3
Bathrooms: 3½
Foundation: Walkout – insulated concrete form
Material List Available: No
Price Category: F

You'll love the charming architectural features and practical contemporary design of this hillside home.

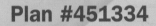

Features:

- Deck: Enjoy basking in the warmth of the sun on this spacious wraparound deck. Or just sit out with friends and enjoy the view on beautiful days or clear, starry nights.

- Kitchen: Efficiently set up, this kitchen includes a raised snack bar as a transition between the kitchen and dining areas, as well as a walk-in pantry for additional storage.

- Master Suite: This window-flanked space features a large walk-in closet and a full bath with his and her sinks.

- Secondary Bedrooms: Two additional bedrooms are located on the second floor for restful quiet. They both include ample closet space and access to a nearby full bathroom.

- Bonus Room: This unfinished space can be anything you dream up, including a home office, an entertainment area, or a study space.

Images provided by designer/architect.

Main Level Floor Plan

MASTER SUITE 13² X 16⁰
GREAT ROOM 16⁰ X 17²
KITCHEN 13² X 11⁶
DINING 13⁶ X 11⁶
COV. DECK 18⁰ X 10⁰
OPTIONAL DECK

Upper Level Floor Plan

TRUSSES
BDRM. #3 11⁴ X 11⁰
OPEN LOFT
BDRM. #2 11⁴ X 11⁰
OPEN TO BELOW
TRUSSES

Lower Level Floor Plan

BASEMENT 13⁶ X 23⁰
BASEMENT 16⁰ X 17²
BASEMENT 13⁶ X 13²

Copyright by designer/architect.

Plan #181172

Dimensions: 26' W x 48' D
Levels: 2
Square Footage: 1,484
Main Level Sq. Ft.: 908
Upper Level Sq. Ft.: 576
Bedrooms: 3
Bathrooms: 2
Foundation: Walkout
Material List Available: Yes
Price Category: B

Images provided by designer/architect.

• **Bedrooms:** The bedrooms situated on the first floor feature a walk-in closet and a near by full bathroom. Two additional bedrooms on the second floor boast wide closets and

ample space for an entertainment center, desk, or sitting area. They share access to a full bathroom with a large whirlpool tub and separate shower.

A great starter home, this cozy space has everything you need. The efficient design makes the house feel larger than it is.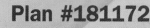

Features:

• **Porch:** This glass-enclosed elevated porch provides extra living space with a view all year round.

• **Living Room:** Spend the evening conversing with family and friends in front of a glowing fire in this sweet sitting room.

• **Kitchen:** This efficient area has plenty of workspace and storage, as well as an angular snack bar that transitions into the living room and the dining room

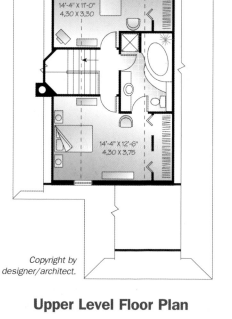

Copyright by designer/architect.

Main Level Floor Plan

Upper Level Floor Plan

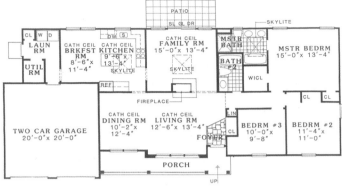

Plan #131001

Dimensions: 72'4" W x 32'4" D

Levels: 1

Square Footage: 1,615

Bedrooms: 3

Bathrooms: 2

Foundation: Crawl space, slab, basement, or walkout

Materials List Available: Yes

Price Category: D

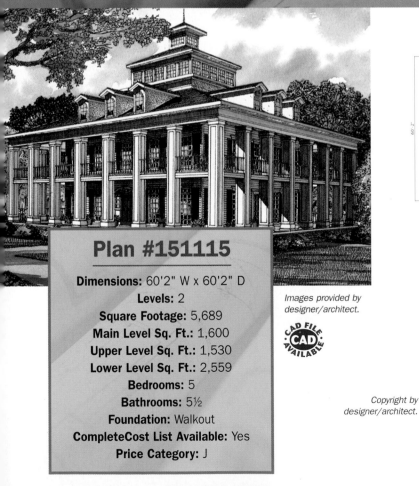

Main Level Floor Plan

Upper Level Floor Plan

Plan #151115

Dimensions: 60'2" W x 60'2" D

Levels: 2

Square Footage: 5,689

Main Level Sq. Ft.: 1,600

Upper Level Sq. Ft.: 1,530

Lower Level Sq. Ft.: 2,559

Bedrooms: 5

Bathrooms: 5½

Foundation: Walkout

CompleteCost List Available: Yes

Price Category: J

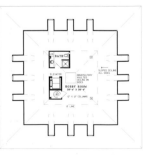

Lower Level Floor Plan

Bonus Area Floor Plan

Plan #271063

Dimensions: 61'4" W x 70' D

Levels: 1

Square Footage: 2,572

Bedrooms: 3

Bathrooms: 2

Foundation: Daylight basement

Materials List Available: No

Price Category: E

Images provided by designer/architect.

CAD FILE AVAILABLE

Optional Lower Level Floor Plan

Copyright by designer/architect.

Plan #321037

Dimensions: 78'8" W x 50'6" D

Levels: 1

Square Footage: 2,397

Bedrooms: 3

Bathrooms: 2

Foundation: Basement or walkout

Materials List Available: Yes

Price Category: E

Images provided by designer/architect.

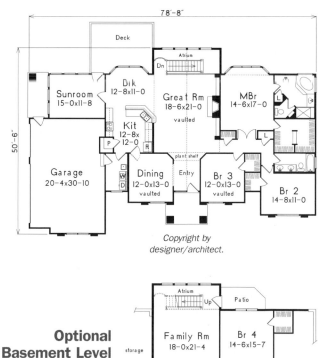

Copyright by designer/architect.

Optional Basement Level Floor Plan

Main Level Floor Plan

Copyright by designer/architect.

Plan #481030

Dimensions: 79'8" W x 64' D

Levels: 2

Square Footage: 3,190

Main Level Sq. Ft.: 1,751

Upper Level Sq. Ft.: 1,439

Bedrooms: 4

Bathrooms: 2½

Foundation: Walkout

Material List Available: No

Price Category: G

Images provided by designer/architect.

Lower Level Floor Plan

Upper Level Floor Plan

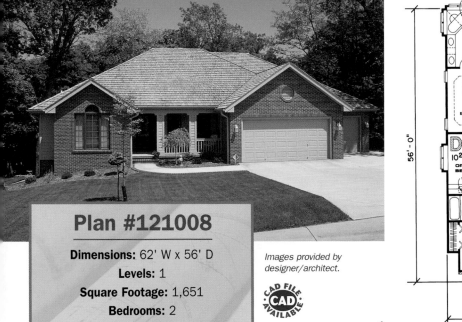

Plan #121008

Dimensions: 62' W x 56' D

Levels: 1

Square Footage: 1,651

Bedrooms: 2

Bathrooms: 2

Foundation: Basement

Materials List Available: Yes

Price Category: C

Images provided by designer/architect.

CAD FILE AVAILABLE

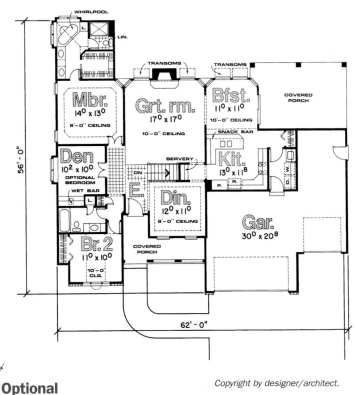

Optional Bedroom

Copyright by designer/architect.

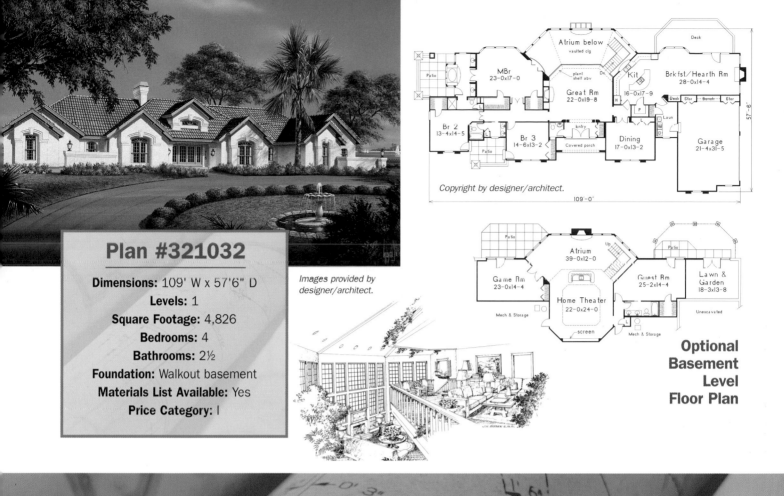

Plan #321032

Dimensions: 109' W x 57'6" D

Levels: 1

Square Footage: 4,826

Bedrooms: 4

Bathrooms: 2½

Foundation: Walkout basement

Materials List Available: Yes

Price Category: I

Images provided by designer/architect.

Optional Basement Level Floor Plan

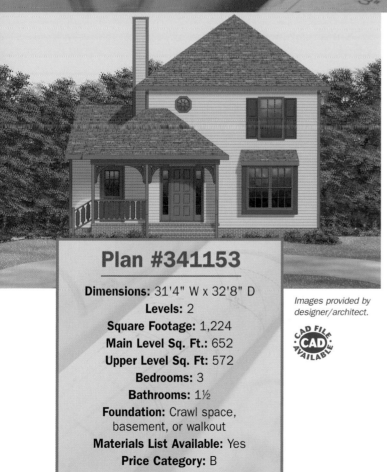

Plan #341153

Dimensions: 31'4" W x 32'8" D

Levels: 2

Square Footage: 1,224

Main Level Sq. Ft.: 652

Upper Level Sq. Ft: 572

Bedrooms: 3

Bathrooms: 1½

Foundation: Crawl space, basement, or walkout

Materials List Available: Yes

Price Category: B

Images provided by designer/architect.

CAD FILE AVAILABLE

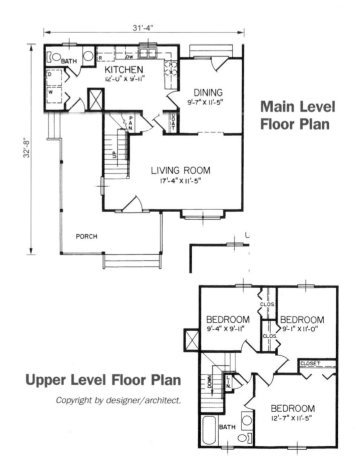

Main Level Floor Plan

Upper Level Floor Plan

Copyright by designer/architect.

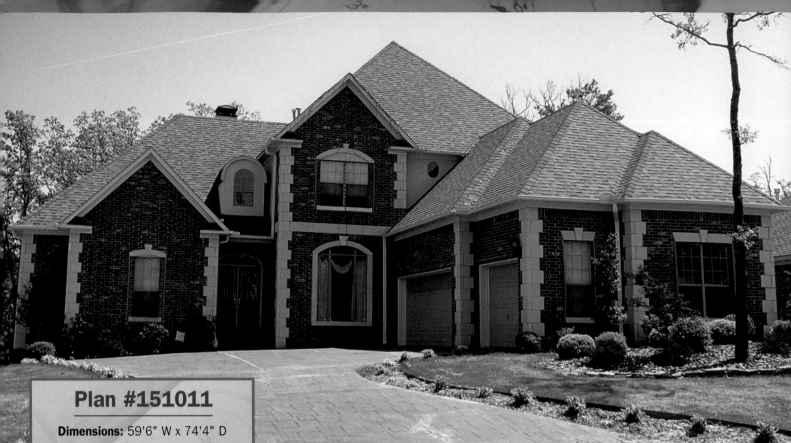

Plan #151011

Dimensions: 59'6" W x 74'4" D
Levels: 2
Square Footage: 3,437
Main Level Sq. Ft.: 2,184
Upper Level Sq. Ft.: 1,253
Bedrooms: 5
Bathrooms: 4
Foundation: Crawl space or slab; basement or daylight basement for fee
CompleteCost List Available: Yes
Price Category: G

Beauty, comfort, and convenience are yours in this luxurious, two-level home.

Features:

- Ceiling Height: 10 ft. unless otherwise noted.

- Master Suite: The 11-ft. pan ceiling sets the tone for this secluded area, with a lovely bay window that opens onto a rear porch, a pass-through fireplace to the great room, and a sitting room.

- Great Room: The pass-through fireplace makes this spacious room a cozy spot,

while the French doors leading to a rear porch make it a perfect spot for entertaining.

- Dining Room: Gracious 8-in. columns set off the entrance to this room.

- Kitchen: An island bar provides an efficient work area that's fitted with a sink.

- Breakfast Room: Open to the kitchen, this room is defined by a bay window and a spiral staircase to the second floor.

- Laundry Room: Large enough to accommodate a folding table, this room can also be fitted with a swinging pet door.

- Play Room: French doors in the children's playroom open onto a balcony where they can continue their games.

- Bedrooms: The 9-ft. ceilings on the second story make the rooms feel bright and airy.

Main Level Floor Plan

Upper Level Floor Plan

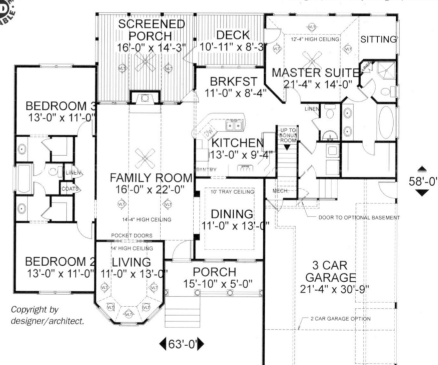

Plan #101006

Dimensions: 63' W x 58' D
Levels: 1
Square Footage: 1,982
Bedrooms: 3
Bathrooms: 2½
Foundation: Crawl space, slab basement, or walkout
Materials List Available: Yes
Price Category: D

Radius-top windows and siding accented with wood shingles give this home a distinctive look.

Features:

- Ceiling Height: 9 ft. unless otherwise noted.

- Family Room: This room is perfect for all kinds of informal family activities. A vaulted ceiling adds to its sense of spaciousness.

- Dining Room: This room, with its tray ceiling, is designed for elegant dining.

- Porch: When the weather gets warm, you'll enjoy stepping out onto this large screened porch to catch a breeze.

- Master Suite: You'll love ending your day and getting up in the morning to this exquisite master suite, with its vaulted ceiling, sitting area, and large walk-in closet.

- Bonus Room: Just off the kitchen are stairs leading to this enormous bonus room, offering more than 330 sq. ft. of future expansion space.

Images provided by designer/architect.

Copyright by designer/architect.

SMARTtip

Art in Pools

The tiled walls and floor of a pool make great canvases for art, so incorporate a serious or whimsical design. Also, make the stairs wide and shallow to form a wading area for kids.

Rear View

Kitchen

Images provided by designer/architect.

Plan #141030

Dimensions: 38' W x 32' D
Levels: 2
Square Footage: 2,323
Main Level Sq. Ft.: 1,179
Upper Level Sq. Ft.: 1,144
Bedrooms: 4
Bathrooms: 2½
Foundation: Basement
Materials List Available: Yes
Price Category: E

This European-style home provides visual excitement, with its many rooflines and multiple gables. Its distinctive design creates a rich, solid appearance.

Features:

- Living Room: Your guests will appreciate the elegance and style that characterize this formal living room.

- Dining Room: A fitting complement to the living room, this formal dining room is well suited for special occasions.

- Kitchen: The well-designed kitchen, with ample cabinet and counter space, makes food preparation a pleasure.

- Master Suite: Enjoy the quiet luxury of this large master suite, sure to become your favorite retreat at the end of the day.

- Bonus Room: This impressive home features an optional bonus room above the garage.

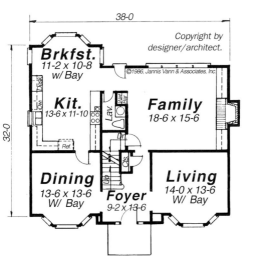

Copyright by designer/architect.
©1986, Jannis Vann & Associates, Inc.

Brkfst. 11-2 x 10-8 w/ Bay
Kit. 13-6 x 11-10
Family 18-6 x 15-6
Dining 13-6 x 13-6 W/ Bay
Foyer 9-2 x 13-6
Living 14-0 x 13-6 W/ Bay
38-0
32-0

Main Level Floor Plan

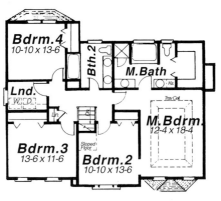

Bdrm.4 10-10 x 13-6
Bth.2
M.Bath
Lnd. W./ D.
Bdrm.3 13-6 x 11-6
Bdrm.2 10-10 x 13-6
M.Bdrm. 12-4 x 18-4

Upper Level Floor Plan

Living Room

Plan #151684

Dimensions: 65'2" W x 63' D
Levels: 1
Square Footage: 1,994
Bedrooms: 3
Bathrooms: 2
Foundation: Crawl space, slab, basement, or walkout
CompleteCost List Available: Yes
Price Category: D

Enter the brick arched entry, and prepare for the perfect home.

Features:

- Great Room: This inviting room, with its romantic fireplace, is a comfortable gathering space, while a formal dining room allows for elegant entertaining.

- Kitchen: This kitchen adjoins the large breakfast room, which has an atrium door leading to the rear grilling porch.

- Master Suite: This suite features a private office and has the ultimate master bath. The corner whirlpool tub is framed by columns and has a large walk-in closet, shower, and private toilet.

- Bedrooms: The two secondary bedrooms feature large closets and share a hall bathroom.

Plan #321016

Dimensions: 88' W x 70'8" D
Levels: 1
Square Footage: 3,814
Main Level Sq. Ft.: 3,566
Lower Level Sq. Ft.: 248
Bedrooms: 3
Bathrooms: 2½
Foundation: Daylight basement
Materials List Available: Yes
Price Category: H

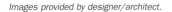

Images provided by designer/architect.

If you're looking for a design that makes the most of a sloped site, you'll love this gorgeous home.

Features:

- **Great Room:** This fabulous room has a vaulted ceiling, sunken floor, and masonry fireplace, and it opens to the two-story atrium.

- **Dining Room:** Both this room and the living room opposite are naturally lit by two-story arched windows.

- **Kitchen:** Open to the hearth room and breakfast room, this kitchen has a central island, too.

- **Hearth Room/Breakfast Room:** A vaulted ceiling, corner fireplace, and door to one deck highlight this angled space.

- **Master Suite:** The bedroom has a coffered ceiling, corner fireplace, door to one deck, and huge walk-in closet. The bath includes a step-down tub with windows and a fireplace, a linen closet, a separate shower, and two vanities.

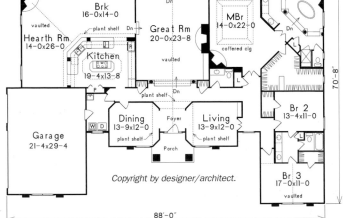

Rear View

Copyright by designer/architect.

Plan #151108

Dimensions: 84'6" W x 58'6" D

Levels: 1

Square Footage: 2,742

Bedrooms: 4

Bathrooms: 2½

Foundation: Crawl space, slab, or basement

CompleteCost List Available: Yes

Price Category: F

Images provided by designer/architect.

The arched entry, with its elegant dual columns, sets the tone for this gracious home.

Features:

- Porches: The covered front porch and a screened rear porch add lounging space.

- Great Room: A fireplace, media center, and French doors to the sunroom are the focal points in this room with a 10-foot ceiling.

- Sunroom: Opening from the great room, one bedroom, and the screened porch, this room is a natural gathering spot.

- Dining Room: Columns define this spacious room with a 10-foot ceiling, where you'll dine in comfort.

- Kitchen: This well-planned work space features a snack bar open to the bayed breakfast nook.

- Master Suite: Atrium doors lead to the screened porch from this suite with two huge closets and a bath with two vanities and numerous amenities.

Copyright by designer/architect.

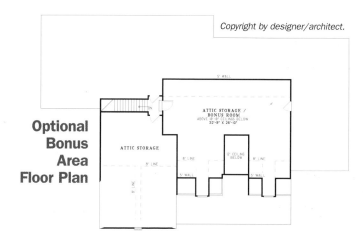

Optional Bonus Area Floor Plan

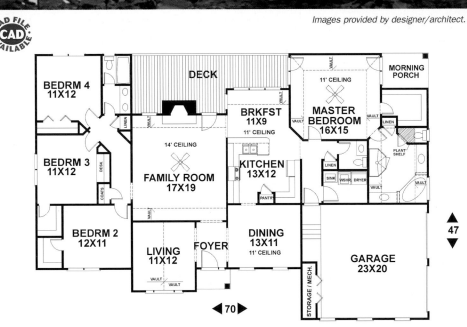

Plan #101010

Dimensions: 70' W x 47' D

Levels: 1

Square Footage: 2,187

Bedrooms: 4

Bathrooms: 2½

Foundation: Crawl space, slab, or basement

Materials List Available: Yes

Price Category: E

Images provided by designer/architect.

This stately ranch features a brick-and-stucco exterior, layered trim, and copper roofing returns.

Features:

- Ceiling Height: 11 ft. unless otherwise noted.

- Special Ceilings: Vaulted and raised ceilings adorn the living room, family room, dining room, foyer, kitchen, breakfast room, and master suite.

- Kitchen: This roomy kitchen is brightened by an abundance of windows.

- Breakfast Room: Located off the kitchen, this breakfast room is the perfect spot for informal family meals.

- Master Suite: This truly exceptional master suite features a bath, and a spacious walk in closet.

- Morning Porch: Step out of the master bedroom, and greet the day on this lovely porch.

- Additional Bedrooms: The three additional bedrooms each measure approximately 11 ft. x 12 ft. Two of them have walk-in closets.

Copyright by designer/architect.

SMARTtip

Using Slipcovers in Your Dining Area

Change the look of your dining room by slipcovering chairs. Short-skirted slipcovers give a more informal appearance; fabrics in graphic patterns, such as checks or floral prints, complement this style of slipcover best. Long-skirted covers are elegant additions to a formal dining room, particularly in solid color or tone-on-tone fabrics. Ties, buttons, or trim can add personality.

Plan #481028

Dimensions: 86'8" W x 53' D
Levels: 1
Square Footage: 3,980
Main Level Sq. Ft.: 2,290
Lower Level Sq. Ft.: 1,690
Bedrooms: 3
Bathrooms: 2½
Foundation: Walkout basement
Material List Available: No
Price Category: H

• **Lower Level:** For fun times, this lower level is finished to provide a wet bar and a recreation room. Two bedrooms, which share a full bathroom, are also on this level. Future expansion can include an additional bedroom.

Rear View

This home, with its Southwestern flair, invites friends and family in for some down-home hospitality.

Features:

• **Foyer:** A 12-ft-high ceiling extends an open welcome to all. With a view through the great room, the open floor plan makes the home feel large and open.

• **Kitchen:** This spacious gourmet kitchen opens generously to the hearth room, which features an angled fireplace. A two-level island, which contains a two-bowl sink, provides casual seating and additional storage.

• **Master Suite:** This romantic space features a 10-ft.-high stepped ceiling and a compartmentalized full bath that includes his and her sinks and a whirlpool tub.

Lower Level Floor Plan

Plan #151188

Dimensions: 63'4" W x 59'10" D

Levels: 1

Square Footage: 2,525

Bedrooms: 3

Bathrooms: 2

Foundation: Crawl space, slab, basement, or walkout

CompleteCost List Available: Y

Price Category: E

Images provided by designer/architect.

CAD FILE AVAILABLE

Copyright by designer/architect.

Plan #321034

Dimensions: 75'8" W x 52'6" D

Levels: 1

Square Footage: 3,508

Bedrooms: 4

Bathrooms: 3

Foundation: Basement, walkout

Material List Available: Yes

Price Category: H

Images provided by designer/architect.

Copyright by designer/architect.

Optional Basement Level Floor Plan

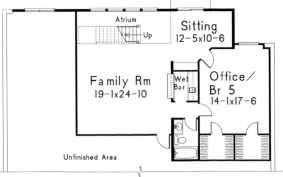

Copyright by designer/architect.

Plan #151007

Dimensions: 54'2" W x 56'2" D

Levels: 1

Square Footage: 1,787

Bedrooms: 3

Bathrooms: 2

Foundation: Crawl space, slab, basement, or walkout

CompleteCost List Available: Yes

Price Category: C

Images provided by designer/architect.

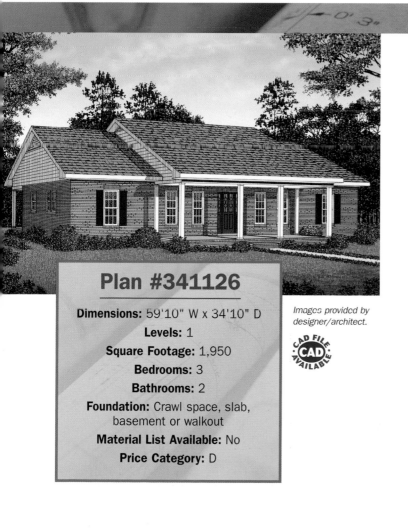

Copyright by designer/architect.

Plan #341126

Dimensions: 59'10" W x 34'10" D

Levels: 1

Square Footage: 1,950

Bedrooms: 3

Bathrooms: 2

Foundation: Crawl space, slab, basement or walkout

Material List Available: No

Price Category: D

Images provided by designer/architect.

Main Level Floor Plan

Deck

Bedroom 13'4" x 11'4"

Dining 10'6" x 12'1"

Kitchen 9'6" x 10'4"

Laun.

Bath

Garage 21'9" x 25'9"

Master Bath

Bedroom 11'4" x 11'5"

Great Room 19'5" x 16'8"

Master Bedroom 12'11" x 15'1"

Porch

70'-2"

50'-8"

Images provided by designer/architect.

Copyright by designer/architect.

Bar

Future Bedroom 12'2" x 11'8"

Unexcavated

Basement

Future Rec. Room 16'4" x 28'10"

Bath

Unexcavated

Lower Level Floor Plan

Plan #161118

Dimensions: 70'2" W x 50'8" D

Levels: 1

Square Footage: 2,154

Main Level Sq. Ft.: 1,483

Lower Level Sq. Ft: 671

Bedrooms: 3

Bathrooms: 3

Foundation: Basement or walkout

Materials List Available: Yes

Price Category: D

MASTER BATH (VAULTED)

STORAGE   STORAGE

DOUBLE GARAGE 22'-0" X 22'-0"

MASTER SUITE 13'-4" X 17'-0"

PORCH

BRK 14'-8" X 7'-4"

UTIL

GREAT ROOM 22'-0" X 17'-4"

KIT

EATING BAR

CL

WET BAR SINK

ISLAND

BATH-2

BEDR'M 2/ STUDY 13'-0" X 13'-4"

FOYER (VAULTED)

DINING 13'-0" X 13'-4"

64'-10"

Main Level Floor Plan

VERANDA

83'-7"

Images provided by designer/architect.

ATTIC

GAMEROOM 19'-10" X 13'-6"

ATTIC

BATH-4

BALCONY

BATH-3

BEDR'M 4 10'-8" X 14'-5"

LANDING   DN

BEDR'M 3 13'-0" X 14'-8"

OPEN TO FOYER

SEAT   SEAT

Upper Level Floor Plan

Copyright by designer/architect.

Plan #241018

Dimensions: 83'7" W x 64'10" D

Levels: 1½

Square Footage: 2,519

Main Level Sq. Ft.: 2,096

Upper Level Sq. Ft.: 423

Bedrooms: 4

Bathrooms: 4

Foundation: Slab

Materials List Available: No

Price Category: E

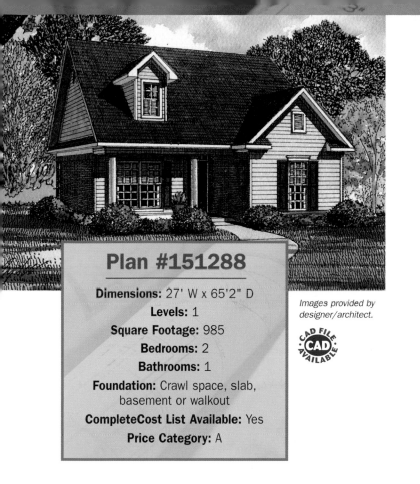

Plan #151288

Dimensions: 27' W x 65'2" D

Levels: 1

Square Footage: 985

Bedrooms: 2

Bathrooms: 1

Foundation: Crawl space, slab, basement or walkout

CompleteCost List Available: Yes

Price Category: A

Images provided by designer/architect.

Copyright by designer/architect.

Main Level Floor Plan

Upper Level Floor Plan

Plan #151100

Dimensions: 69'6" W x 31' D

Levels: 2

Square Footage: 2,268

Main Level Sq. Ft.: 1,168

Upper Level Sq. Ft.: 1,100

Bedrooms: 3

Bathrooms: 2½

Foundation: Crawl space, slab, basement, or walkout

CompleteCost List Available: Yes

Price Category: E

Images provided by designer/architect.

Copyright by designer/architect.

Plan #341063

Dimensions: 50' W x 43'4" D
Levels: 1
Square Footage: 1,566
Bedrooms: 3
Bathrooms: 2
Foundation: Crawl space, slab, basement or walkout basement
Material List Available: Yes
Price Category: C

Images provided by designer/architect.

ready to hold a washer and dryer, as well as anything else you need to maintain the home.

- **Master Suite:** This suite gives you space to make it your own while providing you with what you need: a walk-in closet and sectioned full master bath.

- **Secondary Bedrooms:** Often, the secondary bedrooms are dwarfed by the master suite, but not in this design. The bedrooms give you room to grow. They are both equipped with large closets and share the second full bathroom.

This traditional ranch home, with its charmingly simple design, is ideal for raising a family.

CAD FILE AVAILABLE CAD

Features:

- **Porches:** The covered front porch welcomes guests into your home or onto your stoop as twilight spills over the house. The screened porch, which opens into the kitchen, allows for enjoying breakfast with the morning sun and a warm summer breeze.

- **Living Room:** One thing the budding family needs is space for toys and playpens or entertainment centers and leather recliners. This living room has plenty of space, a blank canvas waiting for your touch.

- **Kitchen:** The L-shaped design in this large space makes room for a convenient dining area. Though the kitchen usually is the "brightest" place in a home, the light streaming in through a wall of windows makes this particularly true with this design. Also attached is the spacious utility room,

Plan #161156

Dimensions: 76' W x 68'1" D

Levels: 1

Square Footage: 2,959

Bedrooms: 3

Bathrooms: 2½

Foundation: Walkout

Material List Available: Yes

Price Category: F

• **Secondary Bedrooms:** Two nicely sized additional bedrooms share access to a private full bath.

Interesting architectural details and a variety of textures make this home's exterior as appealing as its interior.

Features:

• **Great Room:** Perfect for entertaining guests or just cozying up to the glowing, wood-burning fireplace with loved ones, this great room is conveniently located in the center of everything.

• **Kitchen:** This efficiently designed kitchen has enough workspace and storage to please even the most persnickety chef. Easily transition from meal prep to dining in the adjacent breakfast and dining rooms. A covered deck is another fun spot for mealtime.

• **Library:** Flanked by windows, this sunny space is a quiet retreat for study and reflection.

• **Master Suite:** This space is a romantic get-away unto itself. Down a private hallway is the expansive master bath, with his and her sinks, whirlpool tub, stall shower, and large walk-in closet.

Great Room

Plan #151003

Dimensions: 51'6" W x 52'4" D

Levels: 1

Square Footage: 1,680

Bedrooms: 3

Bathrooms: 2

Foundation: Crawl space, slab, or basement

CompleteCost List Available: Yes

Price Category: C

A lovely front porch and bay windows, add sparkle to this home.

Features:

- **Great Room:** Perfect for entertaining, this room features a tray ceiling, wet bar, and a quiet screened porch nearby.

- **Dining Room:** This bayed dining room facing the front porch is cozy yet roomy enough for family parties during the holidays.

- **Kitchen:** This eat-in kitchen also faces the front and is ideal for preparing meals for any occasion.

- **Master Suite:** The tray ceiling here gives an added feeling of space, while the distance from the other bedrooms allows for all the privacy you'll need.

CAD FILE AVAILABLE

Images provided by designer/architect.

This home, as shown in the photograph, may differ from the actual blueprints. For more detailed information, please check the floor plans carefully.

Copyright by designer/architect.

Plan #151006

Dimensions: 54'2" W x 52'10" D

Levels: 1

Square Footage: 1,758

Bedrooms: 3

Bathrooms: 2

Foundation: Crawl space, slab, basement, or walkout

CompleteCost List Available: Yes

Price Category: C

You'll love the expansive feeling of the open, spacious rooms in this home and wonder how you ever did without the amenities it offers.

Features:

- **Foyer:** A foyer with a 10-ft. ceiling provides the perfect transition between the columned front porch and the interior of this home.

- **Great Room:** A fireplace, 9-ft. boxed ceiling, and access to the rear grilling porch and back yard make this room the heart of the home.

- **Dining Room:** The 10-ft. ceiling and boxed columns provide a touch of formality.

- **Kitchen:** Convenience marks this well-designed kitchen that opens to the breakfast room.

- **Master Suite:** With a 9-ft. boxed ceiling, this elegant room will be your favorite retreat. The bath has a whirlpool tub with glass blocks, a shower, and double vanities.

Images provided by designer/architect.

This home, as shown in the photograph, may differ from the actual blueprints. For more detailed information, please check the floor plans carefully.

Copyright by designer/architect.

Plan #161101

Dimensions: 136'3" W x 69' D
Levels: 2
Square Footage: 8,414
Main Level Sq. Ft.: 4,011
Upper Level Sq. Ft.: 2,198
Optional Lower Level Sq. Ft.: 2,205
Bedrooms: 4
Bathrooms: 4 full, 2 half
Foundation: Walkout; basement for fee
Material List Available: Yes
Price Category: L

The grandeur of this mansion-style home boasts period stone, two-story columns, an angular turret, a second-floor balcony, and a gated courtyard.

Features:

- **Formal Living:** Formal areas consist of the charming living room and adjacent music room, which continues to the library, with its sloped ceilings and glass surround. Various ceiling treatments, with 10-ft. ceiling heights, and 8-ft.-tall doors add luxury and artistry to the first floor.

- **Hearth Room:** This large room, with false wood-beamed ceiling, adds a casual yet rich atmosphere to the family gathering space. Dual French doors on each side of the fireplace create a pleasurable indoor-outdoor relationship.

- **Kitchen:** This space is an enviable work place for the gourmet cook. Multiple cabinets and expansive counter space create a room that may find you spending a surprisingly enjoyable amount of time on food preparation. The built-in grill on the porch makes outdoor entertaining convenient and fun.

- **Master Suite:** This suite offers a vaulted ceiling, dual walk-in closets, and his and her vanities. The whirlpool tub is showcased on a platform and surrounded by windows for a relaxing view of the side yard. Private access to the deck is an enchanting surprise.

Rear View

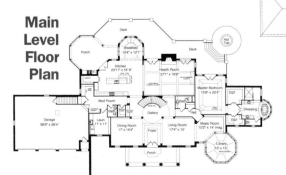

Main Level Floor Plan

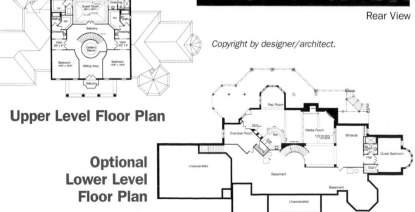

Upper Level Floor Plan

Optional Lower Level Floor Plan

Plan #151031

Dimensions: 60'2" W x 60'2" D
Levels: 2
Square Footage: 3,130
Main Level Sq. Ft.: 1,600
Upper Level Sq. Ft.: 1,530
Bedrooms: 3
Bathrooms: 3½
Foundation: Crawl space, slab
CompleteCost List Available: Yes
Price Category: G

If you love traditional Southern plantation homes, you'll want this house with its wraparound porches that are graced with boxed columns.

Features:

- **Great Room:** Use the gas fireplace for warmth in this comfortable room, which is open to the kitchen.

- **Living Room:** 8-in. columns add formality as you enter this living and dining room.

- **Kitchen:** You'll love the island bar with a sink. An elevator here can take you to the other floors.

- **Master Suite:** A gas fireplace warms this area, and the bath is luxurious.

- **Bedrooms:** Each has a private bath and built-in bookshelves for easy organizing.

- **Optional Features:** Choose a 2,559-sq.-ft. basement and add a kitchen to it, or finish the 1,744-sq.-ft. bonus room and add a spiral staircase and a bath.

CAD FILE AVAILABLE

Images provided by designer/architect.

Main Level Floor Plan

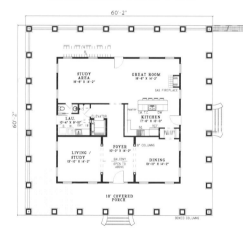

Upper Level Floor Plan

Copyright by designer/architect.

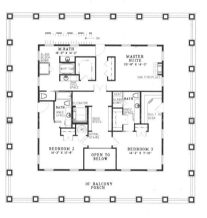

Lower Level Floor Plan

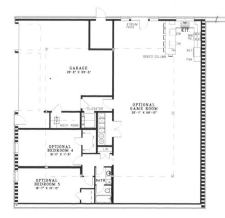

Optional Upper Level Floor Plan

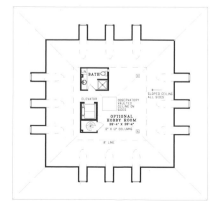

Plan #321065

Dimensions: 80' W x 52' D

Levels: 2

Square Footage: 3,420

Main Level Sq. Ft.: 1,894

Upper Level Sq. Ft.: 1,526

Bedrooms: 4

Bathrooms: 3½

Foundation: Daylight basement

Materials List Available: Yes

Price Category: G

Main Level Floor Plan

Images provided by designer/architect.

80'-0"

52'-0"

Deck

Hearth 14-0x17-8 vaulted

Gallery

Kit 17-5x13-8

Brk

Family 18-0x18-10

Garage 29-4x21-4

Living 14-0x12-0

Foyer

Dining 14-0x12-0

Dn

Up

P

R

OVEN

Up

W

D

Porch

Upper Level Floor Plan

Copyright by designer/architect.

Br 2 14-0x12-0

Br 3 13-4x13-7

MBr 14-0x15-7

Dn

L

Dn

Br 4 11-8x12-0

Foyer

Porch

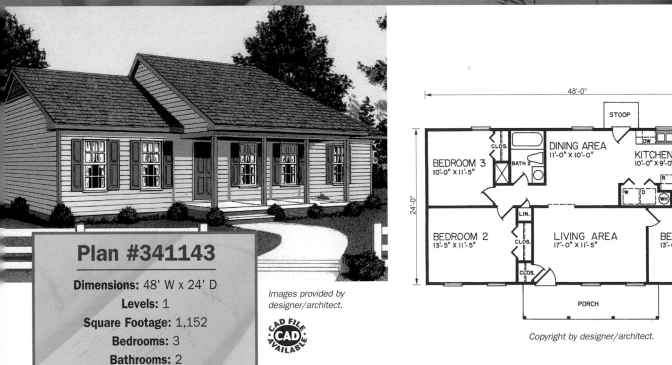

Plan #341143

Dimensions: 48' W x 24' D

Levels: 1

Square Footage: 1,152

Bedrooms: 3

Bathrooms: 2

Foundation: Crawl space, slab, basement, or walkout

Material List Available: No

Price Category: B

Images provided by designer/architect.

CAD FILE AVAILABLE

48'-0"

24'-0"

STOOP

BEDROOM 3 10'-0" X 11'-5"

CLOS.

BATH 2

DINING AREA 11'-0" X 10'-0"

DW

KITCHEN 10'-0" X 9'-0"

BATH 1

BEDROOM 2 13'-5" X 11'-5"

LIN.

CLOS.

LIVING AREA 17'-0" X 11'-5"

W D

WH

CLOSET

BEDROOM 1 13'-6" X 11'-5"

CLOS.

PORCH

Copyright by designer/architect.

Plan #341241

Dimensions: 53' W x 34' D

Levels: 1

Square Footage: 1,176

Bedrooms: 3

Bathrooms: 2

Foundation: Crawl space, slab, basement or walkout

CompleteCost List Available: No

Price Category: B

Images provided by designer/architect.

Copyright by designer/architect.

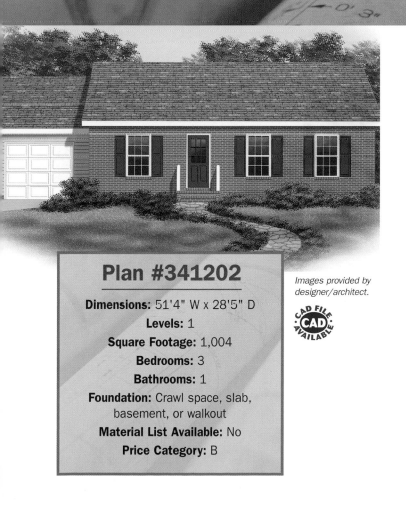

Plan #341202

Dimensions: 51'4" W x 28'5" D

Levels: 1

Square Footage: 1,004

Bedrooms: 3

Bathrooms: 1

Foundation: Crawl space, slab, basement, or walkout

Material List Available: No

Price Category: B

Images provided by designer/architect.

Copyright by designer/architect.

Adding a Room

Do you need more living area? Do your domestic dreams include a home office, a deluxe media room, or perhaps a downstairs hangout for wild and crazy teens? Look no further than under your feet. That's right, your humble basement. In most cases, even the most ambitious project costs only a fraction of what you would spend to build an addition. Estimates for building aboveground average about $150 a foot; remodeling a basement, on the other hand, usually costs only $75 per foot—that's a 50-percent savings.

The lower cost shouldn't surprise you. After all, a basement is fully enclosed and already comes with walls, a floor, and a ceiling. There's no need to spend major dollars breaking ground for an addition or to move to a new house in order to have that special hobby room or that extra bedroom.

What's more, no matter how grand your plan, remodeling your basement provides a major head start over new construction when it comes to heating and cooling the new space, powering a media room or home office, or meeting the

The following article was reprinted from *Design Ideas for Basements* (Creative Homeowner 2004).

A basement space, opposite, can be fun, decorative, and reflective of all of your interests.

Don't settle for a plain living space. Enliven the room with glamour and flavor, left, that will make it unforgettable to guests. Decorate it with an over-the-top theme or exotic accessories.

Adding details to the room, such as an arched median and decorative wallcoverings, below, will leave family and friends wondering whether they are really in a basement.

SMARTtip

Basic Basement Types

The type of basement you have may set up different challenges to overcome in your design, whether it is finishing surfaces, providing sources of ventilation, or choosing windows and doors that may be required by the new International Residential Code (IRC).

A standard basement is surrounded by below-ground walls, with maybe 20 percent of the walls above grade. There might be small windows at the very top or none at all. You can access or exit this basement only through an interior stairway. There is very little light and limited air circulation. A concern may be the coolness of all that concrete, especially in winter.

A walk-out basement has at least one wall that is above grade. This allows more light into the interior. With windows and doors, a walk-out basement has more air circulation than a standard basement. Also, interior and exterior stairs provide greater access into and out of the basement, which makes this space highly usable for bedrooms.

A grand staircase can be a preview, above, of the lush amenities downstairs.

Set the mood, left, with a surround-sound system built into the wall.

A theater-sized screen, opposite, allows you to watch your favorite movie in plush style.

additional plumbing needs of a bathroom or kitchen. The utilities are accessible and can be easily upgraded or adapted to accommodate your design needs.

Heating and cooling are usually a breeze. Basements are naturally cool in summer so air conditioning is often not required. Basements retain some of the residual heat from the furnace that warms up the main and upstairs living space. In colder areas, adding a few panels of baseboard heating can fill in the chilly gaps.

Upstairs, Downstairs

As increasing numbers of people spend more time at home. Experts agree that they see their living space in a new way. People have come to realize that their homes are designable real estate that can meet changing needs and passions, rather than static rooms with rigid roles. And basements are, in

SMARTtip
Future Uses of New Space

People and families change and, along with them, the rooms they inhabit. Before you commit to your basement's final design, make sure that you think through what you might need when the kids move out, you retire, or (gulp) your mother-in-law comes to live with you. The space you use for a playroom now may be converted into a guest suite or a home workshop in the future. Save time and money later by making sure the necessary wiring, plumbing, and mechanical work is roughed in before you cover the walls.

In order to imagine all of the possibilities, do some blue-sky thinking about 5 or 10 years down the line and create a checklist of possible needs for future configurations of your basement space.

many ways, the perfect space for that kind of flexible thinking and designing. The very shape of a basement—a long, shoe-box-like room running the length of the house—is equivalent to a blank slate, beckoning you to leave your design imprint on it, whether your are creating a large space for the entire family or a suite of medium-sized rooms that serve an array of practical purposes.

In fact, the amorphous quality of a basement actually cries out for creativity and the kind of architectural interest and dimension that can transform it from unappealing to inviting.

Think beyond knotty pine paneling and bean-bag chairs, and envision something more sophisticated. You can easily upgrade and enliven a boxy basement, for instance, by varying the height and angle of wall and ceiling planes. Mix materials, textures, and finishes on walls and ceilings. Include a greenhouse bumpout to bring the light and the outdoors into the space.

Let's assume your basement is dry and mold-free. The choice of furniture, accessories, and window treatments can be limitless, and often no different from those you would use in the rest of the house.

SMARTtip

Adding Molding

Keep moldings simple in a basement with lower ceilings. Elaborate moldings around the ceiling or floor can shorten the height of the room.

Stone, ironwork, and rough-hewn beams create an Old World look in this setting, inset.

Dinner is set in this romantic, softly lit wine cellar that was created in a remodeled basement, left.

Rooms of Opportunity

While some designers espouse tying the basement design into the home's overall style, others view basement conversions as a license to be daring. If you've always wanted to try a different look, go for it in the basement. Down-under spaces aren't seen from other levels, so there's no reason to take your design cues from upstairs. Here are some possibilities.

Family Room. This all-purpose living space is probably the easiest and least expensive way to add square footage to your home. You usually won't have to fiddle with or upgrade plumbing or worry about special egress windows. The main concern is keeping the space dry, and selecting finishes for walls, floors, and ceilings that suit your taste and vision. Whether you are looking for space for the kids' toys and games or just a place where you can watch television, listen to music, or dance away the night, a family room is an ideal choice.

Home Office. If you telecommute and need privacy and quiet to get your work done, designing a home office in the out-of-the-way basement is a no-brainer. Just make sure to include enough electrical circuits to power all of your equipment as well as any add-on technology in the future.

Wine Cellar. You might have always wanted one to house your collection of, say, Merlots or Syrahs, but couldn't find the right spot in your main living space. A cool, dark base-

It is essential to have plenty of storage space in a creative work area with a lot of implements, above.

ment provides a perfect climate for your vintage hobby.

Crafts Studio or Home Workshop. Perhaps you have a desire to take up landscape painting, to do some major crafting, or to try woodworking, but don't want to mess up the upstairs rooms or fill the house with paint fumes and dust. A downstairs arts-and-craft studio or home workshop, equipped with a quiet but powerful exhaust fan and a wall of storage bins, can solve both problems and provide the privacy to enable you to complete your masterpiece. You might even combine this space with a laundry room, a trend that's called a "home studio."

Media Room. You don't need a fortune to create a highly entertaining media room for family and friends. It's easy to darken an already dim basement and to increase sound absorption with the right floor, wall, and ceiling materials. If you

are ambitious, include a snack bar or kitchenette, complete with a refrigerator, sink, and microwave oven, so that you don't have to miss a moment of the movie.

Spa or Gym. After a long day's journey back from work, wouldn't it be relaxing to soak in a hot tub or melt away the tension in a sauna? Or reinvigorate yourself with a run on the treadmill or elliptical trainer? Look to your basement, again. The concrete-slab floor requires no additional structural reinforcement to handle the substantial weight of a hot tub, which can weigh more than 4,000 pounds when filled to capacity, or heavy gym machines. Saunas—which usually come as prefabricated packages, complete with walls, floor, and ceiling—are the perfect amenity for a windowless corner of the basement, and can often be tied into existing household circuits.

Bedroom. A basement is perfect for an extra bedroom. It typically has a bare minimum of natural light, and it's cool and quiet—a recipe for a good night's sleep.
Extra Bathroom or Kitchen. Adding an extra bathroom to a basement can free up space and thin out traffic upstairs and,

SMARTtip

Sizing Up Rooms

While there is no perfect-sized room—it depends on your needs and the space you have to work with—the U.S. Department of Housing and Urban Development (HUD) has come up with some recommendations, which are listed below. The minimum net floor area refers to the space within the enclosed walls and excludes built-in features such as cabinets and closets.

	Minimum Area	Minimum Size	Preferred
Master Bedroom	n/a	n/a	12 x 16 ft.
Bedroom	80 sq. ft.	8 x 10 ft.	11 x 14 ft.
Family Room	110 sq. ft.	10.5 x 10.5 ft.	12 x 16 ft.
Living Room	176 sq. ft.	1 x 16 ft.	12 x 18 ft.
Great Room	n/a	n/a	14 x 20 ft.
Bathroom	35 sq. ft.	5 x 7 ft.	5 x 9 ft.

when it's located near water-supply lines and a drain system, is easy and inexpensive to build. For the exact same reasons, adding a small kitchen won't break the bank.

Workout time flies by while watching your favorite TV shows, opposite top.

An extra bathroom in the basement can be glamorous, opposite bottom.

A basement bedroom is the ideal getaway from the upstairs traffic, above.

Plan #161031

Dimensions: 99'8" W x 68'8" D
Levels: 2
Square Footage: 5,381
Main Level Sq. Ft.: 3,793
Lower Level Sq. Ft.: 1,588
Bedrooms: 4
Bathrooms: 3½
Foundation: Basement
Materials List Available: Yes
Price Category: I

Images provided by designer/architect.

If you're looking for a compatible mixture of formal and informal areas in a home, look no further!

Features:

- Great Room: Columns at the entry to this room and the formal dining room set a gracious tone that is easy around which to decorate.

- Library: Set up an office or just a cozy reading area in this quiet room.

- Hearth Room: Spacious and inviting, this hearth room is positioned so that friends and family can flow from here to the breakfast area and kitchen.

- Master Suite: The luxury of this area is capped by the access it gives to the rear yard.

- Lower Level: Enjoy the 9-ft.-tall ceilings as you walk out to the rear yard from this area.

Entry

Rear View

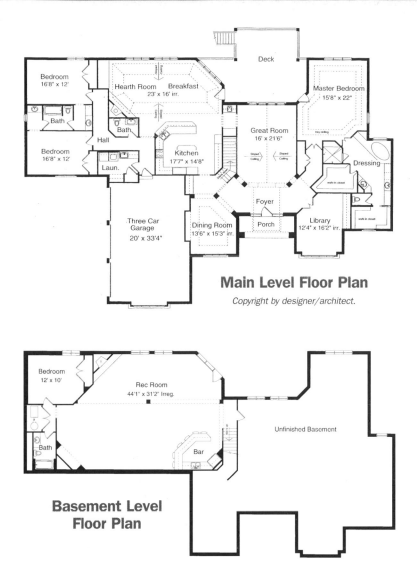

Main Level Floor Plan

Copyright by designer/architect.

Deck

Bedroom 16'8" x 12'

Hearth Room

Breakfast 23' x 16' irr.

Bath

Master Bedroom 15'8" x 22"

Bath

Great Room 16' x 21'6"

Hall

Bedroom 16'8" x 12'

Laun.

Kitchen 17'7" x 14'8"

Dressing

walk-in closet

Three Car Garage 20' x 33'4"

Dining Room 13'6" x 15'3" irr.

Foyer

Porch

Library 12'4" x 16'2" irr.

walk-in closet

Basement Level Floor Plan

Bedroom 12' x 10'

Rec Room 44'1" x 31'2" Irreg.

Unfinished Basement

Bath

Bar

Dining Room

SMARTtip
Paint or Polyurethane Clear Finish?

It usually does not pay to strip the finish off a painted door in the hope of obtaining a wood-grained look. It is extremely difficult to remove all of the paint, and the effort spent stripping, sanding, staining, and sealing isn't worth the time and expense. It is best either to paint the door in a traditional color, such as white, to provide a fresh look, or to coat it with an opaque stain over the existing finish. Consider adding a brass kick plate or letter slot for an elegant touch.

Rear Elevation

Left Elevation

Right Elevation

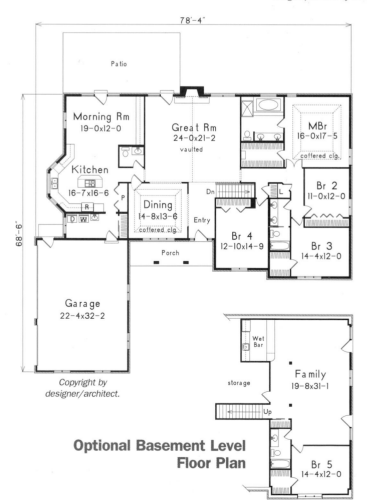

Images provided by designer/architect.

Plan #321036

Dimensions: 78'4" W x 68'6" D
Levels: 1
Square Footage: 2,900
Bedrooms: 4
Bathrooms: 2½
Foundation: Basement
Materials List Available: Yes
Price Category: F

This classic contemporary is wrapped in brick.

Features:

- Great Room: This grand-scale room offers a vaulted ceiling and Palladian windows flanking an 8-ft.-wide brick fireplace.

- Kitchen: This built-in-a-bay room features a picture window above the sink, a huge pantry, and a cooktop island. It opens to the large morning room.

- Breakfast Area: Open to the kitchen, this area features 12 ft. of cabinetry.

- Master Bedroom: This room features a coffered ceiling, and a walk-in closet gives you good storage space in this luxurious bedroom.

- Garage: This area can fit three cars with plenty of room to spare.

Copyright by designer/architect.

Optional Basement Level Floor Plan

Plan #451079

Dimensions: 224'6" W x 112'11" D
Levels: 2
Square Footage: 12,410
Main Level Sq. Ft.: 4,515
Upper Level Sq. Ft.: 7,895
Bedrooms: 7
Bathrooms: 7½
Foundation: Walkout, insulated concrete form
Material List Available: No
Price Category: L

This expansive house is full of cozy, homey details.

Images provided by designer/architect.

Features:

- Foyer: This elegant circular foyer greets you as you enter the home. There is easy access to the library, parlor, dining room, and great room. Circular stairs allow access to the upper level.

- Kitchen: This island kitchen features a circular eating area that adjoins the family room. The large walk-in pantry is just off the garage to ease unloading the car.

- Master Suite: This large retreat features two walk-in closets and a spa area. The master bath spoils you with his and her vanities, a large stall shower, and a separate toilet enclosure.

- Lower Level: This level is dedicated to entertainment and features a game room and a home theater. There are even your own private bowling alley and an exercise room. After all of this excitement you can relax by going for a swim in the indoor pool.

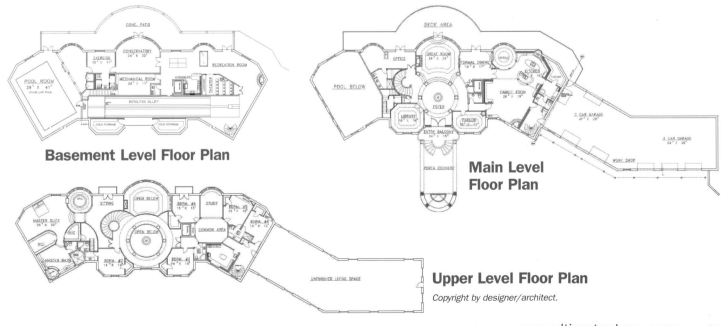

Basement Level Floor Plan

Main Level Floor Plan

Upper Level Floor Plan

Copyright by designer/architect.

Plan #401029

Dimensions: 37'6" W x 48'4" D
Levels: 2
Square Footage: 2,163
Main Level Sq. Ft.: 832
Upper Level Sq. Ft.: 1,331
Bedrooms: 3
Bathrooms: 2½
Foundation: Basement
Materials List Available: Yes
Price Category: D

This two-level plan has a bonus—a roof deck with hot tub! A variety of additional outdoor spaces makes this one wonderful plan.

Features:

- First Level: Family bedrooms, a full bath room, and a cozy den are on the first level, along with a two-car garage.

- Living Area: The living spaces are on the second floor and include a living/dining room combination with a deck and fireplace. The dining room has buffet space.

- Family Room: Featuring a fireplace and a built-in entertainment center, the gathering area is open to the breakfast room and sky lighted kitchen.

- Master Bedroom: This room features a private bath with a whirlpool tub and two-person shower, a walk-in closet, and access to still another deck.

Upper Level Floor Plan

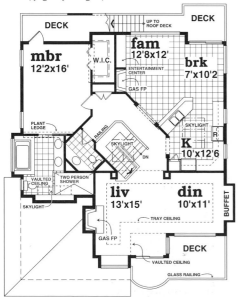

Main Level Floor Plan

Rear Elevation

Dining Room/Kitchen

Plan #271298

Dimensions: 70' W x 61' D
Levels: 2
Square Footage: 2,759
Main Level Sq. Ft.: 2,024
Upper Level Sq. Ft.: 735
Bedrooms: 4
Bathrooms: 2½
Foundation: Crawl space or walkout
Material List Available: No
Price Category: F

Images provided by designer/architect.

This impressive home has an Old World courtyard, but a thoroughly contemporary interior.

Features:

- **Entry:** Welcome guests through wrought-iron gates and into the courtyard as a modest introduction to your gracious home.

- **Living Room:** Treat guests to drinks and conversation in this large, fire-illuminated living room. When you need quality time with your loved ones, enjoy the solace and informality of the family room.

- **Kitchen:** This spacious kitchen is fit for a gourmet chef, with plenty of workspace and storage, as well as a walk-in pantry.

- **Master Suite:** Isolated on the upper level, this master suite has access to a private deck, a large walk-in closet, and a full bath with dual vanities, a spa tub, and a separate shower.

- **Secondary Bedrooms:** Three additional bedrooms are clustered together on the main level, each featuring ample closet space and close proximity to both a powder room and a full bathroom.

Main Level Floor Plan

Upper Level Floor Plan

Copyright by designer/architect.

Plan #161060

Dimensions: 113'10" W x 60'6" D

Levels: 2

Square Footage: 5,143

Main Level Sq. Ft.: 3,323

Upper Level Sq. Ft.: 1,820

Bedrooms: 4

Bathrooms: 3½

Foundation: Basement, walkout basement

Materials List Available: No

Price Category: J

Images provided by designer/architect.

Luxury, comfort, beauty, spaciousness — this home has everything you've been wanting, including space for every possible activity.

CAD FILE AVAILABLE · CAD

Features:

- **Courtyard:** Enjoy the privacy here before entering this spacious home.

- **Great Room:** Open to the foyer, dining area, and kitchen, this great room has a fireplace flanked by windows and leads to the open rear deck.

- **Dining Room:** Situated between the foyer and the kitchen, this room is ideal for formal dining.

- **Library:** Located just off the foyer, this library offers a calm retreat from activities in the great room.

- **Utility Area:** The mudroom, pantry, half-bath and laundry room add up to household convenience.

- **Master Suite:** You'll love the huge walk-in closet, extensive window feature, and bath with a dressing room and two vanities.

Rear Elevation

Upper Level Floor Plan

Copyright by designer/architect.

Main Level Floor Plan

Optional Lower Level Floor Plan

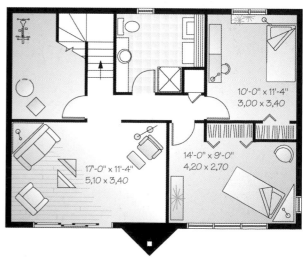

Plan #181124

Dimensions: 32'4" W x 24'4" D

Levels: 2

Square Footage: 1,574

Main Level Sq. Ft.: 787

Lower Level Sq. Ft.: 787

Bedrooms: 3

Bathrooms: 2

Foundation: Walkout

Material List Available: Yes

Price Category: C

Images provided by designer/architect.

This modified A-frame home is as elegantly designed inside as it is out. This house is perfect for remote areas, where you can enjoy the view from the wraparound deck.

Features:

- **Great Room:** This open layout makes the most out of a small space. Entertain guests in front of the fireplace or entertain yourself in front of the television.

- **Kitchen:** This L-shaped kitchen also maximizes space and provides plenty of workspace and storage. The dining area is close enough to be called "eat-in," but far enough to be formal if you prefer.

- **Bedrooms:** Each of the three bedrooms is equipped with a closet and plenty of room for a desk or small entertainment center, as well as additional clothes storage. All three bedrooms are also close to a full bathroom.

- **Basement:** This large space contains two of the three bedrooms and an additional sitting room. Use the upstairs living space for entertaining guests, and hide all of the unattractive family belongings, such as the game consoles and their accessories, downstairs.

Copyright by designer/architect.

Main Level Floor Plan

10'-0" x 11'-4"
3,00 x 3,40

18'-0" x 11'-4"
5,40 x 3,40

13'-0" x 11'-4"
3,90 x 3,40

Lower Level Floor Plan

10'-0" x 11'-4"
3,00 x 3,40

17'-0" x 11'-4"
5,10 x 3,40

14'-0" x 9'-0"
4,20 x 2,70

Plan #451259

Dimensions: 75'2" W x 55'6" D
Levels: 2
Square Footage: 3,798
Main Level Sq. Ft.: 2,485
Upper Level Sq. Ft.: 1,313
Bedrooms: 6
Bathrooms: 6½
Foundation: Walk-out basement
Materials List Available: No
Price Category: H

Images provided by designer/architect.

Classic and gracious outside and functionally elegant inside, this expansive home will be the envy of the neighborhood.

CAD FILE AVAILABLE

Features:

- **Living Room:** Welcome guests into the grand foyer from the portico, through a pair of columns, and into this inviting space. A fireplace and French doors leading out onto the stamped concrete patio are just two special features.

- **Kitchen:** This kitchen features a snack bar and is conveniently located between the breakfast area and the formal dining room, simplifying mealtime transitions.

- **Master Suites:** Yes, "suites"-plural. These two amazing spaces each feature bay windows, walk-in closets, and full baths. The second includes private entry to a patio and a bath with dual vanities and a separate shower.

- **Additional Bedrooms:** The second floor holds three additional bedrooms, all with private access to porches and full bathrooms.

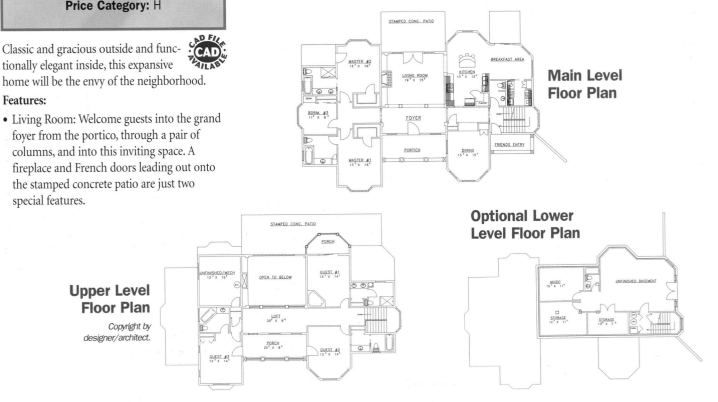

Main Level Floor Plan

Upper Level Floor Plan

Copyright by designer/architect.

Optional Lower Level Floor Plan

Plan #161093

Dimensions: 70'8" W x 64' D
Levels: 1
Square Footage: 4,328
Main Level Sq. Ft.: 2,582
Lower Level Sq. Ft.: 1,746
Bedrooms: 3
Bathrooms: 3½
Foundation: Walkout
Materials List Available: No
Price Category: I

Detailed stucco and stone accents impart warmth and character to the exterior of this one level home.

CAD FILE AVAILABLE

Features:

- **Great Room:** This gathering room, which features a fireplace and a decorative ceiling, offers an extensive view of the rear yard.

- **Kitchen:** Spacious and up-to-date, this extra-large combination gourmet kitchen and breakfast room is an ideal area for doing chores and hosting family gatherings.

- **Main Level:** The extravagant master suite, with its private bathroom and dressing area, the library with built-in shelves, and the formal dining room round out the main floor. Accented by a wood rail, the extra-wide main stairway leads to the lavish lower level.

- **Lower Level:** The two additional bedrooms, adjoining bathroom, media room, billiard room, and exercise room comprise this fantastic finished lower level.

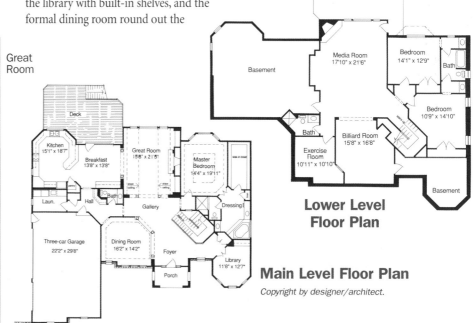

Lower Level Floor Plan

Main Level Floor Plan

Copyright by designer/architect.

Plan #181260

Dimensions: 54' W x 43' D
Levels: 2
Square Footage: 3,251
Main Level Sq. Ft.: 1,536
Upper Level Sq. Ft.: 1,715
Bedrooms: 4
Bathrooms: 3½
Foundation: Basement
Materials List Available: Yes
Price Category: G

Images provided by designer/architect.

CAD FILE AVAILABLE

Main Level Floor Plan

Upper Level Floor Plan

Copyright by designer/architect.

Plan #451387

Dimensions: 131'2" W x 78'4" D
Levels: 1
Square Footage: 4,514
Main Level Sq. Ft.: 2,257
Lower Level Sq. Ft.: 2,257
Bedrooms: 3
Bathrooms: 4½
Foundation: Walkout – insulated concrete form
Material List Available: No
Price Category: I

Images provided by designer/architect.

CAD FILE AVAILABLE

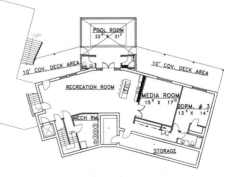

Main Level Floor Plan

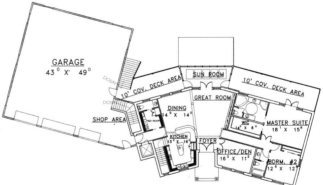

Lower Level Floor Plan

Copyright by designer/architect.

Rear Elevation

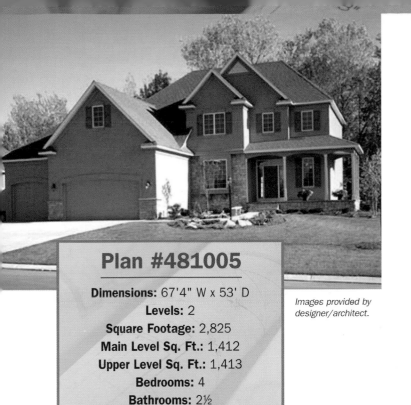

Plan #481005

Dimensions: 67'4" W x 53' D

Levels: 2

Square Footage: 2,825

Main Level Sq. Ft.: 1,412

Upper Level Sq. Ft.: 1,413

Bedrooms: 4

Bathrooms: 2½

Foundation: Walkout basement

Material List Available: No

Price Category: F

Images provided by designer/architect.

Upper Level Floor Plan

Copyright by designer/architect.

Main Level Floor Plan

Plan #271079

Dimensions: 104' W x 55' D

Levels: 1

Square Footage: 2,228

Bedrooms: 1-3

Bathrooms: 1½

Foundation: Daylight basement

Materials List Available: No

Price Category: E

Images provided by designer/architect.

Copyright by designer/architect.

Optional Basement Level Floor Plan

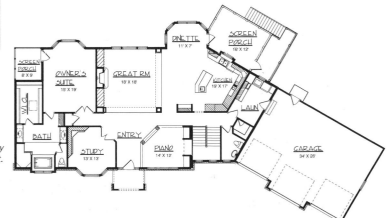

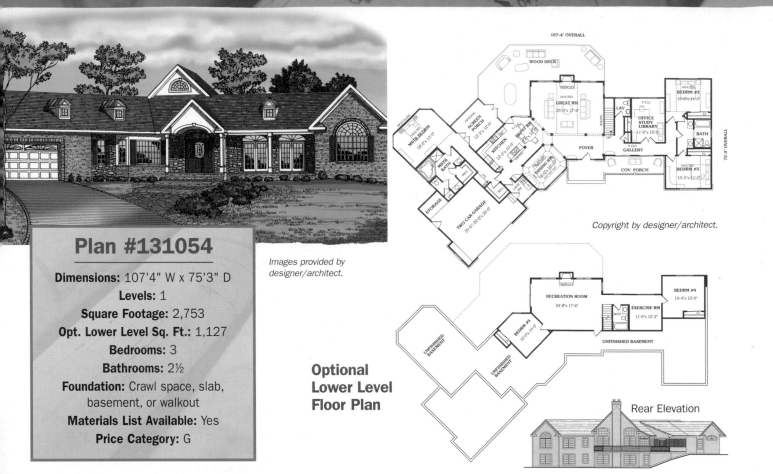

Copyright by designer/architect.

Plan #131054

Dimensions: 107'4" W x 75'3" D
Levels: 1
Square Footage: 2,753
Opt. Lower Level Sq. Ft.: 1,127
Bedrooms: 3
Bathrooms: 2½
Foundation: Crawl space, slab, basement, or walkout
Materials List Available: Yes
Price Category: G

Images provided by designer/architect.

Optional Lower Level Floor Plan

Rear Elevation

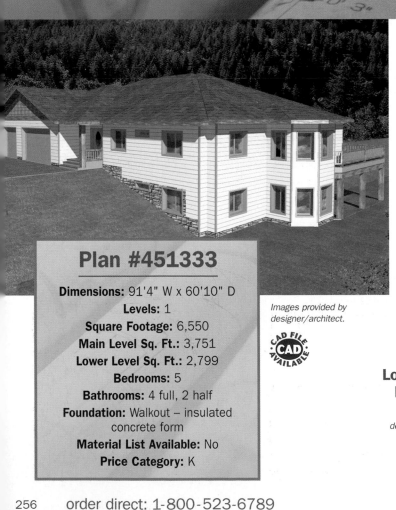

Plan #451333

Dimensions: 91'4" W x 60'10" D
Levels: 1
Square Footage: 6,550
Main Level Sq. Ft.: 3,751
Lower Level Sq. Ft.: 2,799
Bedrooms: 5
Bathrooms: 4 full, 2 half
Foundation: Walkout – insulated concrete form
Material List Available: No
Price Category: K

Images provided by designer/architect.

CAD FILE AVAILABLE

Main Level Floor Plan

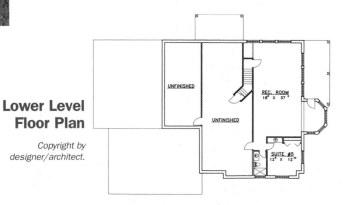

Lower Level Floor Plan

Copyright by designer/architect.

Plan #271060

Dimensions: 72' W x 64'8" D

Levels: 1

Square Footage: 1,726

Bedrooms: 2

Bathrooms: 2½

Foundation: Walkout basement

Materials List Available: No

Price Category: C

Images provided by designer/architect.

CAD FILE AVAILABLE

Copyright by designer/architect.

Optional Lower Level Floor Plan

Plan #181116

Dimensions: 36' W x 34' D

Levels: 2

Square Footage: 1,872

Main Level Sq. Ft.: 1,078

Upper Level Sq. Ft.: 794

Bedrooms: 3

Bathrooms: 2

Foundation: Walkout basement

Materials List Available: Yes

Price Category: C

Images provided by designer/architect.

CAD FILE AVAILABLE

Main Level Floor Plan

Copyright by designer/architect.

Basement Level Floor Plan

Upper Level Floor Plan

Plan #161096

Dimensions: 67'6" W x 75'6" D
Levels: 2
Square Footage: 3,435
Main Level Sq. Ft.: 2,479
Upper Level Sq. Ft.: 956
Bedrooms: 4
Bathrooms: 3½
Foundation: Walkout basement; basement for fee
Material List Available: No
Price Category: G

Images provided by designer/architect.

A stone-and-brick exterior is excellently coordinated to create a warm and charming showplace.

CAD FILE AVAILABLE

Features:

- **Great Room:** The spacious foyer leads directly into this room, which visually opens to the rear yard, providing natural light and outdoor charm.

- **Kitchen:** This fully equipped kitchen is located to provide the utmost convenience in serving the formal dining room and the breakfast area, which is surrounded by windows and has a double-soffit ceiling treatment. The combination of breakfast room, hearth room, and kitchen creatively forms a comfortable family gathering place.

- **Master Suite:** A tray ceiling tops this suite and its luxurious dressing area, which will pamper you after a hard day.

- **Balcony:** Wood rails decorate the stairs leading to this balcony, which offers a dramatic view of the great room and foyer below.

- **Bedrooms:** A secondary private bedroom suite with personal bath, plus two bedrooms that share a Jack-and-Jill bathroom, complete the exciting home.

Upper Level Floor Plan

Rear Elevation

Hearth Room

Main Level Floor Plan

Copyright by designer/architect.

Plan #541031

Dimensions: 57' W x 64'6" D

Levels: 1

Square Footage: 2,803

Main Level Sq. Ft.: 1,670

Lower Level Sq. Ft.: 1,133

Bedrooms: 3

Bathrooms: 2½

Foundation: Walkout; basement for fee

Material List Available: No

Price Category: F

This contemporary-style home, with its sleek lines and steep gables, has crisp, decorative appeal.

CAD FILE AVAILABLE

Features:

• **Entry:** Guests and residents alike are welcomed by a 10-ft.-high ceiling in this distinguished foyer.

• **Great Room:** This impressive great room features a glowing fireplace as well as a 10-ft.-high ceiling, which adds an aura of airiness.

• **Kitchen:** This kitchen exhibits plenty of space for preparing gourmet meals or baking homemade pies. The beautiful room is also accented with an eating bar-a great space for enjoying a light snack, or catching up with friends as you cook.

• **Master Suite:** Enjoy the luxuries of a health resort in your own home in this beautiful master suite. Pamper yourself in this master bath in the generously sized spa, and enjoy dual-vanity sinks. A walk-in closet is ideal for a girl "who can't have too many shoes".

Main Level Floor Plan

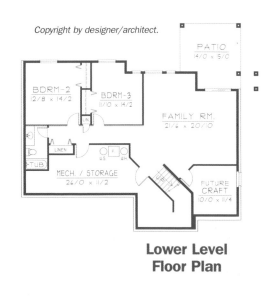

Lower Level Floor Plan

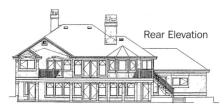

Plan #401023

Dimensions: 76' W x 63'4" D
Levels: 1
Square Footage: 2,806
Bedrooms: 3
Bathrooms: 2½
Foundation: Basement, walkout
Materials List Available: Yes
Price Category: F

The lower level of this magnificent home includes unfinished space that could have a future as a den and a family room with a fireplace. This level could also house extra bedrooms or an in-law suite.

Features:

- Foyer: On the main level, this foyer spills into a tray ceiling living room with a fireplace and an arched, floor-to-ceiling window wall.

- Family Room: Up from the foyer, a hall introduces this vaulted room with built-in media center and French doors that open to an expansive railed deck.

- Kitchen: Featured in this gourmet kitchen are a food-preparation island with a salad sink, double-door pantry, corner-window sink, and breakfast bay.

- Master Bedroom: The vaulted master bedroom opens to the deck, and the deluxe bath offers a raised whirlpool spa and a double-bowl vanity under a skylight.

- Bedroom: Two family bedrooms share a compartmented bathroom.

Rear Elevation

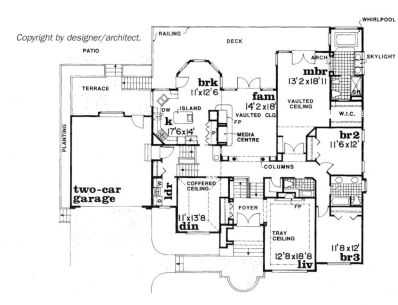

Copyright by designer/architect.

Optional Lower Level Floor Plan

Plan #161103

Dimensions: 89'10" W x 89'4" D
Levels: 2
Square Footage: 5,633
Main Level Sq. Ft.: 3,850
Upper Level Sq. Ft.: 1,783
Bedrooms: 4
Bathrooms: 3½
Foundation: Walkout; basement for fee
Material List Available: No
Price Category: J

Images provided by designer/architect.

The brick and stone exterior, with its arches and balcony overlooking the entry, creates a home that showcases artistic and historic architectural elements.

Features:

- **Kitchen:** The heart of the home centers around this gourmet kitchen, which features a large island and a breakfast area that opens to a delightful terrace. The adjacent hearth room boasts a cozy fireplace.

- **Master Suite:** This main-level retreat has private access to the rear porch and a stepped ceiling in the sleeping area. The master bath will pamper you with amenities such as a platform whirlpool tub and a two-person shower.

- **Secondary Bedrooms:** Three bedrooms are located on the upper level and each have a walk-in closets. Two bedrooms share a Jack-and-Jill bathroom, while the third has a private bathroom.

- **Lower Level:** For fun times, this lower level is finished to provide a wet bar, a billiard room, and a recreation room. Future expansion can include an additional bedroom and an exercise room.

Main Level Floor Plan

Copyright by designer/architect.

Upper Level Floor Plan

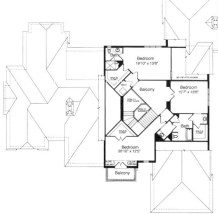

Optional Lower Level Floor Plan

Plan #271084

Dimensions: 51'9" W x 38'9" D

Levels: 1

Square Footage: 1,602

Bedrooms: 3

Bathrooms: 1½

Foundation: Daylight

Materials List Available: Yes

Price Category: C

Images provided by designer/architect.

Copyright by designer/architect.

Optional Lower Level Floor Plan

Plan #271061

Dimensions: 68' W x 52' D

Levels: 1

Square Footage: 1,750

Bedrooms: 1-3

Bathrooms: 1½- 2½

Foundation: Daylight basement

Materials List Available: No

Price Category: C

Images provided by designer/architect.

CAD FILE AVAILABLE

Copyright by designer/architect.

Optional Lower Level Floor Plan

Plan #451226

Dimensions: 98' W x 54' D

Levels: 2

Square Footage: 4,671

Main Level Sq. Ft.: 2,149

Upper Level Sq. Ft.: 385

Lower Level Sq. Ft.: 2,137

Bedrooms: 3

Bathrooms: 3½

Foundation: Walkout

Material List Available: No

Price Category: I

Images provided by designer/architect.

Main Level Floor Plan

Upper Level Floor Plan

Lower Level Floor Plan

Copyright by designer/architect.

Plan #271028

Dimensions: 48' W x 39'6" D

Levels: 2

Square Footage: 2,335

Main Level Sq. Ft.: 1,168

Upper Level Sq. Ft.: 1,167

Bedrooms: 4

Bathrooms: 2½

Foundation: Daylight basement

Materials List Available: Yes

Price Category: E

Images provided by designer/architect.

Main Level Floor Plan

Upper Level Floor Plan

Copyright by designer/architect.

Plan #541034

Dimensions: 79'6" W x 58'3"D

Levels: 1

Square Footage: 3,162

Main Level Sq. Ft.: 2,113

Lower Level Sq. Ft.: 1,049

Bedrooms: 3

Bathrooms: 3

Foundation: Walkout; basement for fee

Material List Available: No

Price Category: G

A combination of stone, shutters, and columns blend to create a magnificent exterior.

Features:

- **Great Room:** A see-through fireplace connects this vaulted gathering area to the kitchen and breakfast nook.

- **Den:** This den has built-in bookshelves and could serve as an additional bedroom.

- **Master Suite:** This fantastic suite features an octagonal sitting area. The private bath includes a separate tub and shower, a walk-in closet, double sinks, and a vanity for applying makeup.

- **Secondary Bedrooms:** Located on the lower level, these two bedrooms share a Jack-and-Jill bathroom.

- **Expansion:** There is no lack of room to expand as the basement allows for a future sunken family room, another bedroom, and an additional bathroom.

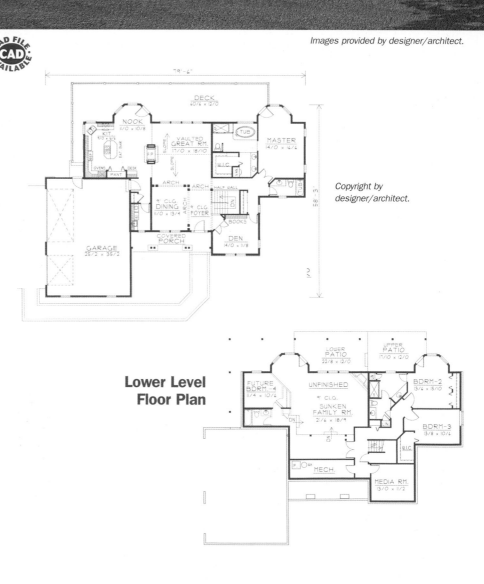

Lower Level Floor Plan

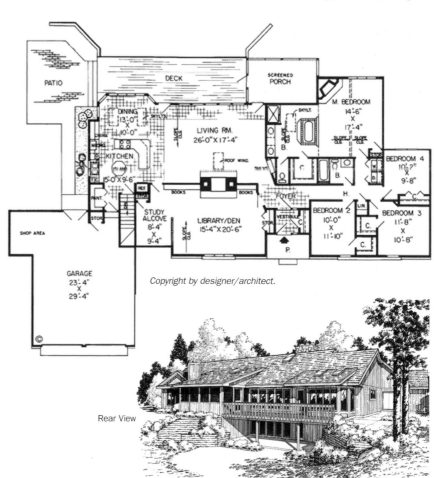

Plan #391156

Dimensions: 96' W x 60'6" D
Levels: 1
Square Footage: 2,450
Bedrooms: 4
Bathrooms: 2
Foundation: Basement or walkout
Material List Available: Yes
Price Category: E

Images provided by designer/architect.

This contemporary home offers many amenities for your family.

Features:

- Entry: This front entry consists of a vestibule, which contains a coat closet, and a separate foyer that leads to the rest of the house.

- Library/Den: This cozy room shares a see-through fireplace with the living room. The room has built-in shelves, a sloped ceiling, and a separate study alcove.

- Kitchen: This modern kitchen, with octagonal island, opens into the dining area. Skylights flood the area with natural light. A large nearby pantry keeps supplies handy and the kitchen neat.

- Master Suite: This private retreat includes a bedroom that is large enough for a comfortable seating area in front of its fireplace. The master bath features a separate room for the toilet, a spa tub, a large shower, and his and her vanities.

Copyright by designer/architect.

Rear View

Plan #161095

Dimensions: 59' W x 49'8" D
Levels: 1
Square Footage: 3,620
Main Level Sq. Ft.: 2,068
Lower Level Sq. Ft.: 1,552
Bedrooms: 3
Bathrooms: 3
Foundation: Walkout basement
Material List Available: No
Price Category: H

This elegant design has everything your family could want in a home.

Features:

- **Dining Room:** This column-accented formal area has a sloped ceiling and is open to the great room.

- **Great Room:** Featuring a cozy fireplace, this large gathering area offers a view of the backyard.

- **Kitchen:** This fully equipped island kitchen has everything the chef in the family could want.

- **Master Suite:** Located on the main level for privacy, this suite has a sloped ceiling in the sleeping area. The master bath boasts a whirlpool tub, a walk-in closet, and dual vanities.

Images provided by designer/architect.

This home, as shown in the photograph, may differ from the actual blueprints. For more detailed information, please check the floor plans carefully.

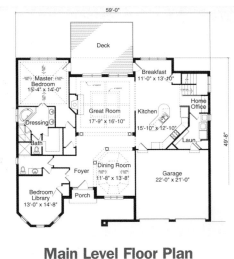

Main Level Floor Plan

Rear View

Lower Level Floor Plan

Copyright by designer/architect.

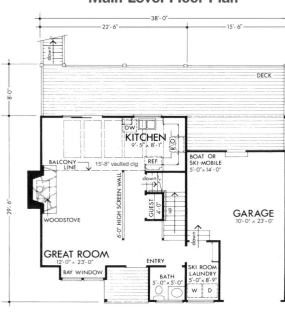

Plan #271468

Dimensions: 38' W x 29'6" D
Levels: 2
Square Footage: 1,312
Main Level Sq. Ft.: 689
Upper Level Sq. Ft.: 623
Bedrooms: 2
Bathrooms: 1 full, 2 half
Foundation: Crawl space or walkout
Material List Available: No
Price Category: B

Images provided by designer/architect.

Contemporary in style, this home has a rustic feel.

Features:

- **Great Room:** This extravagant great room boasts a 15-ft.-high ceiling and a wood stove to warm up your house.

- **Study:** A balcony overlooks the lower level. Use this space as a study, skylights let in plenty of light.

- **Master Suite:** With a sloped-vaulted ceiling peaking at almost 17 ft., this suite encapsulates the definition of luxury. Enjoy his and her closets, a whirlpool tub, and plenty of space to relax.

- **Garage:** This unique garage features a special area that is a wonderful space to store your boat or skimobile.

Rear View

Main Level Floor Plan

Upper Level Floor Plan

Copyright by designer/architect.

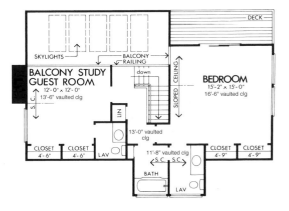

Plan #451267

Dimensions: 82' W x 62'10" D
Levels: 2
Square Footage: 2,723
Main Level Sq. Ft.: 2,016
Upper Level Sq. Ft.: 707
Bedrooms: 4
Bathrooms: 3 full, 2 half
Foundation: Walkout
Material List Available: No
Price Category: F

This is a unique home with a contemporary flair that can be decorated in almost any style.

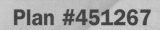
CAD FILE AVAILABLE

Features:

- **Foyer:** A covered entry introduces this foyer, which is open to the second floor. A traditional floor plan allows guests easy access to the formal dining room or the den.

- **Great Room:** An arched opening welcomes you into this large gathering area. The glass doors flanked by windows and the two-story-high ceiling provide an open and airy feeling.

- **Master Suite:** This main-level retreat features a fireplace, which it shares with the great room, a stepped ceiling, and a sitting area. The large master bathroom will pamper you with dual vanities, large walk-in closet, and a separate toilet room.

- **Upper Level:** An unfinished bonus room accompanies two secondary bedrooms and a bathroom. A study overlooks the great room.

- **Lower Level:** A recreation room and a craft area are located on this level. The guest suite will give overnight guests the privacy they need.

Rear Elevation

Main Level Floor Plan

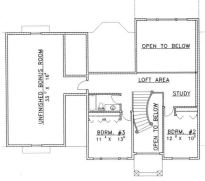

Upper Level Floor Plan

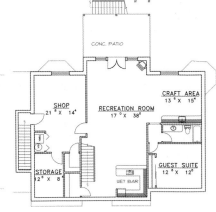

Lower Level Floor Plan

Plan #451399

Dimensions: 116'3" W x 90'11" D

Levels: 1

Square Footage: 3,779

Bedrooms: 3

Bathrooms: 2½

Foundation: Walkout – insulated concrete form

Material List Available: No

Price Category: H

Images provided by designer/architect.

The variations in the exterior texture of this contemporary style home prove uniquely inviting.

Features:

- Kitchen: The angular shape of the home allows for an efficient use of space, especially when it comes to this kitchen. You'll have plenty of room to prepare meals and then serve them in the lovely breakfast nook.

- Sewing/Utility Room: Dreaming of a place to enjoy your hobby? This utility room has plenty of space to relax and enjoy your favorite pastime.

- Master Suite: Tucked away in a cozy corner of the home, this master suite boasts a walk-in closet, whirlpool tub, and plenty of space to relax.

Copyright by designer/architect.

Plan #541033

Dimensions: 70' W x 68'6" D

Levels: 1

Square Footage: 3,057

Main Level Sq. Ft.: 2,017

Lower Level Sq. Ft.: 1,040

Bedrooms: 3

Bathrooms: 2½

Foundation: Walkout; basement for fee

Material List Available: No

Price Category: G

Delight in the spaciousness that the open floor plan of this contemporary style home offers.

CAD FILE AVAILABLE

Features:

- **Entry:** Welcome guests into your home on this roomy porch, or enjoy sunny days from the comfort of your own house.

- **Great Room:** This great room boasts vaulted ceilings that add a lavish feel. A beautiful fireplace is a warming accent to the capacious room.

- **Kitchen:** This charming kitchen features all of the necessities and more. An island in the center of the room is a great space for food

prep and casual conversation. A breakfast nook is placed strategically close to the kitchen for easy access to and from the cooking area, while a vaulted sunroom off of the nook is a cheery retreat for sunny mornings.

- **Master Suite:** These rooms are ideal for the busy couple to get ready in the morning. Featuring his and her walk-in closets, as well as a large bedroom, you'll have plenty of space. After a busy day, relax in the luxurious spa.

Main Level Floor Plan

Lower Level Floor Plan

Plan #271467

Dimensions: 28' W x 42' D
Levels: 1
Square Footage: 1,737
Main Level Sq. Ft.: 1,075
Lower Level Sq. Ft.: 662
Bedrooms: 2
Bathrooms: 2
Foundation: Crawl space or walkout
Material List Available: No
Price Category: C

If you love the outdoors, this home is perfect for you. Tons of windows and a balcony help you enjoy the natural surroundings to the fullest.

Features:

- **Living Room:** Welcome guests into this inviting living room, warmed by streaming sunlight and a rustic wood stove.

- **Kitchen:** This efficient L-shaped kitchen has plenty of workspace and storage for the novice cook and the expert chef alike.

- **Dining Room:** This spacious formal dining room, located between the kitchen and living room, is great for dinner parties. Easily transition between meal prep, dining, and entertaining by the firelight.

- **Bedrooms:** Three bedrooms, each comparable to the next, have wide closets and access to a nearby full bathroom. Since most of the living is done on the upper level, the bedroom on the lower level boasts more privacy and quiet.

Main Level Floor Plan

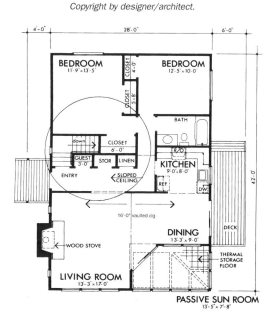

Main Level Floor Plan Option

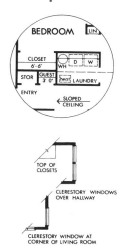

Lower Level Floor Plan

Plan #181680

Dimensions: 86'4" W x 98'4"D
Levels: 2
Square Footage: 9,028
Main Level Sq. Ft.: 3,663
Upper Level Sq. Ft.: 882
Lower Level Sq. Ft.: 4,483
Bedrooms: 7
Bathrooms: 6 full, 2 half
Foundation: Walkout
Material List Available: Yes
Price Category: L

Images provided by designer/architect.

CAD FILE AVAILABLE

There is plenty of room for the extended family in this large home.

Features:

- **Kitchen:** This island kitchen has an abundance of counter space and cabinets. The extended bar makes additional seating available when the dining room is full.

- **Guest Suite:** The entire second level of the home is devoted to this guest suite, complete with a kitchenette. The one-bedroom suite boasts a rear deck with a view of the yard.

- **Master Suite:** There are two master suites in this beautiful home. Each suite features a large walk-in closet and private bath with dual vanities and separate tubs and showers.

- **Lower Level:** Every item on your wish list is located on this level. There are four bedrooms, a home theater room, exercise room, and an indoor pool.

Upper Level Floor Plan

Main Level Floor Plan

Copyright by designer/architect.

Lower Level Floor Plan

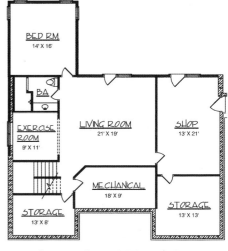

Plan #271078

Dimensions: 83' W x 52' D
Levels: 1
Square Footage: 3,620
Main Level Sq. Ft.: 1,855
Lower Level Sq. Ft.: 1,765
Bedrooms: 2
Bathrooms: 2½
Foundation: Daylight basement
Materials List Available: No
Price Category: H

Sleek lines and a variety of textures make this home's exterior as appealing as its interior.

CAD FILE AVAILABLE

Features:

- **Great Room:** This inviting space is elegantly set apart by a floor-to-ceiling fireplace between the entry and the great room. Go from a romantic candlelit dinner in the adjacent dining room to sitting cozily in front of a glowing fire.

- **Kitchen:** This efficient L shaped kitchen features both a small center island and a larger island with cooktop and snack bar as a room divider. This is a perfect arrangement for multiple cooks.

- **Master Suite:** This sunlit space includes a walk-in closet and compartmentalized bath with his and her sinks, tub, and a large stall shower.

- **Additional Living Space:** The basement floor features an additional bedroom with adjacent full bathroom, a living room, and plenty of space to accommodate storage and hobbies.

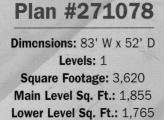

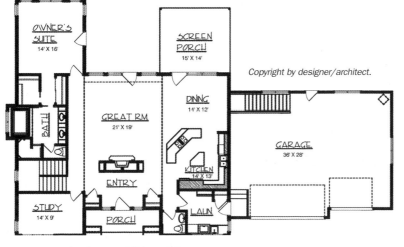

Copyright by designer/architect.

Main Level Floor Plan

Lower Level Floor Plan

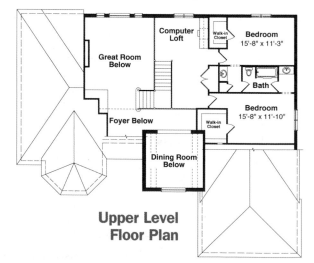

Plan #161097

Dimensions: 70' W x 56'10" D
Levels: 2
Square Footage: 4,594
Main Level Sq. Ft.: 2,237
Upper Level Sq. Ft.: 900
Optional Lower Level Sq. Ft.: 1,450
Bedrooms: 3
Bathrooms: 2½
Foundation: Walkout; basement for fee
Material List Available: No
Price Category: I

The design of this contemporary home complements many rating styles.

Features:

- Foyer: A graceful staircase anchors this traditional foyer. A closet and powder room complete the design. The foyer leads directly to the two-story great room.

- Master Suite: This first-floor retreat includes a circular sitting area with 11-ft.-high ceiling. A super bath adds to the luxurious atmosphere, boasting dual vanities and a private toilet enclosure.

- Loft: Overlooking the first floor, this delightful loft area is perfect for the family computer or as a hobby area. A built-in desk provides a good environment for the kids to do their homework.

- Secondary Bedrooms: These two bedrooms on the second level, each with large walk-in closet and private access to a shared bathroom, complete the exciting family-size home.

Main Level Floor Plan

Upper Level Floor Plan

Hearth Room

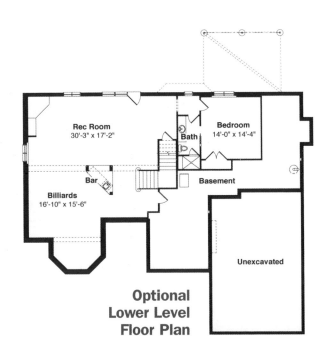

**Optional
Lower Level
Floor Plan**

Rec Room
30'-3" x 17'-2"

Bar

Billiards
16'-10" x 15'-6"

Bath

Bedroom
14'-0" x 14'-4"

Basement

Unexcavated

Dining
Room

Plan #161113

Dimensions: 120'2" W x 60'4" D
Levels: 2
Square Footage: 6,126
Main Level Sq. Ft.: 3,298
Upper Level Sq. Ft.: 1,067
Lower Level Sq. Ft.: 1,761
Bedrooms: 5
Bathrooms: 3½
Foundation: Basement
Materials List Available: No
Price Category: K

Images provided by designer/architect.

A covered entry welcomes friends and family to this elegant home.

Features:

- Library: Just off the foyer is this library, which can be used as a home office. Notice the connecting door to the master bathroom.

- Kitchen: Release the chef inside of you into this gourmet kitchen, complete with seating at the island and open to the breakfast area. Step through the triple sliding door, and arrive on the rear porch.

- Master Suite: This luxurious master suite features a stepped ceiling in the sleeping area and private access to the rear patio. The master bath boasts an oversized stall shower, a whirlpool bath, dual vanities, and an enormous walk-in closet.

- Lower Level: For family fun times, this lower level is finished to provide a wet bar, billiard room, and media room. The area also includes two additional bedrooms and an exercise room.

- Garage: You'll have storage galore in this four-car garage, complete with an additional set of stairs to the unfinished part of the basement.

Lower Level Floor Plan

Copyright by designer/architect.

Main Level Floor Plan

Upper Level Floor Plan

Let Us Help You Plan Your Dream Home

Whether you've always dreamed of building your own home or you can't find the right house from among the dozens you've toured, our collection of affordable plans can help you achieve the home of your dreams. You could have an architect create a one-of-a-kind home for you, but the design services alone could end up costing up to 15 percent of the cost of construction—a hefty premium for any building project. Isn't it a better idea to select from among the hundreds of unique designs shown in our collection for a fraction of the cost?

What does Creative Homeowner Offer?

In this book, Creative Homeowner provides hundreds of home plans from the country's best architects and designers. Our designs are among the most popular available. Whether your taste runs from traditional to contemporary, Victorian to early American, you are sure to find the best house design for you and your family. Our plans packages include detailed drawings to help you or your builder construct your dream house. **(See page 278.)**

Can I Make Changes to the Plans?

Creative Homeowner offers three ways to help you achieve a truly unique home design. Our customizing service allows for extensive changes to our designs. **(See page 279.)** We also provide reverse images of our plans, or we can give you and your builder the tools for making minor changes on your own. **(See page 282.)**

Can You Help Me Manage My Costs?

To help you stay within your budget, Creative Homeowner has teamed up with the leading estimating company to provide one of the most accurate, complete, and reliable building material take-offs in the industry. **(See page 280.)** If that is too much detail for you, we can provide you with general construction costs based on your zip code. **(See page 282.)** Also, many of our plans come with the option of buying detailed materials lists to help you price out construction costs.

How Can I Begin the Building Process?

To get started building your dream home, fill out the order form on page 283, call our order department at 1-800-523-6789, or visit ultimateplans.com. If you plan on doing all or part of the work yourself, or want to keep tabs on your builder, we offer best-selling building and design books available at www.creativehomeowner.com.

Our Plans Packages Offer:

"Square footage" refers to the total "heated square feet" of this plan. This number does not include the garage, porches, or unfinished areas. All of our home plans are the result of many hours of work by leading architects and professional designers. Most of our home plans include each of the following:

Frontal Sheet

This artist's rendering of the front of the house gives you an idea of how the house will look once it is completed and the property landscaped.

Detailed Floor Plans

These plans show the size and layout of the rooms. They also provide the locations of doors, windows, fireplaces, closets, stairs, and electrical outlets and switches.

Foundation Plan

A foundation plan gives the dimensions of basements, walk-out basements, crawl spaces, pier foundations, and slab construction. Each house design lists the type of foundation included. If the plan you choose does not have the foundation type you require, our customer service department can help you customize the plan to meet your needs.

Roof Plan

In addition to providing the pitch of the roof, these plans also show the locations of dormers, skylights, and other elements.

Exterior Elevations

These drawings show the front, rear, and sides of the house as if you were looking at it head on. Elevations also provide information about architectural features and finish materials.

Interior Elevations and Details

Interior elevations show specific details of such elements as fireplaces, kitchen and bathroom cabinets, built-ins, and other unique features of the design.

Cross Sections

These show the structure as if it were sliced to reveal construction requirements, such as insulation, flooring, and roofing details.

Frontal Sheet

Floor Plan

Foundation Plan

Roof Plan

Elevation

Stair Details

Cross Sections

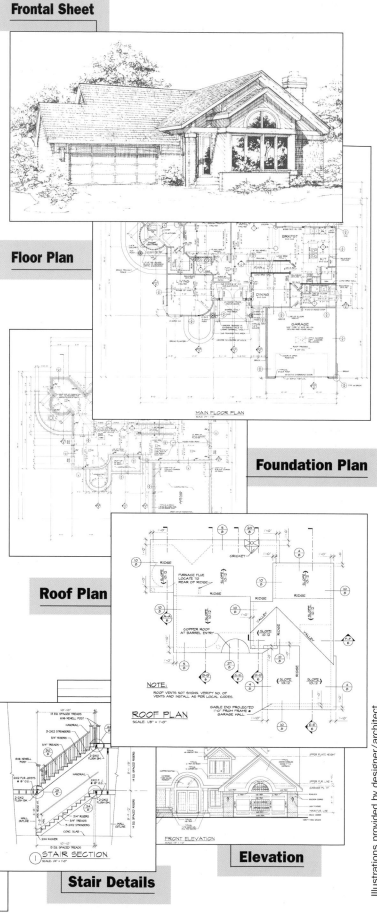

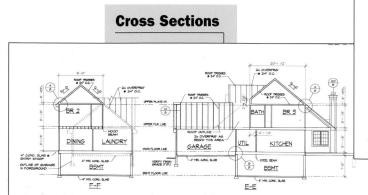

Illustrations provided by designer/architect

Customize Your Plans in 4 Easy Steps

1 **Select the home plan** that most closely meets your needs. Purchase of a reproducible master is necessary in order to make changes to a plan.

2 **Call 1-800-523-6789 to place your order.** Tell our sales representative you are interested in customizing your plan. To receive your customization cost estimate, our modification company will contact you (via fax or email) requesting a list or sketch of the changes requested to one of our plans. There is a $50 nonrefundable consultation fee for this service. If you decide to continue with the custom changes, the $50 fee is credited to the total amount charged.

3 **Fax or email your request** to our modification company. Within three business days of receipt of your request, a detailed cost estimate will be provided to you.

4 **Once you approve the estimate,** a 75% retainer fee is collected and customization work begins. Preliminary drawings typically take 10 to 15 business days. After approval of the design, the balance of your customization fee is due before modified plans can be shipped. You will receive five sets of blueprints, a reproducible master, or CAD files, depending on which package was purchase.

Modification Pricing Guide

Categories	Average Cost For Modification
Add or remove living space	Quote required
Bathroom layout redesign	Starting at $120
Kitchen layout redesign	Starting at $120
Garage: add or remove	Starting at $400
Garage: front entry to side load or vice versa	Starting at $300
Foundation changes	Starting at $220
Exterior building materials change	Starting at $200
Exterior openings: add, move, or remove	$65 per opening
Roof line changes	Starting at $360
Ceiling height adjustments	Starting at $280
Fireplace: add or remove	Starting at $90
Screened porch: add	Starting at $280
Wall framing change from 2x4 to 2x6	Starting at $200
Bearing and/or exterior walls changes	Quote required
Non-bearing wall or room changes	$65 per room
Metric conversion of home plan	Starting at $400
Adjust plan for handicapped accessibility	Quote required
Adapt plans for local building code requirements	Quote required
Engineering stamping only	Quote required
Any other engineering services	Quote required
Interactive illustrations (choices of exterior materials)	Quote required

Note: *Any home plan can be customized to accommodate your desired changes. The average prices above are provided only as examples of the most commonly requested changes, and are subject to change without notice. Prices for changes will vary according to the number of modifications requested, plan size, style, and method of design used by the original designer. To obtain a detailed cost estimate, please contact us.*

Terms & Copyright

These home plans are protected under the terms of United States Copyright Law and may not be copied or reproduced in any way, by any means, unless you have purchased reproducible masters, which clearly indicate your right to copy or reproduce. We authorize the use of your chosen home plan as an aid in the construction of one single-family home only. You may not use this home plan to build a second or multiple dwellings without purchasing another blueprint or blueprints, or paying additional home plan fees.

Architectural Seals

Because of differences in building codes, some cities and states now require an architect or engineer licensed in that state to review and "seal" a blueprint, or officially approve it, prior to construction. Delaware, Nevada, New Jersey, New York, and some other states require that all plans for houses built in those states be redrawn by an architect licensed in the state in which the home will be built. We strongly advise you to consult with your local building official for information regarding architectural seals.

Before Customization

After

Turn your dream home into reality with

UltimateEstimate

When purchasing a home plan with Creative Homeowner, we recommend you order one of the most complete materials lists in the industry.

1 What comes with an Ultimate Estimate?

Quote

- Basis of the entire estimate.

- Detailed list of all the framing materials needed to build your project, listed from the bottom up, in the order that each one will actually be used.

Comments

- Details pertinent information beyond the cost of materials.

- Includes any notes from our estimator.

Express List

- A version of the Quote with space for SKU numbers listed for purchasing the items at your local lumberyard.

- Your local lumberyard can then price out the materials list.

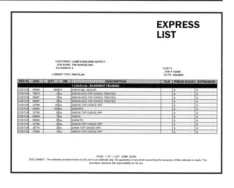

Construction-Ready Framing Diagrams

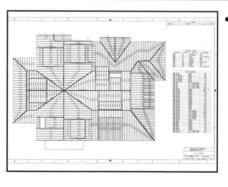

- Your "map" to exact roof and floor framing.

Millwork Report

- A complete count of the windows, doors, molding, and trim.

Man-Hour Report

- Calculates labor on a line-by-line basis for all items quoted and presented in man-hours.

2 Why an Ultimate Estimate?

Accurate. Professional estimators break down each individual item from the blueprints using advanced software, techniques, and equipment.

Timely. You will be able to start your home-building project quickly—knowing the exact framing materials you need to order from your local lumberyard.

Detailed. Work with your local lumberyard associate to complete your quote with the remaining products needed for your new home.

3 So how much does it cost?

Pricing is determined by the total square feet of the home plan—including living area, garages, decks, porches, finished basements, and finished attics.

Square Feet Range	UE Tier*	Price
2,001 to 5,000 total square feet	XB	$299.00
5,001 to 10,000 total square feet	XC	$499.00

*Please see the Plan Index to determine your plan's Ultimate Estimate Tier (UE Tier).
Note: All prices subject to change.

Call our toll-free number (800-523-6789), or visit ultimateplans.com to order your Ultimate Estimate.

4 What else do I need to know?

Call our toll-free number (800-523-6789), or visit
ultimate**plans**.com to order your Ultimate Estimate.

Turn your dream home into reality.

Decide What Type of Plan Package You Need

How many Plans Should You Order?

Standard 8-Set Package. We've found that our 8-set package is the best value for someone who is ready to start building. The 8-set package provides plans for you, your builder, the subcontractors, mortgage lender, and the building department.

Minimum 5-Set Package. If you are in the bidding process, you may want to order only five sets for the bidding round and reorder additional sets as needed.

1-Set Study Package. The 1-set package allows you to review your home plan in detail. The plan will be marked as a study print, and it is illegal to build a house from a study print alone. It is a violation of copyright law to reproduce a blueprint without permission.

Buying Additional Sets

If you require additional copies of blueprints for your home construction, you can order additional sets within 60 days of the original order date at a reduced price. The cost is $45.00 for each additional set. For more information, contact customer service.

Reproducible Masters

If you plan to make minor changes to one of our home plans, you can purchase reproducible masters. These plans are printed on bond or vellum paper that is easy to alter. They clearly indicate your right to modify, copy, or reproduce the plans. Reproducible masters allow an architect, designer, or builder to alter our plans to give you a customized home design. This package also allows you to print as many copies of the modified plans as you need for the construction of one home.

CAD (Computer Aided Design) Files

CAD files are the complete set of home plans in an electronic file format. Choose this option if there are multiple changes you wish made to the home plans and you have a local design professional able to make the changes. Not available for all plans. Please contact our order department or visit our Web site to check the availability of CAD files for your plan.

Mirror-Reverse Sets/Right-Reading Reverse

Plans can be printed in mirror-reverse—we can "flip" plans to create a mirror image of the design. This is useful when the house would fit your site or personal preferences if all the rooms were on the opposite side than shown. As the image is reversed, the letter-ing and dimensions will also be reversed, meaning they will read backwards. Therefore, when ordering mirror-reverse drawings, you must order at least one set of the original plan unreversed. A $50.00 fee per plan order will be charged for mirror-reverse (regardless of the number of mirror-reverse sets ordered). Some plans are available in right-reading reverse, this feature will show the plan in reverse, but the writing on the plan will be readable. A $150.00 fee per plan order will be charged for right-reading reverse (regardless of the number of right-reading reverse sets ordered). Please contact our order department or visit our website to check the availibility of this feature for your chosen plan.

EZ Quote: Home Cost Estimator

EZ Quote is our response to one of the most frequently asked questions we hear from customers: "How much will the house cost me to build?" EZ Quote: Home Cost Estimator will enable you to obtain a calculated building cost to construct your home, based on labor rates and building material costs within your zip code area. This summary is useful for those who want to get an idea of the total construction costs before purchasing sets of home plans. It will also provide a level of comfort when you begin soliciting bids. The cost is $29.95 for the first EZ Quote and $19.95 for each additional one. Available only in the U.S. and Canada.

Materials List

Available for most of our plans, the Materials List provides you an invaluable resource in planning and estimating the cost of your home. Each Materials List outlines the quantity, dimensions, and type of materials needed to build your home (with the exception of mechanical systems). You will get faster, more-accurate bids from your contractors and building suppliers. A Materials List may only be ordered with the purchase of at least five sets of home plans.

CompleteCost Estimator

CompleteCost Estimator is a valuable tool for use in planning and constructing your new home. It provides more detail than a materials list and will act as a checklist for all items you will need to select or coordinate during your building process. CompleteCost Estimator is only available for certain plans (please see Plan Index) and may only be ordered with the purchase of at least five sets of home plans. The cost is $125.00 for CompleteCost Estimator.

Ultimate Estimate (See page 280.)

Order Toll Free by Phone
1-800-523-6789
By Fax: 201-760-2431

Orders received 3PM ET, will be processed and shipped within two business days.

Order Online
www.ultimateplans.com

Mail Your Order
Creative Homeowner
Attn: Home Plans
24 Park Way
Upper Saddle River, NJ 07458

Canadian Customers
Order Toll Free 1-800-393-1883

Mail Your Order (Canada)
Creative Homeowner Canada
Attn: Home Plans
113-437 Martin St., Ste. 215
Penticton, BC V2A 5L1

Before You Order

Our Exchange Policy

Blueprints are nonrefundable. However, should you find that the plan you have purchased does not fit your needs, you may exchange that plan for another plan in our collection within 60 days from the date of your original order. The entire content of your original order must be returned before an exchange will be processed. You will be charged a processing fee of 20% of the amount of the original order, the cost difference between the new plan set and the original plan set (if applicable), and all related shipping costs for the new plans. Contact our order department for more information. Please note: reproducible masters may only be exchanged if the package is unopened and CAD files cannot be exchanged and are nonrefundable.

Building Codes and Requirements

At the time of creation, our plans meet the building code requirements published by the Building Officials and Code Administrators International, the Southern Building Code Congress International, the International Conference of Building Officials, or the Council of American Building Officials. Because building codes vary from area to area, some drawing modifications and/or the assistance of a professional designer or architect may be necessary to comply with your local codes or to accommodate specific building site conditions. We strongly advise you to consult with your local building official for information regarding codes governing your area.

Blueprint Price Schedule

Price Code	1 Set	5 Sets	8 Sets	Reproducible Masters	CAD	Materials List
A	$315	$360	$415	$560	$950	$85
B	$395	$455	$505	$630	$1,100	$85
C	$450	$525	$580	$680	$1,200	$85
D	$515	$590	$640	$745	$1,300	$95
E	$580	$650	$695	$810	$1,400	$95
F	$640	$715	$760	$870	$1,500	$95
G	$705	$780	$820	$935	$1,600	$95
H	$800	$870	$915	$1,030	$1,700	$95
I	$900	$975	$1020	$1,135	$1,800	$105
J	$1,010	$1,080	$1,125	$1,250	$1,900	$105
K	$1,125	$1,210	$1,250	$1,380	$2,030	$105
L	$1,240	$1,335	$1,375	$1,535	$2,170	$105

Note: All prices subject to change

Ultimate Estimate Tier (UE Tier)

UE Tier*	Price
XB	$299
XC	$499

* Please see the Plan Index to determine your plan's Ultimate Estimate Tier (UE Tier).

Shipping & Handling

	1-4 Sets	5-7 Sets	8+ Sets or Reproducibles	CAD
US Regular (7–10 business days)	$18	$20	$25	$25
US Priority (3–5 business days)	$25	$30	$35	$35
US Express (1–2 business days)	$40	$45	$50	$50
Canada Express (1–2 business days)	$80	$80	$80	$80
Worldwide Express (3–5 business days)	$100	$100	$100	$100

Note: All delivery times are from date the blueprint package is shipped (typically within 1-2 days of placing order).

Order Form
Please send me the following:

Plan Number: _____ **Price Code:** _____ (See Plan Index.)

Indicate Foundation Type: (Select ONE. See plan page for availability.)

❏ Slab ❏ Crawl space ❏ Basement ❏ Walk-out basement

❏ Optional Foundation for Fee _____ $_____
(Please enter foundation here)

Please call all our order department or visit our website for optional foundation fee

Basic Blueprint Package	Cost
❏ CAD Files	$_____
❏ Reproducible Masters	$_____
❏ 8-Set Plan Package	$_____
❏ 5-Set Plan Package	$_____
❏ 1-Set Study Package	$_____
❏ Additional plan sets: __ sets at $45.00 per set	$_____
❏ Print in mirror-reverse: $50.00 per order	$_____

Please call all our order department or visit our website for availibility

❏ Print in right-reading reverse: $150.00 per order $_____

Please call all our order department or visit our website for availibility

Important Extras

❏ Ultimate Estimate (See Price Tier above.)	$_____
❏ Materials List	$_____
❏ CompleteCost Materials Report at $125.00 Zip Code of Home/Building Site _____	$_____
❏ EZ Quote for Plan #_____ at $29.95	$_____
❏ Additional EZ Quotes for Plan #s_____ at $19.95 each	$_____

Shipping (see chart above)	$_____
SUBTOTAL	$_____
Sales Tax (NJ residents only, add 7%)	$_____
TOTAL	$_____

Order Toll Free: 1-800-523-6789 By Fax: 201-760-2431
Creative Homeowner (Home Plans Order Dept.)
24 Park Way
Upper Saddle River, NJ 07458

Name _____
(Please print or type)

Street _____
(Please do not use a P.O. Box)

City _____ State _____

Country _____ Zip _____

Daytime telephone ( ) _____

Fax ( ) _____
(Required for reproducible orders)

E-Mail _____

Payment ❏ Bank check/money order. No personal checks.
Make checks payable to Creative Homeowner

❏ VISA ❏ MasterCard ❏ AMERICAN EXPRESS Cards ❏ DISCOVER

Credit card number _____

Expiration date (mm/yy) _____

Signature _____

Please check the appropriate box:
❏ Licensed builder/contractor ❏ Homeowner ❏ Renter

SOURCE CODE CA550

Copyright Notice

All home plans sold through this publication are protected by copyright. Reproduction of these home plans, either in whole or in part, including any form and/or preparation of derivative works thereof, for any reason without prior written permission is strictly prohibited. The purchase of a set of home plans in no way transfers any copyright or other ownership interest in it to the buyer except for a limited license to use that set of home plans for the construction of one, and only one, dwelling unit. The purchase of additional sets of the home plans at a reduced price from the original set or as a part of a multiple-set package does not convey to the buyer a license to construct more than one dwelling.

Similarly, the purchase of reproducible home plans (sepias, mylars) carries the same copyright protection as mentioned above. It is generally allowed to make up to a maximum of 10 copies for the construction of a single dwelling only. To use any plans more than once, and to avoid any copyright license infringement, it is necessary to contact the plan designer to receive a release and license for any extended use. Whereas a purchaser of reproducible plans is granted a license to make copies, it should be noted that because blueprints are copyrighted, making photocopies from them is illegal.

Copyright and licensing of home plans for construction exist to protect all parties. Copyright respects and supports the intellectual property of the original architect or designer. Copyright law has been reinforced over the past few years. Willful infringement could cause settlements for statutory damages to $150,000.00 plus attorney fees, damages, and loss of profits.

Index
For pricing, see page 283.

Index

For pricing, see page 283.

Plan #	Price Code	Page	Total Finished Area Square Feet	Materials List Available	Complete Cost	UE Tier
181106	C	207	1648	Y	N	XB
181107	D	204	1879	Y	N	XB
181116	H	257	3930	Y	N	XB
181120	B	196	1480	N	N	XB
181123	B	205	1482	Y	N	XB
181124	C	251	1574	Y	N	XB
181128	C	194	1634	Y	N	XB
181132	B	206	1437	Y	N	XB
181133	D	199	1832	Y	N	XB
181159	D	155	1992	Y	N	XB
181172	B	211	1484	Y	N	XB
181232	B	145	1325	Y	N	XB
181243	E	181	2219	Y	N	XB
181260	G	254	3251	Y	N	XB
181669	E	159	2348	Y	N	XB
181673	G	172	3392	Y	N	XB
181680	L	272	9028	Y	N	XC
181708	F	149	2800	Y	N	XB
191023	C	168	1785	N	N	XB
221121	J	120	5140	N	N	XC
241013	G	19	3033	N	N	XB
241018	E	226	2519	N	N	XB
261011	I	172	4042	N	N	XC
271028	H	263	3620	N	N	XB
271050	B	200	1188	Y	N	XB
271051	D	193	1920	Y	N	XB
271054	F	29	2654	N	N	XB
271056	F	37	2850	N	N	XC
271058	F	16	2924	N	N	XC
271059	C	31	1790	N	N	XB
271060	C	257	1726	N	N	XB
271061	C	262	1750	N	N	XB
271063	E	213	2572	N	N	XB
271064	F	157	2864	N	N	XB
271073	D	46	1920	N	N	XB
271076	D	49	2188	N	N	XB
271077	C	85	1786	N	N	XB
271078	H	273	3620	Y	N	XB
271079	E	255	2228	N	N	XC
271084	C	262	1602	Y	N	XB
271086	D	195	1910	Y	N	XB
271087	F	197	2734	N	N	XB
271089	E	101	2476	N	N	XB
271090	F	93	2708	N	N	XC
271091	F	103	2854	N	N	XB
271092	F	109	2636	N	N	XC
271125	C	110	1776	N	N	XB
271214	C	145	1612	N	N	XB
271298	F	249	2759	N	N	XC
271362	F	120	2645	N	N	XB
271467	C	271	1737	N	N	XB
271468	B	267	1312	N	N	XB
281009	B	104	1423	Y	N	XB
281014	C	157	1677	Y	N	XB
281031	B	10	1493	Y	N	XB
291023	D	174	2047	N	N	XB
321001	C	20	1721	Y	N	XB
321009	E	25	2295	Y	N	XB
321010	C	50	1787	Y	N	XB
321016	H	220	3814	Y	N	XC
321024	B	23	1403	Y	N	XB
321025	A	192	914	Y	N	XB
321029	E	47	2334	Y	N	XB
321031	G	148	3200	Y	N	XC
321032	I	215	4826	Y	N	XC
321034	H	224	3508	Y	N	XC
321035	B	201	1384	Y	N	XB
321036	F	246	2900	Y	N	XC
321037	E	213	2397	Y	N	XB
321065	G	234	3420	Y	N	XB
341063	C	228	1566	Y	N	XB
341064	B	158	1418	Y	N	XB
341071	C	41	1500	Y	N	XB
341073	B	43	1486	N	N	XB
341081	B	48	1365	N	N	XB
341084	B	51	1429	N	N	XB
341105	D	64	1822	N	N	XB
341121	B	48	1429	Y	N	XB
341126	D	225	1950	N	N	XB
341143	B	234	1152	N	N	XB
341153	B	215	1224	Y	N	XB
341170	C	38	1704	Y	N	XB
341176	D	27	2170	Y	N	XB
341190	B	208	1440	N	N	XB
341202	B	235	1429	Y	N	XB
341206	B	147	1348	N	N	XB
341214	D	168	1806	Y	N	XB
341216	D	22	1881	N	N	XB
341224	C	46	1534	N	N	XB
341234	B	152	1476	N	N	XB
341241	B	235	1176	N	N	XB
341251	E	153	2254	Y	N	XB
341282	B	96	1404	N	N	XB
341284	E	169	2384	Y	N	XB
341285	B	33	1481	Y	N	XB
341287	B	32	1217	Y	N	XB
341291	D	58	2147	Y	N	XB
341294	B	17	1418	N	N	XB
341305	B	173	1362	N	N	XB
381046	C	65	1605	Y	N	XB
391156	E	265	2450	Y	N	XB
401023	F	260	2806	Y	N	XC
401029	D	248	2163	Y	N	XB
441011	F	178	2898	N	N	XB